POLITICS
AND
GOVERNMENT

POLITICS AND GOVERNMENT

Compiled & Edited
by
Dr. R.K. Pruthi

DISCOVERY PUBLISHING HOUSE
NEW DELHI-110002

First Published-2005

ISBN 81-8356-011-3

Published by

DISCOVERY PUBLISHING HOUSE
4831/24, Ansari Road, Prahlad Street,
Darya Ganj, New Delhi-110002 (India)
Phone: 23279245 • Fax: 91-11-23253475
E-mail:dphtemp@indiatimes.com

Printed at:
Arora Offset Press
Laxmi Nagar, Delhi 110 092.

Preface

Politics is the art of possible and the structure which exercises power and control is termed as government. In modern times the organisation of politics and government has become complex. Their power has increased. But still we need the government to organise social relations, to contain and resolve conflicts and to achieve common goals of the society.

Why do we need the government? How is it organised? What are its forms and functions? In this book an attempt has been made to select best possible material, especially for the use of our students and teachers.

We take this opportunity to acknowledge the authorities which have directly and indirectly influenced us in preparing this book.

We thank all those librarians and their staff members who have been very kind and co-operative.

My publisher and his staff members have rendered every possible assistance and help. We shall all feel amply rewarded if our readers find the book useful to them.

R.K. Pruthi

Contents

1

Government

Aristotle's famous work is entitled by one of its translators, William Ellis, *A Treatise on Government*, and, in fact, almost the whole of it consists of discussions upon government. After giving the ideal of the State as a City, as the best form of civil society, and briefly dealing with the citizens, the family, and domestic government, he proceeds, in Book II, to seek for the most perfect form of Government, and glances over special forms existing in the world of his day. In Book III, with equal brevity, he speaks of the City and the Citizen, and, in Chapter vii, reaches his famous definitions, that "every form of Government or administration, for the words are of the same import, must contain a supreme power over the whole State, and this supreme power must necessarily be in the hands of one person, or a few, or many"; thus there are Kingdoms, Aristocracies, and "States"; in any one of these, if the holder of power apply that power to the common good, the State (he uses the word "State" of all governed communities as well as designating by it Government by "the citizens at large") is well-governed; if the power be applied in the interest of its holder, then is the State ill-governed. He concludes this brief survey, which occupies Chapter vii, by saying:

> Now the corruptions attending each of these governments are these: A kingdom may degenerate into a tyranny, an aristocracy into an oligarchy, and a State into a democracy. Now a tyranny is a monarchy where the good of one man only is the object of Government, an oligarchy considers only the rich, and a democracy only the poor; but neither of them has a common good in view. (Book III, chap. vii, p. 93.)

The rest of Book III discusses the nature of each of these, with illustrations from Greek conditions and history. On these lines discussions in the West have proceeded.

A BIRD'S-EYE VIEW

Taking Government as the supreme power in a State, and looking over the past and the future, we may discover by such a bird's-eye view that Humanity has passed through a period of childhood, in which, as in a family, the Elders governed as a matter of course; then through a period of youth, in which innumerable experiments were tried by States at various stages of their development; now, in early manhood, the most civilised States are reaching, or have reached, the conclusion that the interests of all are best served by power being vested in the hands of all, and are seeking methods by which that consummation may be reached in a self-disciplined and justly-ordered State. Many will be the struggles and the failures and the renewed efforts to attain that condition, before Humanity reaches its Golden Age; but the main outline is clear: Individualism is passing, in the most advanced States, out of its combative self-assertion—a necessary condition for its development—and will pass into the associative stage, wherein the common good will be sought by mutual co-operation instead of by compctition, and Democracy in its true, and in its Aristotelian, sense, will be the form of Government, a Socialism of common agreement, not of compulsion and confiscation applied to the rich by the poor for the benefit of the latter, but of wisely adapted and mutually beneficial and enjoyable adjustment of capacities and functions, willingly worked for and adopted by all, when the ideal of Proudhon shall be attained, and the rule shall be for every citizen: "From each according to his capacity; to each according to his need." This is obviously a return, at a more complicated social stage, to the principle of the family; therein are elders, equals, youngers, marking out stages of capacity; but this is reversed when we come to needs, for the needs of the younger are greater in proportion to their helplessness, their lack of capacity; the needs of the equals and elders diminish with increase of capacity. Hence the principle that the most unskilled work, the unpleasant drudgery, being devoid of honour and enjoyment, should be the shortest and best paid, while much of the remuneration of the equals should be in the interest, the enjoyment, in their work, and that of the elders in honour.

Gradually, and very slowly, the regulations necessary to accomplish this will fall into desuetude, having become unnecessary, and human society, by the consent of the Will to Good, embodied in many wills, shall reach the harmony of external nature, the perfect reign of Law, but Law springing from within, no longer from without. Put into a sentence: "Human evolution consists in bringing the separated wills of men into perfect accord with the Will of God, the individual wills with the Universal Will; the Will of God is first an external compulsion, finally an internal impulsion; outer laws give way to the inner Law." After all, what is this but the vision of the Prophet: "And they shall teach no more every man his neighbour and every man his brother, saying, Know the Lord; for they shall all know me, from the least of them unto the greatest of them" (*Jeremiah*, xxxi, 34). In this state will it be realised that God's "service is perfect freedom," because that which a man *ought* to do is that which he *wishes* to do, the Universal Will is one with the individual will.

Age must succeed age ere this great consummation can be reached. Yet we can see the grand unifying principle running like a golden thread through all the tangle of human efforts and struggles; we can see the most superficially opposing elements continuing to bring Humanity to the ultimate goal; we can discern the "soul of good in things evil," the purpose of each institution which appears and disappears as the great stream rolls on. In autocracy and tyranny, we can see a contribution to human progress, to be swept away when outgrown; in the most selfish Individualism, we can see the necessary development of strength; in the crudest Socialism, the germ of human Brotherhood; in the criminal actions of the modern anarchist the wild groping after the theory of philosophic Anarchism, as held by such men as Kropotkin and Tolstoy—the substitution of inner for outer authority, the rule of the omnipotent Divinity within each child of man.

From such a bird's eye view we may gain understanding, tolerance, encouragement, and we may see the Star of Hope shining over the dark tossing waves of conflict and of suffering. For in each imperfect stage the good survives and remains, while the evil perishes, for "Truth alone conquers, not falsehood". The mortal forms die, but the Eternal Spirit lives.

From this high flight of vision into the far, far-off future, let us come down to the ground of past and present happenings, and study Government in its nature and its general forms. The detail of the forms must come later.

THE NATURE OF GOVERNMENT

Government is the supreme Power in the State, incarnating its Sovereignty, its Authority, whencesoever that authority may be derived. It may base its claim to govern on "the Grace of God" or on the "Will of the People," or on any authority intermediate between these two poles. It is the embodied Will of the State, the executive activity, which carries out the plan laid down by the Wisdom of the State, embodied in the Legislature. Theoretically, the word Government should apply both to legislation and administration, since both have to do with the creation and working of the machinery of the State; but by a convention which we must understand, even if we disagree with it, the word is confined to the executive functions, and hence Aristotle makes Government and Administration synonymous (see above). If we look on the State as an organism, a body, then the Government is the organ of State Action, the arms which guide, the feet which move it. All State activities must be carried out by the Government, all State organisation must be effected by it; whatever its form, in whomsoever the Power of the State is embodied, the carrying out of the conclusions arrived at by the brain of the body politic must rest in the Government, hence rightly called the Executive. The whole administration of the State, from its highest to its lowest officer, is merely the machinery by which the Executive acts. But whether Government and executive should be equivalent terms we shall consider presently.

Hence it is said that the essence of Government resides in the power of compulsion; hence, again, it is said that Government rests on force. And this remains true, whatever the form of the Government, whencesoever its power is derived. The Government exercises external pressure on all who are within its jurisdiction; it compels obedience. Dr. Wilson puts this clearly and well:

> The essential characteristic of all Government, whatever its form, is authority. There must in every instance be, on the one hand, governors, and, on the other, those who are governed. And the authority of governors, directly or indirectly, rests in all cases ultimately on *force.* Government, in its last analysis, is organised force. Not necessarily or invariably organised, armed force, but the will of a few men, of many men, or of a community prepared by organisation to realise its own purposes with reference to the common affairs of the community. Organised, that is, to rule, to dominate. The machinery of government necessary to such an organisation consists of instrumentalities fitted to enforce in the conduct of the common affairs of a community the will of sovereign men: the sovereign minority, or the sovereign majority. (*loc. Cit.*, Chap. xiii, § 1387.)

This "force," Dr. Wilson points out, need not be armed force, nor force which is patent. "But there is a force behind them (governments) none the less because it never shows itself." That force may be "the free consent of the governed," "the force of an agreeing majority":

> The overwhelming nature of this force is evident in the fact that the minority very seldom challenge its exercise. It is latent just because it is understood to be omnipotent. There is force behind the authority of the elected magistrate, no less than behind that of the usurping despot, a much greater force behind the President of the United States than behind the Tsar of Russia. The difference lies in the display of coercive power. Physical force is the prop of both, though in the one it is the last, while in the other it is the first, resort. (*Ibid.*, § 1388.)

"SOVEREIGNTY"

Bluntschli apparently prefers to use the word "Sovereignty," or even "State" in preference to "Government". He says:

> The State is the embodiment and personification of the national power. This power, considered in its highest dignity and greatest force, is called Sovereignty... Gradually the name ceased to be given to mere branches of administration, and came to be

limited to the one highest ruling power in the State, and the conception was applied only to the concentrated power of the State. (*Loc. cit.*, Book VII, chap. i, p. 493)

Bluntschli, however, places this concentrated power not in what other writers call Government, but in the Legislature: "The legislative power is the normal manifestation of the Sovereignty of the State" (*Ibid.*, p. 509). His central conception is not "Government" but "Sovereignty". The Legislature is the normal manifestation of Sovereignty, and "all public powers depend in principle upon it: thus the constitution and legislation limit and arrange all other expressions of sovereignty" (*Ibid.*, Chap. iii, p. 509).

It will be seen that Bluntschli is here dealing with the question of the source of power, not of Government itself. No confusion need arise in the mind of the reader, if he understands that Bluntschli is not, in this, dealing with what other writers call Government, but with the source whence Government derives its power, and for this source the word Sovereignty is well employed. "Government" to him, as to Aristotle is "Administration". Legislation, he says, belongs "to the whole body politic," whereas other functions have special organs (*Ibid.*, Chap. vii, p. 520), hence it is the superior power; this is true, but rather as exercising thought, as the brain of the State, as the embodiment of such Wisdom as the State has reached. The "particular powers" with him are four: (1) Government or Administration; (2) Judiciary; (3) Care of the intellectual elements of civilisation; (4) Care of the material interests (*Ibid.*, pp. 521, 524). Government to him also, is the ruling power (*Ibid.*, p. 523). The student will do well to master Bluntschli's analysis, as it is suggestive, without binding himself to its terms. It is essential to grasp principles, differences and likenesses, and then words cease to confuse.

Seeley defines Government as "a power of constraint, or compulsion, exercised by means of punishment" (*Loc. cit.*, Lecture v, p. 109). Hence he makes Government the opposite of Liberty. He considers "the essence of it to lie in the imposition of his will by one man upon another, so that A does under fear of punishment not what A but B wills to do" (*Loc. cit.*, Lecture vii, p. 153). This is a very general view of the meaning of Government, though it is seldom put quite so sharply and lucidly. I think we need a very different view, if we are to meet the needs of the Nations.

WHAT IS "GOVERNMENT"?

Let us consider what is the object of Government, as a help to defining Government. Some say, the establishment of Justice among the citizens. Others say, the Welfare of the State. The word "welfare" is obviously inclusive, since justice and other elements of peaceful and happy living are all included therein. The Common Weal is the object of Government. Let us join with this the idea that Government is the Will of the State, and remember that Will is expressed in the outer world by Activity. Let us see in the Legislature, the law-making wisdom of the State; in the Judiciary, the calm and balanced Intellect of the State. Then as in a man, the Spirit, the Unit of Consciousness, expresses its Self in three ways, by Will, by Wisdom, by Intellect, and these have their manifestation in the physical body as Action, Emotion, and Thought, so in the organic life of men as a State, the Spirit, the source of the Sovereignty of the State, is the People—more or less imperfectly vocal in fractions thereof—and that Sovereignty expresses its Self in the same three ways, Will, Wisdom, Intellect, and these have their manifestation in the body politic as the Executive, the Legislature, the Judiciary. All three might rightly be called the Government of the State, for all, as a matter of fact, do govern, and each is a branch of Government, not the whole of it. The executive carries out the laws made by the Legislature, the Judiciary decides, when dispute arises, the meaning of the laws. Each is a function of Government, an expression of the Sovereignty of the People. Hence I should prefer to use the word "Government" for this Triplicity in Unity, and designate as the "Executive" the embodiment of the Will, the Power, of the People in Action, and I shall use the word here as denoting the group of persons exercising that function of Activity in a Nation, and using the machinery of administration. Taking this view, the pair of opposites stated by Seeley, Government and Liberty, disappears.

It is interesting to note that this triplicity in a Government is recognised by Aristotle, although he speaks, in one place, of

Government being equivalent to Administration. In Book IV, Chapter xiv, he speaks of the principles belonging to all Governments, and says:

> The first of these is the public assembly; the second the officers of the State... the third the judicial department.

The Public Assembly determines war and peace, enacts laws, calls the officers to account, etc. The officers are chosen in various ways, by vote, by lot, etc., and carry on the business of the State. The Judges are also chosen in a similar way. We have here the Legislature, with unlimited powers; the Executive responsible to it; the Judiciary. We have here the Legislature identified with Sovereignty, since the citizens as a whole formed the legislative body. It is interesting to notice that this body calls the officers "to account, for their behaviour when in office," i.e., he rightly regards the Executive as responsible to the Legislature.

The triplicity of the Government has also been recognised in later times. Montesquieu is quoted by Bluntschli as the first to enounce the modern principle (of the separation of functions) with emphasis and effect. He demands in the name of civic freedom and security that different public functions should be exercised by different persons. "If (says Montesquieu) legislative and executive powers are united in the same person, or even in the same body of magistrates, there is no liberty, because people are afraid that the monarch or the senate may make tyrannical laws in order to administer them tyrannically. There is no liberty, again if the judicial power is not separated from the legislative and executive; if it is joined to the legislative power, the life and death of the citizens may be arbitrarily disposed of, for the judge will be legislator; if it be joined to the executive power, the judge may have the force of an oppressor." (*Esprit des Lois,* xi, 6, quoted by Bluntschli, Book VII, Chapter vii, p. 518.)

Montesquieu makes the threefold division into Legislature, Executive and Judiciary, and it is widely accepted by writers on Political Science. In England the independence of the Judiciary is acknowledged by all parties; in India, though under British rule, the Executive and Judicial functions are united in the magistracy, and hence, for the reasons given by Montesquieu, "there is no liberty," and politics are imported into the lower magistracy, and the opponents of the bureaucratic form of government are harried by the bureaucrat as magistrate. This is one of the abuses that the National Congress has worked at from the beginning of its career, and which has been condemned in the House of Commons, but continues to exist. So also laws are made by the "machinery of autocracy" (Montague-Chelmsford *Report*, para 289), and administered by another part of the same machinery, to the manifest danger of the public. It is well that you should recognise that the principle of government admitted in all civilised countries is disregarded here.

In the Republic of the United States of America, this principle is embodied in the Constitution. There is a Congress which makes the laws; a President, who is the Executive; and a Supreme Court which determines the legality of the actions of the citizen, and the local (State) and Federal Governments. The machinery of Government is created by statute, but no statute can go outside the Constitution.

The three functions of Government, the making of laws, the decision of laws, the execution of laws, may all be exercised by one person, the Ruler of the State—Aristotle's "one person". Or they may be lodged in a group of persons, his "few". Or in a varying majority of, or all, citizens, his "many," the "citizens at large". These we shall consider.

THE SPHERE OF GOVERNMENT

On the "sphere of Government" endless disputes have arisen. What is the sphere of the Government, or collective, action, and what the sphere of individual action? It should be obvious that this must depend on the conditions existing in each State. The common answer seems to me to be: Everything which, under existing conditions, can be better done collectively than individually, should be done by the Government; everything which can be better done individually than collectively should be done by the individual. By "better done" is meant "conduces to the greater welfare of the Nation".

There is not likely to be an immediate unanimity of opinion on the relative superiority in a particular case of collective or individual action. But the principle may be laid down. Unanimity can only be reached by experience. Under "government by the people" much more can with advantage be done collectively than under an oligarchy or a bureaucracy. For instance in a country where free institutions prevail, it is a great convenience to have State postal and telegraphic services. In a country ruled by a bureaucracy, which suspects its subjects, opens their letters, and suppresses letters and telegrams at its whim, to injure those whom it dislikes or to pry into their private affairs, private services run for profit—side by side with the State services—would be preferable, because more reliable.

The representatives of the people in the Legislature must, of course, decide on the services in which, considering all the actual conditions, collective action would conduce to the benefit of all better than individual action. The greater the approach to the Ideal State, in which every adult has a voice in choosing the Government, the safer and more beneficial becomes collective action. So long as there is class representation and class legislation, so long is collective action liable to injure the unrepresented classes.

INDIVIDUALISM AND SOCIALISM

In modern western States the tendency is towards an increasing socialisation of the State, i.e., the substitution of collective for individual control. Individualism, regarding Government as opposed to Liberty, minimises executive action as far as possible, and therefore prefers to leave in private hands the means of production, land, capital, and labour. It would not restrict private ownership in land and capital, and would leave the owners of these to complete for labour—land and capital being unproductive and unremunerative without labour. The labourers, having neither land nor capital, cannot utilise their labour for themselves, but can only sell it to the highest bidder. Competition thus becomes necessary, and the State remains in a condition of perpetual internal conflict, of class war, the landlord and the capitalist in one army—few but all-powerful, because holding the means of subsistence and the landless and capital-less on the other—numerous but helpless, their choice being between acceptance of the price offered for their labour and death by starvation. There is, of course, a third possibility: owing to their immense numerical superiority, they can rise in revolt, and seize the means of subsistence. But against this method of remedying their ills have to be set the facts that the few control the armed force of the Nation, that many of themselves would side with the owners in the hope of bettering their own condition without danger of being massacred, and the most fatal obstacle of all, their own ignorance, and consequent inability to produce without direction and supervision, even if they had seised both land and capital. It may be said also, in passing, that capital is not so easy to seize, consisting very largely as it does of credit, not of bullion, and even bullion not being immediately edible, whereas hunger is immediate. As this last inability gradually disappears through the spread of education, the maintenance of the Individualistic system becomes more difficult. The system connotes the co-existence of great wealth and terrible poverty, of palaces and slums, of idleness and overwork, and thus contains within itself the seed of its own disintegration. It is also very costly and wasteful, the continual competition between class and class, individual and individual, entailing continual unnecessary expenditure and ceaseless friction; it is, as often said, a perpetual State of social war, sometimes open, as in strikes and lock-outs, sometimes under the surface, smouldering hatreds and suspicions.

The opposite system is that of Socialism, ranging from the taking over by the Executive, on behalf of the Nation, of the ownership of land, working capital and the means of communication, to the negation of all private property. Its many schools must be studied later; the general indication may suffice for the moment. In this direction the modern world is moving. There has been much municipalising of town conveniences in England in the most progressive towns; water has long been supplied and a tax levied for it; gas or electric lighting has been added in many; public baths exist in many places; this addition of new conveniences has been quietly going on for many years, and

"Municipal Socialism" is largely accepted. Municipalities are concerning themselves with medical relief, child welfare, the care of mothers, and the like, it being recognised that the improvement of the conditions of the poor is a National necessity; human Brotherhood, or human solidarity, is being acknowledged as a fact in Nature, that Nations ignore at their peril.

The War, in these matters, has worked a revolution in men's minds. Under the stern pressure of necessity, the Executive has taken over the control of National resources, of means of transit, and largely of the production and distribution of the necessaries of life, and of all things needed for the maintenance of National defence. That which has been learned in time of War and found to be useful is likely to be practised also in time of Peace.

FORMS OF STATES

To return to States and their Governments. We have seen the distinction on which so much stress is laid by western writers between the City State and the Country State: in the first, the citizens ruled through an Assembly consisting of themselves, the Ecclesia; in the second, two forms of Government necessarily arose, local and National. The Country State grew by aggregations of villages into districts, provinces or shires—larger and larger areas—and thus into Kingdoms like the English Heptarchy, and then into a larger Kingdom or Empire. In these, the older Governments became local as the central and more inclusive Government was established. Seeley agrees in the division of Country States into two chief forms, the "unitary" and the "federal," but divides each of these into two: the unitary into the "centralised," and the "decentralised" according as the local government exercises important functions or is reduced almost to impotency; the federal into two—the "Federal State" and the "System of Confederate States". The United States of America is a Federal State, in which there is a strong central Government, with clearly defined functions, presiding over well-organised States, each of which has its own State Government. In the second, the Central Government is feeble and shadowy, and the System cannot rightly be called "a State". The Holy Roman Empire is given as an example. He gives a convenient summary of these divisions:

I. The City State—Local Government none.

II. The Country State.

(a) Centralised Unitary—L.G. small.

(b) Decentralised Unitary—L.G. considerable.

(c) Federal State—L.G. predominant.

(d) System of Confederate States—L.G. all-powerful. (*Loc. cit.*, 1st series, Lecture iv, pp. 88-100.)

Professor Seeley (*Loc. cit.*, Lecture vii, pp. 156-167) regards the City State as governed by its citizens, and the Country or Nation State as governed by representatives, and speaks of the latter as Government by majority, and speaks of representation as "scarcely known to the ancient world" —an extraordinary blunder, due to his unfortunate ignorance of the East. The principle of representation was, in fact, inherent in Aryan social life. The Gramani represented his village in certain functions; the father represented the family, bound it by his contracts and could be sued for its debts; the priest represented the worshippers, acted on their behalf; it therefore came quite naturally to the Aryan to utilise this principle in matters of Government, the moment that participants in a function became inconveniently numerous.

FORMS OF GOVERNMENT

No country, perhaps, has made so many experiments in Forms of Government as has India. The immense age of her civilisation, its stability through millennia, despite wars, invasions, forays and raids; its survival down to the present day, after a century and a half of a foreign yoke; all these testify to the genius of the Indian peoples for Self-Government and to their vitality as a Nation.

We have seen that the Village Council, the unit of local self-government, endured from an unknown period before the Christian era down to nineteen centuries after it; this had developed naturally from the Patriarchal Family.

Of this, Dr. Banerjea writes:

> From very early times, the reverence for family ties was firmly established and held sacred in India. The family was like a small communistic society, bound together by the tie of natural affection, holding in joint possession the means of production, and enjoying the fruit of labour in common. All acquisitions were joint property, and all expenses were paid out of the common fund. The Joint Family was, in fact, very similar to the *societas universorum bonorum* of the Romans. The father was the head and protector of the family. But just as the dependent members owed their duties to the father, so the father was bound by obligations to the rest of the family. Unlike the Roman *paterfamilias*, the father of the Indian family had no powers of life and death over the subordinate members. The family was not his property. Every individual member of the family had a *locus standi* in the law courts and the other departments of the State; and the government could, if it thought fit, deal direct with every member of the family without the intervention of the head. As regards the family property, the father was the manager, rather than the owner of it. The family collectively was the owner, and the father had powers to deal with it only as the representative of the family; but even here, his powers were not unlimited. The members of the family were the father, the mother, sons, daughters, daughters-in-law, brothers, sisters, and other dependent relations. (*Loc. cit.*, Chap. ii, pp.24, 25.)

This Joint Family still persists, but is gradually breaking up under the stress of western influence and individualism. It shows an essential difference between Indian and European society; the Indian idea of society is an enlarged family, but a family in the Indian sense, not in the European, which was based on the Roman family. In the latter, the father was an absolute Monarch, owning the family and its property. In the former the father was the head and the administrator, but the family was a system of mutual obligations, by which each member was equally bound, and the father was legally, as well as morally, held responsible for his administration. This fundamental difference runs through the systems of Government. The family was the unit, not the isolated member; the family had rights, the members duties, obligations. The family was continuous: it had existed in the past, was existing in the present, would exist in the future; the members were ever changing. The family inherited from the past, preserved and increased in the present, bequeathed to the future. It is the true model for National organisation, and the idea is revived in Modern Socialism. Europe is returning in Modern Socialism to the old Indian ideal of the State.

The position of the Monarch in India and in Europe grew out of this same difference between Indian and Roman thought. In India, the "absolute Monarch" was an excrescence and an exception, as we shall see; his duties, as laid down were burdensome and his power limited: he was to act only with his Council; he had a right only to a share of the produce of the land in exchange for protection; and, if he proved too troublesome, he was dethroned. In Europe, the Monarch was the owner of the land, could give a portion of it to any subject, it being his by conquest by himself or his ancestors, and the early village communities were gradually ousted—though not completely—and first the barons, then the burghers, then the masses, had to acquire rights by conflict, limiting the royal power. Europeans, coming to India, brought with them their ideas based on feudalism, and ascribed to Indian Monarchs the absolutism and property in land never sanctioned by Indian law nor by Indian custom, though occasionally usurped by bad Monarchs, and frequently punished by their overthrow.

The word "janah," or "kula," was originally used for family, but gradually was applied to the tribe or Nation, and the Aryans, invading India and settling in the north, were spoken of as the "Pancha-janah," five tribes, or five Nations. These were divided into clans, the vishah, and these again into branches, shakhah or gotrah.

The first two are mentioned by Dr. Banerjea (p. 15). Baden-Powell (*Loc. cit.*, p.p. 194, 195) has a useful sketch, mentioning these terms, but using "shakkah" as equivalent to "vishah," and calling the sub-division of the clan, blood relations, "janman," quoting Zimmer. He mentions also the Gramani, head of a village, the Vishpati, chief of a clan, the Raja, or Monarch, who is evidently not independent of some great popular assembly; and affairs seem generally to have been managed by councils of the tribe—of the clan or of smaller groups, for more than one distinct term is used. The Sabha apears to be the council of the minor clan, or other limited group; the Samiti would be a larger gathering of the clan or tribe over which the King presides—rather, however, as *primus inter pares*.

The Kingship, he says, was hereditary, but sometimes elective. As he points out, the transition to later forms of Monarchy is natural. The King, as territories expand, is the central authority; the Chiefs take charge of districts; the frontiers are guarded by the 'Senapati, the Commander of the army.

As families became grouped and settled down together into villages, the heads of the households naturally formed the Council, for managing the common affairs of the village, till they grew too numerous for business meetings. Then, as we have already seen—*pace* Professor Seeley—the quite natural and obvious device of choosing representatives was adopted, and the whole village elected them, either by a unanimous vote, by acclamation, or by a majority, the minority yielding, or by lot out of the duly qualified persons. When the village became inconveniently large for management by a single body, executive committees were formed as already stated. As villages were grouped into districts, and as districts grew numerous, some formed Republics, while larger groups consolidated into Kingdoms. In both, however two types of Government persisted, the General Assembly of the citizens, the "Samiti," and the smaller Executive Council, the Sabha. Questions of general policy were referred to and decided by the Samiti—"that that which concerned all should be judged by all," as Edward I of England wisely said; in fact reference to the Samiti was a kind of referendum, as used in modern times; but it had also an inherent power of legislating, though the great body of law had been laid down in the ancient Smritis, and a new law was only needed where quite new circumstances had arisen. Where Kings were elected, they were elected by the Samiti, as says a shloka in the *Atharva Veda*: "All the Vishah elect you......The Assembly makes you King" (Raja). Even where Kingship was hereditary in a family, and the King chose his successor from among his own sons, his choice was, sometimes at least, submitted to the Assembly, as in the choice of Shri Ramachandra by his father, King Dashratha called first his princes and nobles, and asked their opinions, lest his affection should have swayed his judgement, and then the citizens were called together, and the Brahmanas, the chiefs of the army and the citizens took counsel together, being warned by the King not to allow his wishes to sway their decision. Their final answer was:

> Speedily instal thy son, endowed with noble qualities, resembling the God of Gods, ever intent upon the welfare of the whole State. (*Ramayana*, Ayodhyakandam, § ii.)

Only then did the King order the enthroning, and inform his son of the decision of himself and his councillors.

In his very valuable *Introduction to Hindu Polity,* Mr. Kashi Prasad Jayaswal, M.A. (Oxon.), has the following:

> In Vedic times the Hindu Society was divided into tribes, or jana, and the members of the tribe were called Visah (visha:), from which the word vaisya (one of the people—the commoner) is derived. The entire corpus of the Visah used to meet together (samiti) to deliberate on public matters in their folk-assembly, the samiti. In the assembly all the visah were taken to be present, for there, the principle of representation was not operative. (*Loc. cit.*, p. 2. Reprinted from the *Modern Review.*)

The writer speaks of:

> Another association, which was smaller than the Samiti, and which seems to have differentiated from the Samiti. It was called the Sabha. In a song of the *Atharva Veda*, Samiti and Sabha are described as two sisters. It seems that the Sabha, on behalf of the assembly or the folk (abhijana) looked after certain public matters. (*Ibid*).

Out of the villages and districts, as just said, Republics and Kigdoms were formed, but Councils are found in both.

The same dual system of Councils prevailed also in the West, but modified in various ways. The large body elected by the people, or by a part of the people, became the House of Representatives, and a second House, or Senate, was composed in Kingdoms of nobles and distinguished men chosen by the Ruler, or of representatives of local bodies, or restricted electorates, under Republics. Some form of bi-cameral Legislature is almost universal.

We shall proceed to consider briefly these two main forms of Government, Republics and Kingdoms, in East and West, by "one," "few" or "many".

We proceed to consider the two chief Forms of Government in East and West, again taking India as representing the East.

THE EAST

Republics

On the general question of the existence of Republics in India, there can be but one answer, but few recognise how widely republican forms of Government had spread. In speaking of the dynasties before Alexander, 600 B.C. to 323 B.C., Mr. Dutt (*Ancient Civilisation in India*, p. 144) recalls Mr. Vincent Smith's statement:

> The settled country between the Himalayan mountains and the Narbada river was divided into a multitude of independent states, some monarchies and some tribal republics, owing no allegiance to any paramount power, secluded from the outer world, and free to fight among themselves.

He also notes that in Huen Tsang's account of Kapilavastu, we find the remark that there was no King in the country, but that each town appointed its own ruler.

Republics are called Sangha or Gana; some of the latter are also termed Gana-rayani, "States ruled by the whole community". Mr. Jayaswal points out that translators and commentators have used the word Gana as corporation, and also as associations of craftsmen and traders, though the latter are called by other and specific names. He quotes from the *Mahabharata* (Shanti Parva, cvii, 6—8 and 19), showing that Ganas conquer enemies, gain allies, use espionage, shape policy, and collect revenue for the exchequer—all actions of States, not of associations within States

(*Loc. cit.*, p. 3, note). Kautilya (*Loc. cit.*, Book XI, Chap. I, pp. 455—459) speaks of Sanghas of warriors in Khambhoja, Sanrashtra and other countries living by agriculture, trade and wielding weapons, and of the Sanghas of Licchivika, Vrijika, Mallaka and others which claim the title of raja; these are known to have been Republics, and to have called their citizens Rajana: king-people. Kautilya advises Kings to ally themselves with these, as the acquisition of their help "is better than the acquisition of an army, a friend, or profits" (p. 455 § 376). Mr. Jayaswal mentions Panini as speaking of Yandheyas as a Sangha "living by the profession of arms," and "these Yandheyas we know from numismatic and lithic inscriptions to have been a republican community" (*Loc. cit.*, p. 4). He quotes the *Kasika Commentary* as mentioning Kshudrahas, Malavas, and Mallas as Sanghas, and these are known to have been Republican. He refers also to the Republics mentioned by Greeks (spoken of in Lecture II, p.28, and Lecture III, p.59), and then quotes Indian testimony. The Republic of the Yadavas, he says, was called "Svarajya," or "Svarat," "one's own State", and he notes that Shri Krshna was objected to by Shishupala as being present among crowned heads though not a King. The *Aitareya Brahmana* (VII, iii, 14) speaks of the Bhoja and Svarat constitutions as Vairrajya or Kingless, and says that amongst the Uttara Kurus and the Uttara Madras "the whole community is consecrated to rulership"; Monarchy is said to be confined to the Middle Country and the East. The Lord Buddha speaks of "the free communities (of His neighbourhood) with admiration and affection," and gave similar advice to the Vajjians and to His own Bikkhus, His Sangha being modelled on their lines. The Republics had Councils of Elders, and some had families who held hereditary functions—aristocracies and oligarchies, to borrow the Greek terms. They had also General Assemblies, the Lord Buddha advising full and frequent gathering of these. Kautilya and other statesmen disliked them, and endeavoured to incorporate them in Kingdoms and Empires, and they gradually disappeared, a few lingering to about 300 Vikrama Samvat. (Summarised from pp. 3—7 of Mr. Jayaswal's monograph.) Dr. Banerjea also puts the disappearance of Republican forms of Government at the fourth century A.D.

Very interesting are the remarks of the Lord Buddha on the Vajjian Sangha, or Republic. When Ajatashatru sent to Him to ask His advice, when he thought of attacking the Vajjians (Vrijikas), the Lord asked Ananda: "Have you heard, Ananda, that the Vajjians hold full and frequent assemblies?" "Lord, so have I heard," said he. "So long, Ananda," rejoined the Blessed One, "as the Vajjians hold full and frequent assemblies, so long may they be expected not to decline but to prosper. So long, Ananda, as the Vajjians meet together in concord and rise in concord, and carry out their undertakings in concord, so long as they enact nothing not already established, abrogate nothing that has been established, and act in accordance with the ancient institutions of the Vajjians as established in former days—so long as they honour, esteem and revere and support the Vajjian Elders and hold it a point of duty to hearken to their words... so long may the Vajjians be expected not to decline, but to prosper." (Quoted from the *Mahaparnibbana Suttanta*, by Dr. Banerjea, *loc. cit.*, Chap. viii, pp. 95, 96.)

Some further useful indications are gathered by noting the methods of voting in the Buddhist Sangha, so obviously modelled on the political Sanghas. (It is a matter of extraordinary interest that the Lord Buddha seems to have strongly approved of popular Government, and his whole religion is profoundly democratic in character. We have already noted His remarks on the Vajjian Republic, and we have now to see how the arrangements for the management of affairs in His Sangha followed most closely those of the Republics around Him in the conduct of public business.) When a question arose in the Sangha for discussion, and a resolution to take action was proposed, the vote thereupon had to be taken three times, those approving keeping silence, those opposing speaking. When all kept silence, it was declared to be passed. If any spoke, then the vote was decided by a majority, the procedure being called "Ye-bhuyyasikam," "Those-more-procedure" —"The majority procedure". (Here again we may note the falsity of the statement that the Greeks invented the majority vote, for we find it used here in the time of the Lord Buddha, and used, not as a new thing but as a well-established custom.) The voting was done by coloured tickets, usually made of wood, and might be open or secret.

"According to the larger number of the Bhikkus who are guided by the Dhamma shall speak, so shall the case be decided" (*Challavagga*, IV, xiv, 24). A teller was appointed who distributed the tickets and collected them. Minute rules are given for contingencies, and it is noticeable that the Lord Buddha used all the technical terms of the Republican Sanghas in His directions, as being evidently well known. (Summarised with the exception of the sentences within brackets, from Jayaswal, pp. 8-10.) Mr. Jayaswal concludes this part of his exposition by noting that the Kurus and the Panchalas formed themselves into Sanghas, their old dynasties having disappeared, by the fourth century B.C., and that the Videhas became a Republic after having been a Kingdom, in the sixth century, B.C.

Thus we have about the sixth to fourth centuries B.C. the stage when Republics were *founded designedly*, that is, the primitive "tribal stage" had been long passed over—a conclusion to which we would be brought also by the principles underlying the procedure and the principle of the separation of functions and powers. (*Ibid*., p. 11.)

MONARCHY

As Republics grew readily out of villages and groups of villages, in the well-watered and mountain-subdivided tracts of northern and western India, where communications were difficult, so did Monarchy readily develop from the larger village-groupings of the plains, and the heads of small tribes easily became nobles of the strongest among them, who took the title of Raja, King. The rise of Monarchy, according to Indian traditions from very ancient times, was due to the prevalence of oppression of the weaker by the more powerful. Then the people appealed to Vaivasvata Manu, and He became their King. We read of Divine Kings and happy peoples, and in the Smriti find kingdoms minutely organised and evidently of long standing. Manu's *Institutes*, after the brief statement that when "creatures, being without a King, through fear dispersed in all directions, the Lord created a King for the protection of this whole" (*Loc. cit*., Chap. vii. 3), plunge into the importance and the duties of a King. He cannot govern alone, but must have ministers (55-59); if he oppresses his Kingdom, he and his relatives will soon lose life and Kingdom (111, 112); his taxes must be moderate, the eighth, sixth, or twelfth part of the crops (128-132); mechanics, artisans and manual labourers should give one day a month to the King, and those who live by traffic a "trifle, annually" (137, 138). His duties were exacting and almost endless; for he was the Chief of the Executive, and responsibility, though not full power, was on him finally for good government.

The existence of a Council was held to be vital—Kautilya says: "Kingship is possible only with assistance. A single wheel can never move. Hence he shall employ ministers, and hear their opinion" (*Loc. cit.*, Book I, Chap. vii, § 13, p.14) —but opinions differ on the best number of councillors; the school of Manu say twelve, of Brihaspati sixteen, of Ushanas twenty, but Kautilya concludes in favour "of as many members as the needs of his dominion require" (*Loc. cit.*, Book I, Chap. xv, § 29, pp. 32, 33). The final decision rested nominally with the King, who sent his order in writing to the officials, but the order bore his seal, without which it was not valid: "For it was the signet which was king, and not the personal king," quotes Mr. Jayaswal from the *Panchatantra*, ii, 290. He points out that the seals of the departmental ministers were also necessary, and that "the royal order was thus the order of the ministers" (*Loc. cit.*, p. 19).

The *Shukranīti* gives details on this:

> The King, after seeing and studying the document, should place his handwriting wherever he likes. The Mantri, Chief Justice, Learned Adviser as well as Ambassador should write: "This document has been written with my consent." The Amatya should write: "Well-written is this." The Sumantra then should write: "Well considered." The Pradhana should write: "True." The Pratinidhi is to write: "It can now be approved." The Crown Prince should write: "It should be accepted." And the Priest is to write: "Approved." They should put down their seals over it at the end of the writing. And the King is to write and sign: "Accepted." As it is not possible for the King to see fully all details owing to the pressure of work (multiplicity of duties), the documents are generally to be examined by the Crown Prince and other advisers,

who are to write upon it with their seals. And the King should at once write: "Seen." (*Loc. cit.*, Chap. ii, 729-744.)

(The *Shukranīti* dates from the eighth century A.D., not from an early age. Megasthenes gives somewhat the same testimony as to ministerial power in the fourth century B.C.)

It will thus be seen that the Ministers were in a position to go counter to the King, and cases are on record in which they over-ruled the King's wish, showing that their power was a real one and was exercised. It is, of course, possible that a head-strong King might go against his Ministers, but it must also be remembered that the Ministers could, and sometimes did, depose him. On this Mr. Jayaswal writes:

> A more effective bridle to royal despotism consisted in the Council of Ministers. The origin of the Hindu ministry is unique in social history. *It was not a creation of the monarch.* Ministers are already in existence when the king is elected. The king-elect, it is laid down in the *Shatapatha Brahmana* and elsewhere, had to go to the house of the respective Ratnins or High Functionaries, Treasurer, Master of Forests, etc., to offer them *havi*. These are addressed by the king-elect, "O you kings." They are also called *king-makers*, rajakrita, a term which is applied to ministers in the early Buddhist sutras and *Ramayana*. Hindu ministers are the Vedic Ratnins, who were an outcome of the Vedic Sabha to the Samiti. The Mantri, or mantri-Sabha or mantri-parishat thus was a popular institution of the Hindus in its origin and throughout Hindu history it maintained its independence and integrity in a wonderful manner. The history of the council of ministers is the purest, to my mind, among our social institutions.
>
> It is a law and a principle of Hindu politics that the king cannot act without the approval and co-operation of the council of ministers. The law-sutras, the law-books, the political treatises are unanimous on the point. Even in the edicts of Ashoka, the highest type of Hindu despot, we find the parishat (which I take to have been the mantri-parishat, Rock Edict VI[2]) mentioned as a body and probably as opposing the king. Edicts addressed to royal princes as governors of provinces are addressed to the Prince-and-his-ministers. All the grants published in Ceylonese inscriptions are made by His Majesty and his council of ministers. When the

> ministers found a worthless monarch on the throne they deposed him and put another in his place. When King Dasharatha is dead (according to the view prevalent in the first century B.C.), the ministers are said to hold a council and decided that some one of the Ikshvakus must be appointed King immediately (A. 67.8). Instances of their opposition to illegal tendencies in the king are numerous. Radhagupta closed the treasury to Ashoka when he wanted to squander away public money on Buddhist monasteries in his senility. Rudradaman in his inscription states that his council and ministers for public works opposed the proposed repairing of the Sudarshana lake at Girnar, whereupon he had it repaired out of his private purse. I could give you other interesting instances if time allowed. (*Loc. cit.*, pp. 18, 19.)

Dr. Banerjea takes much the same view. He regards the Hindu kingdom as a "limited monarchy".

The King had to abide by the law as laid down in the Shastras or embodied in the customs of the country. In the practical work of administration he was guided by his ministers, who occupied an important position in Society and wielded the real power in the State. Then there was the influence of the learned Brahmanas as a class, who were looked upon by the people as the natural guardians of society. With these checks operating on the governmental system it was very difficult for a king to have his own way in the administration of the country. (*Loc. cit.*, Chap. v, p. 50.)

Again:

> The Council was the chief administrative authority in the kingdom. The King was supposed not to do anything without the consent of the Council. All ordinances were perhaps sanctioned by the Council. It possessed immense powers and enjoyed a great deal of independence. In exceptional cases it had even the power to elect the King. (*Loc. cit.*, Chap. viii, p. 103.)

In the Kingdom of Kerala there were five Assemblies, of the People, of Priests, of Physicians, of Astrologers, of Ministers (*Ibid.*, p. 105).

The rule of the Monarch, whether in Empire or Kingdom, was thus hedged round with many limitations. First, there were the

Shastras, the Law above the King; then there was his Council; public opinion was a very real check. Then there was his election, or confirmation of hereditary claim by the people, at his coronation. There was his self-pronounced curse, if he became a tyrant, that he invoked the destruction of all the good he had done, of his place in heaven, his life and his progeny "if I oppress you" (*Aitareya Brahmana*). There was his Coronation oath:

I shall see to the growth of the country, considering it always as Brahma. Whatever law there is here, and whatever is dictated by dharma, and whatever is not opposed to policy, I will act according to. I shall never act arbitrarily. (*Mahabharata*, Shanti Parva, lix, 106-7.)

Moreover the carrying out of the oath was by no means disregarded. Brihadratha, says Mr. Jayaswal, was removed from the throne, for being weak in his oath; and Naga-dasaka was deposed for parricide (*Loc. cit*., p. 17). Kautilya mentions the names of eleven Monarchs who were put to death for various crimes, "these and other several kings" (*Loc. cit*., Book I, Chap. vi, pp.12, 13). Manu mentions five others (*Loc. cit*., Chap. vii, 41). Mr. Dutt, in his *Civilisation of Ancient India* (Vol. I, Chap. iv, p. 221) gives the following quotation from the *Mahavamsa* (translated by George Turnour, revised by L.C. Wyesinha, 1889.) It shows a peculiarly detestable family, which finally outwore the patience of the people over whom it ruled, and was put an end to, by no means too soon. The quotation runs:

Udayibhaddaka, the perfidiously impious son of Ajata Satru, having put his parent to death reigned sixteen years. Anirudhaka, the son of Udayibhaddaka, having put him to death; and the son of Aniruddhaka, named Munda having put him to death; these perfidious, unwise princes in succession ruled. In the reigns of these two monarchs eight years elapsed. The impious Nagadasaka, son of Munda, having put his father to death, reigned twenty-four years. The populace at the capital, infuriated at such conduct, designating this a "parricidal race," assembled, and formally deposed Nagadasaka; and desirous of gratifying the whole nation, they unanimously installed in the sovereignty the eminently wise minister, bearing the historically distinguished appellation of Susunaga. He reigned eighteen years. His son Kalasoka reigned twenty years. Thus, in the tenth year of the reign of King Kalasoka, a century had elapsed from the death of Buddha.

Nor was drastic treatment of a bad King merely due to popular indignation. The *Shukraniti* lays it down as a principle, that:

> If the king be an enemy of virtue, morality and strength, people should desert him as the ruiner of the State. In his place, for the maintenance of the State, the priest with the consent of the ministers, should instal one who belongs to his family and is qualified. (*Loc. cit.*, Chap. ii, § 549-552, p. 89.)

Again:

> The king who does not perform his civic duties well has undoubtedly to rot in hell. (*Ibid.*, Chap. IV, section v, 16, 17.)

The idea in § 549 above is still carried out among the Lushai, a Tibeto-Burman tribe; for Mr. Baden-Powell quotes a paper by Captain Shakespear, as saying: "An incompetent village chief is removable by the voice of the villagers; or rather the villagers will desert the chief, and build a new village (the bamboo structures are easily replaced), on another site." (Baden-Powel, *Loc. cit.*, Chap. IV, section i, p. 144.)

Hindu history and Hindu laws are apparently quite unknown to western writers, who blandly inform us that, until the British came, Indians had only known absolute Monarchs. Indians have had bad Monarchs, like every other people, and have sometimes endured them—did not England put up with Henry VIII?—sometimes put them to death, sometimes merely deposed them. It may be admitted that Indians, at least, should know something of Political Science, as deduced from their own history and practised in their own country.

In such an Empire as that of Chandragupta Maurya, in the fourth century B.C., we see the detail of administration as carefully organised as in the eighth century A.D. and on the same general lines. There were two great branches of the Central Government, Military and Civil. The Military Department, according to Megasthenes, had a Council of 30 members, divided into 6 Boards of 5 members each, respectively controlling: Admiralty; Transport and Commissariat; Infantry; Cavalry; War-Chariots; Elephants. On the Civil side was a similar organisation, that of the Municipality of Pataliputra being described: Six Boards, supervising industrial matters, wages, etc.; looking-after foreigners, Vincent Smith remarks on the provision of Consuls, showing that the Empire "was in constant intercourse with foreign States; next, registration of births and deaths as a basis of taxation; then trade, and keeping the standard weights and measures, compulsory on all; next, superintendence of manufactures; lastly, collectors of tithe-tax on value of all goods sold. Markets, harbours, temples, etc., were in charge of the Municipality. The States grew in size, as said, in the plains, and the idea of a paramount Sovereign over many States, which were ruled by their own Kings, was well recognised by the horse-sacrifice, mentioned in the Itihasa. Such a Sovereignty was of the nature of a compliment acknowledged by the paying of tribute, rather than of the extension of a central administration, Dr. Banerjea regards it as a kind of offensive and defensive alliance among the Kings, with the strongest as a nominal Suzerain (*Loc. cit.*, Chap. v, p. 4-8), and it seems to have been little more; Professor Seeley would probably classify it as a System of Confederate States. Mr. Jayaswal calls it "the First Imperial System of the Hindus" (*Loc. cit.*, p.14), and regards it as pre-classical, i.e., before 1,500 B.C. In the *Aitereya Brahmana* (100 B.C.), he recognises a second type of Empire, a "Monarchical Imperialism," stretching over the Gangetic plain to the Bay of Bengal, "a single Monarch up to the ocean," and he thinks it originated in Magadha, and aimed at the inclusion of a number of States predominantly Shudra, i.e., inhabited by mixed Aryan-Kolarian races (*Loc. cit.*, pp. 14, 15). This aimed at an effective central authority, and had gone far along the road to it from Mahapadma Nanda, the founder of the Nanda dynasty in Magadha to the overthrow of its last Monarch, and the placing on the throne of Chandragupta Maurya, under whom, with the help of his Minister Kautilya, or Chanakya, we have the picture of an Imperial Administration, improved still more by Bindusara and Ashoka. Dr. Banerjea says:

> The home province was under the control of the central Executive, while distant provinces were administered by Viceroys or Governors sent out from the capital. In Asoka's time there were four or five such provinces, besides Magadha, which formed the home province. The provinces were divided into districts and sub-districts, with suitable officials in charge of them. (*Loc. cit.*, Chap. v, p. 49.)

The plan was not so very different from that of the British Empire now, except that every office was filled by an Indian, and the rule was so good that as Megasthenes remarked:

> It is accordingly affirmed that famine never visited India, and that there has never been a great scarcity in the supply of nourishing food. (Quoted by Dr. Banerjea, *Loc. cit.*, Chap., iii, p. 32.)

Elsewhere Megasthenes speaks of two, and even three, crops a year, in consequence of the fertility of the soil, and the abundance of water.

In Southern India, while we find highly developed local government and the village at its best, historians have not, so far, unburied past Republican Governments, so far as I know. Research on these lines has dealt with Northern and Middle India more than with Southern. But we have, in Southern India, great and prosperous Kingdoms of high civilisation, huge wealth and marvellous stability. The history of the Kingdoms of the South of India must also be studied with the above in detail. Suffice it here to say that the great Kingdoms of Andhra, Pandya, Chola, Kerala and Satyaputra flourished exceedingly and traded largely, especially with Egypt and Rome.

The extraordinary stability of civilisation, and prosperity in India, despite invasions and local wars, is, I think, due to the recognised superiority of Law over individuals, over Monarchs as well as subjects. It was the Supreme Governor alike of Prince and Peasant, and was largely accepted even by foreign invaders who settled permanently in the country and founded Kingdoms or Empires therein. The settled polity of the country was not changed by them; local government continued on the old lines, customary law was respected, and methods of rule were assimilated largely to the pre-existing types. The goodwill of the Hindu majority was thus cultivated, and the conquerors became part of the Nation, and ceased to be foreigners. Taxation and property in land remained much as before, and the masses of the people—when the rush and turmoil of conquest was over—remained much as before.

Hence when the European Companies came to India in the seventeenth century, they found a country rich in natural resources, with an educated people, a flourishing internal and external trade, and astonishingly wealthy. They came to "shake the pagoda tree," and shook it with success. It is for Economic Science to investigate the causes of India's past wealth and present poverty. Political Science has but to trace the history of institutions, leaving their value to be judged by their results. India need not fear the test.

THE WEST

The Free Cities of Greece have been already spoken of in Lecture V, with the City and Empire of Rome, and the growth of Teutonic villages and towns, and the Free Towns. These practically rank as Republics, widening in the case of the Villages into districts and Kingdoms. Sometimes the process was one of internal growth, subject to invasions, as in the Saxon Heptarchy, the transformation of War-Chiefs into Kings. On the Continent a whole Nation organised for War under a King would invade a neighbouring Nation, conquer it and settle down permanently, as with the Franks. Then the Feudal System appeared, with its King and Barons. Mr. Baden-Powell gives us an interesting glimpse of Welsh families and tribes, strangely similar to the parallel State of affairs in India, mentioned in the last lecture. He says, in dealing with the subdivisions of a clan, single families or households forming the latest groups:

> Let us take, merely for the purpose of comparison and illustration, such a standard as the Welsh tribe, which has recently been examined by Dr. Seebohm. Speaking first of the grouping of the *people*, not of their mode of ownership, we find (1) a close-kindred, or group of

immediate relations recognised, and also (2) a wider-kindred. The former answers to the family, the latter very much to the minor-clan. Outside that, again, is the general group of the clan, still held together by the common lien of loyalty to the chief and of obligation to general service and defence, as well as by certain customs of co-aration and common pasturage. In Wales the close-kindred was called a *wele* or *gwely*; it consisted of the purely natural group of the individual clansman, and his father, grandfather, and great-grandfather; direct inheritance went no further. And this group of close-kindred would naturally also suggest a wider group; but I will quote Dr. Seebohm's own words. "The eldest living ancestor, as chief of the household, occupying the principal homestead, or *tyddyn*, and seated by the ancestral hearth, might well live to see growing up around it a family group, extending to great-grandchildren. On the other hand, looking backward to his own childhood, he might well recollect his own grandfather sitting as head of the household at the same hearth, just as his great-grandchildren would hereafter remember him. Thus the extreme natural reach of the knowledge of the head of the household might cover seven generations. Finally, if family tradition went back two stages further than actual memory, then it would embrace the larger kindred." (*Loc. cit.*, Chapter vi, pp. 233, 234.)

Mr. Baden-Powell shows the same succession among the Hebrews, as the narrowing down by lot from the wider-kindred to the son of the close-kindred, the individual sought. The same carefully preserved succession is found among the ancient Greeks, and in Manu's *Institutes* among the Brahmanic Aryans. The cake in the Shraddha ceremony is offered to three ancestors and the three preceding them, thus the offerer is the seventh, and his son is not partaker in the oblations. The offerer remembers his father, grandfather and great-grandfather, and beyond them are the great-grandfather's father, and grandfather and great-grandfather. The offerer in turn may see his son, grandson and great-grandson, again seven generations; the relationship sapinda ceases with the seventh person, and all are thus related who offer the pinda and the water to the same ancestors. Mr. Baden-Powell thinks that these groupings, found in regions so far apart, point to "a feeling common to all early tribes, and founded in human nature itself." (Summarised from *Loc. cit.,* pp. 234 to 236.)

The City-State of the Greek grew very naturally out of the families and the villages; but there was no further aggregation; as we saw in Lecture V, p. 111, the Greek City generated other Greek Cities, but each remained independent, a separate City; there was no aggregation into a more complex State. Most of these Cities were Republican, governed by the body of citizens. But they were aristocratic in spirit not democratic, for they were based on slavery. The early Greeks, living in families a somewhat isolated life, formed the "City" of Homer's day, and a King was the head of all these little family Republics, each having its own laws and customs, its worship, its property, its responsibility for all its members. Each of these "gens" had a representative in the King's Council, and the confederated gentes formed a City. Many a migration went out; Miletus for instance had eight daughter Cities, and the eighth, seventh and tenth centuries B.C. saw the Hellenising of the Mediterranean. Who does not know the names of Chalcis, Tarentum and Syracuse, and how southern Italy became Magna Grecia? Aristocracy too often became an Oligarchy; many a colony was founded by hands of men seeking for freedom; Democracies gave place to Tyrannies. Many changes followed each other. Leagues and Confederacies were formed, but lasted only for short periods. Macedon created an Empire which invaded the East, and laid the foundation of the Eastern or Greek Empire with its capital at Byzantium, named Constantinople after the Emperor Constantine.

Meanwhile Rome monarchical had arisen, had tired of Kingship, and had become a fighting Republic in 509 B.C. Two Consuls were elected by the Assembly, the Comitia Centuriata, an enlargement of the less popular Curies, in which only the Patricians, descended from the Gentes, could vote. Rome conquered, and built her conquests into alliance with herself, becoming a Country State, centralised in Rome, and developing into an Empire at the beginning of the Christian era. Then followed gradually the supremacy of the army, militarism triumphed, establishing a despotism. The division of the Empire followed into Eastern and Western, and Rome in the fifth and following centuries fell under the assaults of the Teuton peoples, while Constantinople lasted on until the fifteenth century.

Rome, with its family organisation, which made the father the despot of the family, the owner of its members as well as of its property, developed throughout its Republican career the root of despotism. Papal Rome followed Imperial Rome in its autocracy, and the Bishop of Rome, gathering up the magic of her great name, became the despot of Western Europe. Though Charlemagne recreated at the beginning of the ninth century the name of the Holy Roman Empire—Holy as Catholic, Imperial as Rome—it exercised but a shadow of power, though Roman Law became the basis of European Common Law.

While these changes were going on, the free Teuton peoples had invaded and colonised northern and western Europe. We saw the growth of their village system in Lecture V, pp. 119 *et seq*., and found in it the basis of the free institutions of Britain. We saw the establishment of the more arbitrary royal power buttressed by the feudal system. But the buttress ceased to support, and the Barons wrung from King John the old Saxon liberties in Magna Carta, and King Edward I created the house of Commons to pit burgesses against nobles, and to fill his empty purse. Edward IV broke the power of the Barons, and cleared the way for Tudor despotism. The growing power of Parliament faced the Monarchy, struck it down, and beheaded the King for treason to the Nation. The Revolution of 1688 changed the Monarch into a constitutional King, created by Parliament, and power was transferred more and more to the Commons House. The Reform Bills of 1832 and 1867, made real by the Educational policy inaugurated in 1870, transferred power to the Nation in ever-increasing measure, until, in 1917, universal adult suffrage was established for men, and for all women over thirty years of age.

—Annie Besant

Notes

1. A minister siding with the king as against the people's interest was "hated." *Panchatantra*, I, 142.

2. Amusing guesses have been made by scholars about the meaning of the Parishat. The Parishat had become a technical term denoting the Council of Ministers in the Artha-Shastra.

2

Classification of the Form of Government

CLASSIFICATION OF PLATO AND ARISTOTLE

Distinction between State and Government

The first point to be noted in the classification of state and government is the distinction between the state and government. In many books the classification of the forms of government is entitled the "forms of the State". Strictly speaking all states are the same. The student must bear this in mind: the "form of state" is really the form of government. It is true that we might classify states according to the type of mind evident in the state, or according to population or territory. Such classifications, however, would be of little value. It would not be helpful, for example, to divide states according to the size of their population, making the classification of large, medium and small.

Many classifications of the forms of government have been by writers of Political Science. The most common bases are (1) the number of people in whom the supreme power rests, and (2) the form of the state organisation or government. As we shall see, it is extremely difficult to find a satisfactory basis for the classification of modern governments. While certain general characteristics are common to some governments, we often find along with these common elements marked dissimilarity. Moreover, the forms of government change very quickly, so that while a classification may be satisfactory at the present moment it may be quite unsuitable a generation hence.

The Classification of Plato and Aristotle

The most famous of all classifications of forms of constitution or government is that given by Aristotle in his *Politics*.

Aristotle's classification is not, however, an original classification. He himself was a pupil of Plato, and Plato's classification, though not so well known, is almost of equal value and importance.

Plato's Classification

Plato's classification has not the definiteness of that of Aristotle. His views, moreover, are not consistent. He gives a different series of forms in the *Republic* and the *Statesman*. In the *Republic* he gives the forms which are noted below in connection with the cycles of political change. From the *Statesman* may be extracted a logical classification, which bears a striking similarity to the later classification of Aristotle. As Aristotle borrowed from Plato, so did Plato borrow from Socrates. According to Socrates the three main forms of government are monarchy, aristocracy and democracy. Monarchy and tyranny each is the government of a single person, but in monarchy, as contrasted with tyranny, there is respect for law. Aristocracy is contrasted with plutocracy, or government by the few rich. In aristocracy the capacity to rule is recognised: in plutocracy mere wealth is the test of rule. Democracy is the rule of ignorance. Socrates held that "only those who know shall rule."

Plato adopts the Socratic criterion of knowledge as the supreme test of goodness in government. Working with this principle he gives three grades of state:

1. The state of perfect knowledge, where the real sovereign is knowledge. No such state exists, but this is the best state of all. It does not count in ordinary classifications, but it is the ideal state, and other states are to be judged by it. Plato seems to regard this ideal state sometimes as a monarchy, or the rule of an all-wise one, sometimes as an aristocracy, or the rule of the best (the original meaning of aristocracy). It may best be termed Ideocracy, the state of the sovereign idea or reason.

2. States where there is imperfect knowledge. In such states laws are necessary, because of man's imperfection, and these laws are obeyed.

3. States where there is a lack of knowledge: states of ignorance, where laws exist and are not obeyed.

Deducting the first class, which does not exist, we have two classes left—states where law is obeyed, and states where it is not obeyed. With this basis, we also have the Socratic basis of the rule of one, of few and of many. Thus we have:

	States in which law is obeyed	States in which law is not obeyed
Rule of One.	Monarchy.	Tyranny.
Rule of Few.	Aristocracy	Oligarchy.
Rule of Many.	Moderate Democracy	Extreme Democracy

Plato classifies these also in order of merit. Monarchy is best: tyranny is worst. Aristocracy and oligarchy are intermediated. Democracy in states in which law is observed is the worse type: but in non-law states it is the better. It is the weakest for virtue and also the weakest for vice.

Aristotle's Classification

Aristotle's classification likewise adopts a double basis. The first is that of Normal and Perverted. The criterion in this case is the end of the state. As a moral entity, the state pursues, or should pursue, the good life. Therefore every state which pursues the end of the good life is a Normal or True State. States which do not pursue this end are Perverted. Thus Normal, or True, and Perverted is the first basis. The second is the basis of number, as in Plato's classification, or the constitution, which determines the government. Thus we have:

Form of Constitution.	Normal forms in which the rulers unselfishly seek the common welfare.	Perverted forms, in which the rulers seek their own welfare.
Rule of One.	Monarchy.	Tyranny.
Rule of Few.	Aristocracy	Oligarchy.
Rule of Many.	Polity.	Democracy.

"Polity" is a Greek word used to designate this particular type of government given by Aristotle. Its nearest modern equivalent is constitutional democracy. It is the unselfish rule of the many for the common welfare.

Aristotle's classification is thus founded on (a) the end of the state, and (b) the constitution, or number of persons who actually hold power. It is important to remember the first of these bases, because many critics have rejected Aristotle's classification on the ground that it is based purely on number or quantity, as distinct from quality. Obviously, however, Aristotle accepted number only as a secondary standard. His chief standard for the definition of all things was the end, hence his distinction of normal and perverted, which is a distinction of quality.

Aristotle's classification may be called the fundamental classification of the forms of government. The classification is not sufficient for modern forms of government, but it has provided the historical basis of practically all classifications made hitherto. Even in modern classification the general ideas of Aristotle are frequently adopted.

Cycles of Political Change: Plato's Cycle

In addition to their classifications of government, both Plato and Aristotle, give what in their opinions are the cycles of political change. Plato's cycle starts from the highest form. Ideocracy, the form which is the result of the highest type of mind. Plato classified states according to the qualities of mind shown in them, and his cycle of political change follows the same procedure. The highest type of state is that which has the highest type of mind as its basis, that is, the state where reason is supreme. The constitution resulting from this is Monarchy or Aristocracy, or, preferably, in the Platonic language, Ideocracy, the rule of the idea or reason. Ideocracy degenerates in time into the type of state where spirit replaces reason. This type of government is known by Timocracy. Timocracy means government by the principle of honour or spiritedness. It is a military type of state. In the Timocratic state there are still elements of reason, but it also contains the element of desire, because of private property. Private property leads to money-making and in time timocracy gives way to Oligarchy. In Oligarchy the wealthy classes rule. Gradually the people revolt against wealth and the oppression which wealth brings. This leads to Democracy. In Democracy the ordinary man-in-the-street is the characteristic type. It is the negation of order and freedom. There is no justice in Democracy, and no unity. Gradually Democracy passes into the hands of demagogues, and ultimately the most powerful demagogue seizes the reins of government and becomes sole ruler. This form of government, tyranny, is the worst type possible.

Aristotle's Cycle.

According to Aristotle, the cycle of political change starts from monarchy. The first governments, he considers, were monarchical. In early communities men of outstanding virtue were created kings. Gradually other persons of virtue and merit arose and tried to have a share in political power. This led to aristocracy. By the deterioration of the ruling class, aristocracy passed into oligarchy; from oligarchy the form of government changed into tyranny, and from tyranny the change was to democracy. Aristotle's theory of political change is based on the end of the government, just as was his classification of states. Plato's theory of political change is founded on the type of mind prevailing in the state.

OTHER CLASSIFICATIONS

Many other attempts at the classification of the forms of government have been made by political theorists of all ages. Machiavelli, the Italian writer, who ends the mediaeval era and heralds the modern, adopts the Aristotelian classification, and adds the mixed form of government, which he says, is the best. The mixed form is given by both Cicero and Polybius. Machiavelli is mainly concerned with monarchies and democracies: different circumstances, according to him, require different forms of governmental organisation. John Bodin, the first comprehensive political philosopher of modern times, bases his classification solely on the number of men in whose hands sovereignty rests. When the sovereign power is in the hands of an individual, the state is monarchic; when the sovereignty is in the hands of less than a majority of the citizens, the state is aristocratic; and when sovereignty rests in the majority, it is democratic. Monarchy, again, is classified by Bodin into three species—*(a)* Despotism, in which the monarch, like the ancient patriarch, rules his subjects as the *pater familias* rules his slaves; *(b)* Royal Monarchy, in which the subjects are secure in their rights of person and property, while the monarchy, respecting the laws of God and of nature, receives willing obedience to the law he himself establishes; and *(c)* Tyranny, in which the prince, spurning the laws of nature and of nations, abuses his subjects according to his caprice. Of these three species, Bodin regards Royal Monarchy—if the matter of succession is firmly fixed on the principle of heredity, primogeniture and the exclusion of the female line—as the best form of state or government. Thomas Hobbes is a close follower of Bodin and adopts Bodin's classification unreservedly. John Locke gives a new classification: according to him "the form of government depends upon the placing the supreme power, which is the legislative." When the "natural" men first unite by compact into political society, the whole power of the community resides naturally in the majority. If this majority exercises that power in making laws for the community from time to time, and in executing those laws by officers of their own appointing, then the form of government is a perfect democracy; if the power of making laws is put into the hands of a few select men, and their heirs or successors, it is an oligarchy; if it is put into the hand of one man, it is a monarchy. Locke is careful to point out that there can be forms of government, but not forms of state. Montesquieu, the great French writer, classifies governments into (1) Republics, with their two varieties of democracy and aristocracy, (2) Monarchies (of the West), and (3) Despotisms (of the East). Each form has its peculiar principle—of democracy, public service; of aristocracy, moderation; of monarchy, honour; of despotism, fear. The duration of any of these forms depends upon the persistence in a given society of that particular spirit which is characteristic of the form. According to Rousseau, the famous contemporary of Montesquieu, a government is called a democracy, an aristocracy, or a monarchy, according as it is conducted by a majority or a minority of the people or by a single magistrate. There are, again, three forms of aristocracy—natural, elective and hereditary—of which the elective aristocracy is the best, and the hereditary one is the worst. Rousseau also allows for the existence of the "mixed" form of government, in which the various elements are combined.

Bluntschli accepts Aristotle's classification as fundamental, but he considers that a fourth form is necessary. This fourth form is Theocracy. Its perversion Bluntschli calls Idolocracy. There is no real necessity for this additional form of government. It is useful, indeed, to have the term theocracy to describe that form of government in which the ruler is supposed to interpret the will of God or in which God himself is actually supposed to rule, but theocracies can be classified under either monarchy, aristocracy or democracy. The modern Political Scientist is not concerned with the intervention of God in politics. His duty is to decide where in the last resort the supreme power in the government lies, and that supreme power, so far as he knows, must always lie in either one person or a number of persons.

The German writer, Von Mohl, tries to classify states on a historical basis. His classification is (1) patriarchal states; (2) theocracies; (3) patrimonial states (in which sovereignty and the ownership of the land both belonged to the ruler); (4) classic states, such as those of Greece and Rome; (5) legal states; (6) despotic states. Von Mohl gives other types in addition to these and sub-divides classic states into Monarchy, Aristocracy and Democracy. His classification is based on no single principle and it makes no attempt to distinguish the state from government.

The "Mixed State"

Many other classifications have been given, particularly by German writers of last century. But not one of them gives a satisfactory basis on which to classify modern governments. Before proceeding to the classification of modern forms of government, we may first dismiss the common form of state called "mixed state". In addition to monarchy, aristocracy and democracy, Aristotle himself speaks of this mixed type. The Stoics considered the mixed type as a good type of state, and Cicero and Polybius both speak of the Roman state as a mixed form, composed of monarchic, aristocratic and democratic elements. There is really no such form of state. The mixture of monarchy, aristocracy and democracy does not make a mixed state. The state is sovereign and cannot be mixed. The form of government, however, may contain elements of monarchy, aristocracy and democracy but to say that there is a mixed state is to confuse the state with government.

Mr. Marriott's Basis of Classification

For the classification of modern forms of government. It is hardly possible to adopt any single basis. Mr. J.A.R. Marriott, the modern English writer, adopts a tripartite basis. While accepting Aristotle's classifications as fundamental, he regards monarchy, aristocracy and democracy as somewhat inadequate for modern governments. Thus, to take five examples, England is a monarchy, Germany (before the War) was a monarchy, France is a democracy, Russia (before the War) a monarchy, and the United States a democracy. Yet Germany, nominally a monarchy, was really more akin to the United States, which is a democracy, than it was to England, which is a monarchy. England, a monarchy, is really more akin to France, nominally a democracy, than England was to the monarchical Russia. This comparison suggests a principle. If we take the pre-war Russia, France, Spain, Italy and Great Britain, they agree in this respect, that they are simple or unitary governments. Germany, the United States, Switzerland, the old Austria-Hungary, Canada, Australia and South Africa are complex, federal or composite. This is one basis of division. In a unitary type of government the local organs, such as provincial and county bodies, are created by the central government; the central government preserves power to abolish or alter these bodies as it wishes. In a federal government, both the central or federal authority, and the provincial or state authorities derive their powers from a constitution. In a federal government, each authority holds its power in such a way that the powers cannot be altered without the alteration of the constitution. So long as the constitution remains as it is, neither can affect the powers of the other.

The next basis is that of rigid and flexible constitutions. In a rigid constitution there is a marked distinction between the ordinary law-making powers and the constitution making powers. In a flexible constitution, the ordinary legislature has constitution-making powers. In this way we may classify the United Kingdom and the old Austria-Hungary and all despotisms (where the will of a single individual is the law-making power) as flexible, and the United States, France, Germany—in fact all other governments—as rigid.

The third basis of classification is Monarchical or Presidential government on the one hand, and Parliamentary, Responsible, or Cabinet government on the other. This is undoubtedly the most important basis of classification for modern governments. The criterion in this case is the relation of the executive to the legislature. Executive power in government may either be co-ordinate with, superior to, or subordinate to the legislature. Where the executive is superior to the legislature, the type of government may be called despotic. The executives in practically all modern democratic states are either co-ordinate with or subordinate to the legislature. In the United States, the executive is theoretically co-ordinate with the legislature. In France, Italy, Great Britain, the British self-governing Dominions and many other countries, the executive is subordinate to the legislature. Where the executive is subordinate to the legislature, the type of government is called *responsible* government, because the executive is responsible to the legislature. This type is also called Cabinet government. The name Cabinet government owes its origin to the English system where the Cabinet, which is the executive, is responsible to the House of Commons.

Thus we have, according to Marriott, three bases of division: (1) Simple or Unitary and Composite or Federal, or simply, unitary and federal; (2) Rigid and Flexible; (3) Monarchical, Presidential, Non-responsible or Non-parliamentary and parliamentary, Responsible or Cabinet government. Applying these criteria, we find that Great Britain is unitary, flexible and parliamentary. The United States is federal, rigid and presidential. France is unitary, rigid and parliamentary, Germany, before the War, was federal, rigid and presidential, or rather monarchical. The present Germany is federal, rigid and parliamentary. Austria-Hungary was composite, but not federal, flexible and parliamentary. The British self-governing Dominions, Canada, Australia, New Zealand and South Africa are federal, rigid and parliamentary. India, at present, is difficult to classify, because it is in a transitional state. Its constitution is partly flexible, partly rigid; according to the Government of India Act of 1919, it is partly parliamentary and partly non-parliamentary. At present India is more unitary than federal, but the future organisation of India as a whole, including British India and the Native States, is likely to be federal.

Dr. Leacock's Classification

Professor Leacock of McGill University, Montreal, gives almost a similar classification. Professor Leacock adopts as the fundamental distinction despotic and democratic. Democratic states he subdivides into Limited Monarchy, in which the nominal headship of a personal sovereign is preserved, and Republican Government, in which the head of the executive is appointed by the people. Each of these kinds, he subdivides into unitary and federal, and in turn each of these he subdivides into parliamentary and non-parliamentary. Professor Leacock's classification is best explained by his own table:

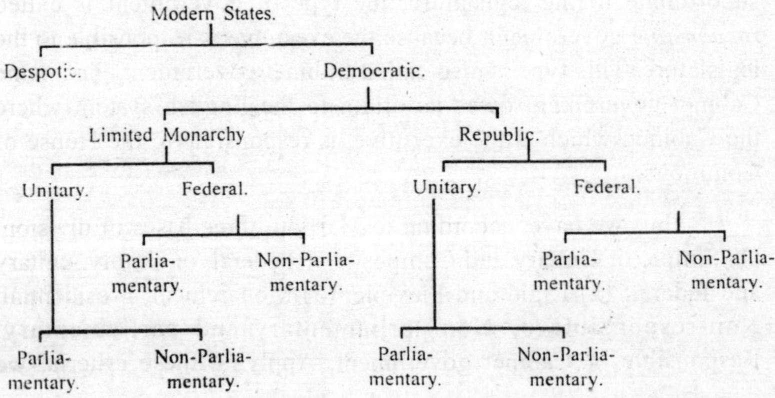

MONARCHY, ARISTOCRACY AND DEMOCRACY

The classification of Aristotle we have seen to be applicable only in a very general way to modern forms of government. The manifold new developments of modern democracy, and of government organisation in general, have materially altered the traditional classification. We have now to adopt new bases of classification, but, mainly for historical purposes. We must analyse shortly the Aristotelian forms of government by themselves.

Monarchy

1. Monarchy is the oldest type of government known. It is the type invariably found in early societies. In connection with the origin of the state, we have already seen how from both the religious and civic senses of early man evolved a monarchical form of government. Whatever may be said against the various historical types of monarchy, there is no doubt that in the ruder stages of social development, the monarchical system was the most beneficial. Monarchy is marked by singleness of purpose, unity, vigour and strength. It secures order and strong government. The monarch in early societies combined in himself the functions of law-maker, judge and executive, and was thus able to hold together by his own personal force a society which otherwise might have broken up into many elements.

Hereditary and Elective Monarchy

Monarchy may be classified in various ways. The most usual classification is Absolute Monarchy and Limited or Constitutional Monarchy. Another classification is Elective Monarchy and Hereditary Monarchy. Hereditary monarchy is the normal type, but there are several historical examples of elective monarchy. In early Rome the kings were elected, as also were the emperors in the Holy Roman Empire. The Polish kings used also to be elected. In early societies, too, there was a considerable element of election. Sometimes the crown fell to the lot of the ablest general of the royal family, who was elected by the chief men of the tribe or people. All modern monarchies are hereditary, although sometimes, as in the United Kingdom, the legislature regulates the succession to the throne.

Absolute Monarchy

Absolute Monarchy means that ultimately the monarchy is the final authority in making, executing and interpreting law. His will is the will of the state. There are many historical examples of absolute monarchies. The most notable is the French monarchy under Louis XIV., who declared "The state is myself." Absolute monarchy is still common in parts of Asia and Africa, but with the spread of enlightenment it is rapidly dying out.

Hobbe's Views

Hobbes is of opinion that of all forms of government absolute monarchy best answers the purpose for which sovereignty is instituted, and that for the following reasons:

1. A monarch's private interest is more intimately bound up with the interests of his subjects than can be the case with the private interest of the members of a sovereign assembly.
2. A monarch is freer to receive advice from all quarters, and to keep that advice secret than an assembly.
3. Whereas the resolutions of a monarch are subject only to the inconstancy of human nature, those of an assembly are exposed to a further inconstancy arising from disagreement between its members.
4. A monarch "cannot disagree with himself out of envy or interest, but an assembly may, and that to such a height as may produce a civil war."

Theocracy

Absolute Monarchy is sometimes combined with theocracy. In theocracy, the ruler is supposed to be either the interpreter of the will of God or the direct instrument of God. Such a theory of government can have only one organisation, and that is absolute monarchy. If the ruler is directly equivalent to God, then there is no appeal against his will. History gives many examples of theocratic government. The Jews considered themselves directly governed by God whose instrument was the King. The only states that can be called theocratic at the present day are the Mahommedan states, the fundamental law of which is the Koran. But in the modern Mahommedan states absolute monarchy is gradually being tempered by constitutional elements.

Limited Monarchy

By Limited Monarchy is meant a monarchy that is limited by a constitution. Sometimes constitutional rights have been wrested by the people from unwilling monarchs: sometimes monarchs have granted constitutions on their own initiative. Limited monarchy is thus a constitutional type of government, and as such is the same in principle as the republican type of government. The only difference between the limited monarchy and a republic is that in a republic the chief executive is elected, whereas in a monarchy the chief executive is hereditary. One of the chief merits of limited monarchy is that it secures continuity in the executive head of government. The main defect is that the hereditary principle is not a sound basis for the selection of the head of an executive. As a matter of fact, in modern limited monarchies, the monarch as a rule has only nominal powers. In the United Kingdom, for example, the chief executive, though nominally the king, is really the Cabinet. For every public act of the king the ministers are actually responsible.

Limited Monarchy in the United Kingdom

The limited monarchy of the United Kingdom occupies a special place. For one thing, the monarchy has been continuous, with only a slight break, ever since England became a nation. The institution is ingrained in the popular mind, and when other monarchies have been attacked or destroyed, no voice has been raised against the English kingship. The constitutional position of the king makes him powerless in government affairs, nevertheless by his personality he is able to exert considerable influence on his ministers. But the chief virtue of the English monarchy is the sense of security which it fosters among the people. Monarchy, too, has the virtue of impressiveness. The pomp and dignity surrounding a throne not only attract the people, but give additional impressiveness to both the institution of monarchy and the personality of the monarch. The usefulness of the king's personality was amply demonstrated in the Great War, when by practice and precept he encouraged, guided and warned the people.

The English monarchy is also invaluable as an Imperial asset. The king is the chief bond of union in the vast empire: as Professor Lowell has pointed out, "the Crown is the only visible symbol of the union of the Empire, and this has undoubtedly had a considerable effect upon the reverence felt for the throne." General Smuts, the South African statesman, recently expressed identical sentiments when, speaking of the Empire, he said: "We are an organic union forming one whole with the king as the connecting link."

Aristocracy

2. Aristocracy may be of various kinds; it may be aristocracy of wealth, of heredity, of intellect, or it may be military aristocracy. The real meaning of Aristocracy is the government of the best (the word "aristos" is a Greek word, meaning best). According to Aristotle's classification, aristocracy is a normal type of government, the perversion of which is oligarchy, or the rule of a few for their own interests. Unfortunately, aristocracy is very frequently confused with oligarchy, hence the sinister meaning usually associated with the word aristocracy. Aristocracy is popularly regarded as equivalent to the rule of the higher classes in their own interest. Throughout the history of political thought the aristocratic type of government has been held up as the ideally best type. To avoid the word aristocracy, some writers use the term "aristo-democracy," which means that form of democratic government in which the best types of men wield the power.

Merits of Aristocracy

Although aristocratic government, in the sense of the rule of the higher classes, is a thing of the past, it is not to be thought that aristocracy is essentially evil. Its chief quality is that it is conservative. It does not like change, and strongly resents rapid change. It reveres custom and tradition and tries to prevent the quick inrush of new ideas into government or society as a whole. In every government for the sake of stability there should be a certain amount of conservatism. The best principle of both social and political progress is the principle of conservative innovation. This means that every reform should be integrally connected with past institutions. A reform which is either too new or too unexpected distributes popular feeling and as such is a danger to the stability of government. It is, therefore, of the greatest importance in social and political progress that the principle of progress or liberalism should always be joined to the principle of stability or conservatism.

We shall see in connection with the organisation of the legislature that most modern governments attempt to preserve a certain amount of aristocracy in government by the system of Second Chambers. For Second Chambers the basis of selection is sometimes aristocracy of birth, sometimes aristocracy of wealth, sometimes aristocracy of intellect. Where the Second Chambers are elected, the elections are usually so arranged as to make the Second Chamber representative of the best minds in the nation. Such a system, therefore, is aristocratic in the best sense.

Weakness of Aristocracy

The chief weakness of aristocracy is that division of the people into classes please nobody. It is impossible for any man or body of men to divide a people into social classes by any satisfactory criterion. A very common basis of classification is property or wealth. In any society the propertied or wealthy class is relatively small, and rule by this class is resented by the large or non-propertied classes as oligarchical (oligarchy literally means the rule of the few.) it is equally impossible to divide any community into classes by intellectual or moral qualifications.

Democracy

3. Democracy is pre-eminently the modern type of government. It is the type of government to which all other types are

moving. Democracy literally means the rule of the people (the Greek word "demos" means the people), or popular government. It is the government of the people, by the people and for the people. It is of two kinds: (1) pure or direct democracy, and (2) representative or indirect democracy.

Direct Democracy

In the first type, pure or direct democracy, the will of the state is expressed directly through the people themselves. Such a type of democracy is possible only where the area of the state is very small,—where the people of the state can all meet and deliberate together to make laws. This type of democracy existed in all the Greek city-states. It must be remembered that in these city-states, only the citizens were allowed to take part in the proceedings of the Legislative Assembly. Not all the inhabitants were citizens. The citizens were often in a minority of one to two; the majority was made up of slaves. The direct democracy of the ancient Greeks was possible only because the manual work in the state was done by slaves. In modern democracy the very class which was excluded in Greece—the workers—is the most important. Greek democracy was a democracy in relation to the citizens in the state, but it was a very close aristocracy in relation to the total population in the state.

Indirect or Representative Democracy

Modern Democracy is indirect or representative. In modern large nation states it is physically impossible for all the citizens to meet together and deliberate. Even if it were possible, the work of legislation would be so great that the ordinary industrial and commercial life of the country could not be carried on. Modern democracy, therefore, rests on the principle of representation. Instead of everybody attending the Legislative Assembly the people elect representatives by vote. These representatives attend the Legislative Assembly and act on behalf of the citizens. If the citizens are not satisfied with their representatives they may reject them in the next elections. This system of representative democracy combines the principle of aristocracy—in the sense of the rule of those best qualified to rule—with that of democracy.

Virtues and Dangers of Modern Democracy

Representation is only an approximate way of expressing the will of the people. As yet no perfect system of representation has been found. The chief defects of democracy are due to the fact that up to the present time, it has been found impossible to make a perfect organisation for democracy. In theory democracy is the best form of government. It is the government of the people as distinct from the government of an individual or of a class of people. It makes all the citizens interested in their country by giving them a voice in legislation. It educates and enables the individual citizen: it gives each a sense of personal responsibility which gives a new meaning to his personality.

Another virtue of democracy is that it is less liable to revolution than other forms of government. Popular government is government by common consent. From its very nature, therefore, it is not likely to be revolutionary. On the other hand there is always the danger in democracy that it may develop into what Aristotle regarded as the perversion of democracy, namely, mob rule or ochlocracy. The Greek writers continually bring before us the danger of demagogues and this danger is as marked in modern democracy as it was in ancient democracy. The work demagogue literally means a leader of the people: actually it means one who tries to stir up popular passion against either the government or the higher social classes.

The Rule of Ignorance

The greatest of all the dangers of Democracy is, as Plato pointed out, that it may be the rule of ignorance. Democracy, it is often said, pays attention to *quantity* and not to *quality*. The business of government is highly technical. It requires expert administrators, and expert legislators. Not everyone can be a profound thinker on government matters, but every citizen should acquaint himself with current problems so as to pass an intelligent opinion on them. The danger of democracy is that the citizens may not be sufficiently educated to appreciate the meaning of the issues which come before them at elections. They may be misled either by demagogues or by class passions. Great responsibility is thrown on them at every election, for upon the type of representatives they choose will depend the future course of legislation. The popular vote must be given to the best men. Both in Britain and in America it would be possible to show that the best thinkers of their time, if indeed they wished to be elected to the Legislative Assembly, could have been elected. In modern democracies, on the whole the popular vote has proved a good selective agency. The modern "demos" has not proved so lacking in judgement as many of the opponents of democracy would have us believe.

The only certain antidote to demagogy is the sound education of the masses: in fact the back-bone of all democracies is sound education. Where each individual has a voice in government, he should be instructed in public mattes to make his voice intelligent. In modern democracy the necessity of a sound educational system as a rule has been recognised. Democracy is the result of popular education, and sound popular education is the chief need of democracy.

CABINET OR RESPONSIBLE GOVERNMENT AND PRESIDENTIAL OR NON-RESPONSIBLE GOVERNMENT

It is necessary to give a little more attention to the above types of government because either they are, or they are tending to become the prevailing types of government at the present day. The Cabinet system of government owes its origin to Great Britain, and the present system of government in Great Britain is the best existing example of Cabinet government. The government of the United States provides the best example of Presidential or non-responsible government. The Great War has tested both these systems of governments and enables us to pass certain definite judgements upon them.

Cabinet Government in the United Kingdom

In the English system the Cabinet is the head of the executive as well as the directing power in the legislature. The Cabinet is chosen from the political party which commands the majority in the House of Commons. The head of the Cabinet, the Prime Minister, is appointed by the king and after his appointment he selects his ministers who also are technically appointed by the king. The Cabinet is representative of both the House of Lords and the House of Commons, but is responsible only to the House of Commons. As a rule it includes the heads of the great executive departments of the government. Indirectly it may be said that the Cabinet is chosen by the House of Commons for, although the Prime Minister can exercise his own will in the matter of choice, he is bound to select the chief men of the political party in power. The Cabinet is jointly responsible to the House of Commons for the action of its individual members and in the case of defeat by the House, the Cabinet must resign. The Cabinet, moreover, has the power, through the Prime Minister, to advise the king to dissolve the House of Commons. Although the Cabinet is but a committee of the legislature, it really is master of the legislature.

The Cabinet system in Great Britain is a direct contradiction of the theory of the separation of powers of which we shall speak later. The theory of the American constitution is that the legislative, executive and the judicial branches of government should be independent of each other, but in the English constitution, both the legislative and the executive control lies in the Cabinet. The Cabinet links together the executive and the legislature. In theory the king is the head of the executive, but in actual practice the king is not responsible for the acts of his ministers. The Cabinet also is a permanent link between the people as a whole, and the legislature. In virtue of its power to recommend a dissolution of Parliament, it helps to preserve harmony between the will of the people and the legislature. Further, during the War, by the Defence of the Realm Act, the Cabinet was able to interfere with the ordinary rights of the citizens as enjoyed in peace time. During the war the Cabinet was able to circumvent the fundamental fact of English liberty, namely, the rule of law. This action was necessary in order to strengthen the executive, as a strong executive is essential for the conduct of war.

Presidential Government in the United States

According to the American Constitution, the President of the United States is the independent executive head. The founders of the constitution recognised that an essential of good government is a vigorous head of the executive. To make the executive independent from interference, the Americans adopted the theory of the separation of powers. They established an independent legislature, an independent executive and an independent judiciary. The President is head of the American executive. He is elected for four years and, according to the custom of America, cannot be elected more than twice. His powers are definitely limited by the constitution. Some of his executive authority he holds in conjunction with the Senate: the greater part of his authority he exercises by himself. He appoints his own ministers and can remove them. His ministers are not members of the legislature nor are he and his ministers responsible to the legislature for their acts. The limits on the power of the President are: (*a*) the limits laid down in the Constitution; (*b*) the limits laid down by the statute law of the land (if the President or any of his ministers exceed their legal authority their acts will be nullified by the courts); and (*c*) the political limits. The President is elected by the people. He is the nominee of a political party and as such to a certain extent must try to please the party, but as no President may be re-elected more than once the political limit is only temporarily effective.

Comparison

In time of peace Cabinet government has several advantages. In the first place, it secures men of outstanding ability as leaders in the legislature and in the executive. In modern democracies it is difficult for men without ability to rise to cabinet rank. The Prime Minister especially must have qualities which mark him out above his fellow-men. Not only is the Prime Minister responsible for the making and the execution of the laws, but he is also the leader of his own party. As a leader of his own party his policy very largely is the policy of the party. The Prime Minister must therefore be a man of commanding personality; and it is to his advantage to have round him the ablest men we can find.

In the second place, the Cabinet system of Great Britain is educative. The party system, on which it is founded demands high organisation, and the duties of party organisations are to win elections. To win elections means securing the votes of the people and, as each party is as keen as the other to win, the people have always before them the various sides of the questions before the country. In America, too, the party system prevails, but in the Cabinet system of Great Britain the responsibility of the Cabinet to the House of Commons, or its ability to secure the majority of votes in the House gives an additional *zest* to party politics. In America the executive, once in office, cannot be turned out by any party till his period of office is over. In Britain the Cabinet may be turned out of office by an adverse vote at any time.

In the third place, the Cabinet, by virtue of its position as head of the executive and as directing power in the legislature, is above to carry through measures which *for executive reasons* are necessary or advisable. In America Congress need not carry through a single measure recommended by the President.

In the fourth place, the Cabinet is continuously responsible for its executive actions. The members of the House of Commons by means of questions, motions, etc., exercise continual supervision over the executive departments.

In the fifth place, the debates in the House of Commons are party debates. They give both sides of the question at issue, and, to avoid defeat, the Cabinet has to present as sound a case as possible before the House.

The Great War has shown also that the Cabinet system is flexible. It is well known that in times of crisis, such as a great war, one directing head is better than many heads. The government in England was able to adapt itself to the new situation created by the war by evolving from within itself a small body whose special duty it was to conduct the war. But the advantage of flexibility was more than discounted by the lack of unity which became apparent in England soon after the beginning of the War. Undoubtedly the greatest defect of Cabinet government is that it cannot *at once* adapt itself to meet great emergencies, such as wars. For emergencies a dictator is more useful than a council. One bad general, as Napoleon said, is better than two good ones.

The Experience of the Great War

Presidential government is shown at its best in time of war. Once war was declared in America, President Wilson became a dictator. He was able to direct all resources of the United States without any interference to one end. It is true, particularly in the very early stages of the War, that the Cabinet was able to do very much the same for Great Britain, but as the War progressed, it became more and more necessary to concentrate the power of direction in the hands of fewer men. Throughout the whole War, the Cabinet in Great Britain was subject to the will of the House of Commons. If the House of Commons had so cared, it might have turned the Cabinet out of office at any critical period in the War. As a matter of fact, in the later stages of the War it is well known that there were considerable dissensions in the Cabinet and in Parliament itself. One Prime Minister had to resign, and several appointments were made not for purely executive reasons, but from the desire to conciliate the party leaders in the House of Commons. While the President of the United States belongs to a political party, he is completely independent while he holds office. In war he is an autocrat. He dictates to Congress legislative measures necessary for the conduct of the war, and in the executive conduct of the war he can carry on his work without fear or favour.

It may be said that a dictatorship of this kind is a danger to public liberty. The liberty of the American citizens was no more adversely affected during the War than the liberty of the British. In both Britain and America everything had to be subservient to success in the struggle, and the old ideas of individual liberty were completely submerged for this end.

It is clear, then, that in times of war the presidential is the better system. Although both the Cabinet and the president are the result of party elections, yet the president is able to shake himself free from party ties more easily than the Cabinet. In Cabinet government, too, a great deal of time may be lost in useless discussion. During the War a considerable part of the time and energy of those responsible for the conduct of the War, was taken up by meeting objections to various points raised by members of the legislature. While discussion in times of peace is one of the benefits of Cabinet government, in time of war it is one of its greatest defects.

Presidential government of the type existing in the United States, although it is more beneficial in war, does not appear to be so beneficial in time of peace. Thus in the United States of America, the great presidents have been those men who have had to cope with national crises. The history of the United States has been marked by relatively few national crises, so that the good qualities of presidential government have not been frequently tested. In times of peace the president's general duties are to execute the laws as efficiently as possible. His executive work is largely done by his ministers, and if he is careful in his choice of ministers, the tenure of his office may be uneventful and easy. The only statesmanlike act which the president is called upon to do in normal times is to review the position of the country in his presidential messages to Congress. These messages may be or may not be acceptable to Congress. The president has no power to compel Congress to pass any law. The future of his messages is entirely at the mercy of the good feeling of Congress. By the party system in the United States, the president usually belongs to the same political party as the majority in Congress for the time being. But although the party organisation in the United States is the strongest in the world, the actual dividing lines between the parties in matters of political opinion or proposed legislation are so indistinct that the party similarity of President and Congress is no guarantee that the president's views will prevail.

To sum up, the English Cabinet system compares favourably with the presidential system in times of peace, but unfavourably with it in times of war.

3

Forms of Government

Some writers on Political Science classify the forms of government as the forms of the State. But this is wrong. There can be no forms of State. All States are alike in their nature and all combine the same essential elements—population, territory, organisation and unity. Differences in population and territory do not make any difference in their status of Statchood. A distinction is, no doubt, sometimes made between a city-State, a nation State, and a world empire. But this distinction has no practical value in Political Science, for classification of States on the basis of territory and population is a mere historical description, and an act of a fallacy coming from Aristotle's time when no distinction was made between the State and government. To classify States on the basis of unity is also impossible. All States are sovereign and all sovereign States are equal. Accordingly, it is illogical to classify the equals.

But States do differ in their organisation. The organisation of the State is its government and it is through the instrument of the government that the State formulates, expresses, and realises its purpose. The purpose of every State is the same, the well-being of its people, and the form of government is the expression of the way in which the purpose of the State is to be realised. This involves the problem of determining in whose hands is vested the legal authority of the State, to what extent is actual use made of it, what are the instrumentalities or organs employed in its use, and what rules and procedure are followed by such organs in performing their functions. These differences are wide from State to State and matter a good deal in differentiating the organisation of one State from another. The form of government is, therefore, the actual basis of division.

Aristotle's Classification. The traditional classifications of governments follow the course set by Aristotle. Aristotle, however, was not original. He borrowed from Plato as Plato had borrowed from Socrates. Aristotle based his classification on two principles:

1. the number of persons who exercise supreme power; and
2. the ends they serve.

Applying the first principle, Aristotle said if the supreme power is vested in one single person it is a *monarchy*. If it is rule of the few, it is *aristocracy*, and if the supreme power is vested in many, it is a *polity*.

Aristotle, then, proceeds to distinguish between what he calls the "normal" and the "perverted" forms of government basing his conclusions on the ends which the rulers serve. A *normal* State is that which always aims at the good of the community as a whole. It becomes a *perverted* form when the ruler or rulers become selfish and he or they exercise power vested in him or them for his or their own benefits rather than for the benefits of the community as a whole. *Monarchy, aristocracy* and *polity* are the normal forms of government. In their perverted form they become *tyranny, oligarchy* and *democracy*. Tyranny, Aristotle said, was the degenerated form of monarchy, oligarchy as the degenerated shape of aristocracy and democracy as the degenerated form of polity. Tyranny placed in the hands of the monarch arbitrary control over the lives and fortunes of the citizens. In oligarchy, the wealthy few ruled for selfish ends and used their powers and privileges for the oppression of the common people. Democracy meant mere mob rule, wherein the interests of none were safe and there was confusion and chaos all round.

Two points about this classification deserve attention. First, Aristotle draws a clear distinction between aristocracy and oligarchy. But modern usage does not differentiate between the two and we often use them synonymously. Secondly, democracy for

Aristotle has not the same meaning as it has for us. He regarded it as a perverted form, a mob rule, whereas we regard democracy as the best form of government. The perverted form of democracy, according to the modern use, is *mobocracy* or *ochlocracy*. Moreover, the modern sociologists have clearly shown that there is no government of the many, that all governments are governments of the few, or, in fact, oligarchies. Nowhere in the world do the people or even substantial number of them rule. In all States the exercise of government is left to a few hands, while the determination of policy is actually in the hands of a yet smaller minority, the political leaders. The Cabinet in England is the supreme directing authority, "the magnet of policy", as Barker calls it, and it now consists of sixteen members.

The distinction between Aristotle's different forms of government may be stated in the following tabular form:

I Test	II Test	The end they serve
Form of Constitution.	Normal—when the rule is for the benefit of the community as a whole.	Perverted—when it becomes selfish and rulers exercise authority for their own benefit.
Rule of one	Monarchy	Tyranny
Rule of two	Aristocracy	Oligarchy
Rule of many	Polity	Democracy

Cycle of Aristotle's political change. Like his teacher Plato, Aristotle, too, subjects his forms of government to cyclic political changes. Just as the wheels of a cycle revolve, so do the forms of government according to Aristotle. His cycle of political changes starts from monarchy. The first government, he says, was kingship. With the degeneration of the character and aims of the monarches, it became tyranny when government was no longer directed towards the public good. But a tyrannical government could not continue for long. It was overthrown and substituted by a government of the few talented persons who were prompted by the ideas of the common good. With the lapse of time, they also degenerated. The ideals of public spirit which inspired them in the beginning disappeared. Aristocracy, thus, lapsed into oligarchy. But the people could not for long tolerate a government the aim of which was the benefit of the ruling class alone. The citizens as a whole made a successful revolt against such an authority and established a polity, the supreme power being vested in the hands of the mass of the people and used by them for the common good. When polity became perverted it was substituted by democracy.

Democracy, according to Aristotle's terminology, is a rule by the mob which is always an intolerable confusion. There is neither certainty nor stability. It is at this stage that some powerful warrior-statesman comes to the forefront declaring himself a king and, thus, runs the course of Aristole's political changes. "The first governments," says Aristole, "were kingships, probably for this reason, because of old, when cities were small, men of eminent virtue were few. They were made kings because they were benefactors, and benefits can only be bestowed by good men. But when many persons equal in merit arose, no longer enduring the pre-eminence of one, they desired to have a commonwealth and set up a constitution. The ruling class soon deteriorated and enriched themselves out of the public treasury; riches became the path to honour, and so oligarchies naturally grew up. These passed into tyrannies, and tyrannies into democracies; for love of gain in the ruling classes was always tending to diminish their number, and so to strengthen the masses, who in the end set upon their masters and established democracies."

Criticism of Aristotle's Classification. Such is Aristotle's classification. The cycle of political changes given by him is fully corroborated by the history of the Greek city-States in the centuries preceding the Peloponesian war. Recent history, too, provides examples of a similar political progression. The last phase of political anarchy to be suppressed by a military autocracy is a common feature of our own times and it reminds us of various *coup d'etats*, the most recent being one led by General Naguib in Egypt, Brigadier Kassem in Iraq, General Ayub in Pakistan, Lt.-General Ibrahim Abboud in Sudan and many other such very recent examples.

In spite of this, Aristotle's classification has been subjected to severe criticism. It is urged that his classification is not based on any scientific principle as it emphasises quantitative rather than qualitative aspect; his division is mechanical and not spiritual in character. This criticism does not hold good. Aristotle, no doubt, ignores the various stages in the development of political consciousness of the people, but his test is ethical and spiritual whether the form of government is monarchy or aristocracy or polity. Aristotle might have differed in his political philosophy from his teacher, yet his, as it was with Plato, true test of a good government was knowledge, spiritual and ethical. The determining factor of his classification lies in the character of the one, or the few or the many. Burgess has rightly said that Aristotle's classification is organic or spiritual rather than numerical.

'It is further maintained that Aristotle confuses the State with government and his classification is really that of forms of government and not of forms of State. This is true. Aristotle never differentiated between the two. In fact, no Greek did it. The distinction between the State and government is of recent political growth. Burgess is of the opinion that Aristotle's classification is sound and logical if only we substitute his 'State' and 'sovereignty' by 'government' and 'rule'.

Moreover, Aristotle's classification does not embrace modern forms of government like constitutional monarchy, unitary, and federal governments, parliamentary and presidential types. The city-States of Aristotle, as Seeley says, do not fit in with modern 'country-States.' Perhaps Aristotle could not conceive, at the time when he flourished, the various forms into which a government might develop. Nor do we use democracy in the same sense in which Aristotle used it. Aristotle's classification into monarches, aristocracies, and politics is also not satisfactory according to our norms of division. If we accept his classification, are we to class Great Britain as a monarchy or a democracy and how is it to be differentiated from the government of the United States? Finally, Aristotle definitely distinguishes between aristocracy and democracy (polity). But the attempt to distinguish between the two is futile in our times for it is not easy to find out where one ends and the other begins.

Other Classifications. In spite of these defects Aristotle's classification was accepted as fundamental till quite modern times. The modern writers dropped the ethical or qualitative basis and classified governments on quantitative basis alone. Three-fold classification of governments—Monarchies, Aristocracies and Democracies—became the generally accepted norm till the end of the First World War when Democracy merged others, except for subject countries, colonies dependencics or trust territories and others where dictatorships were established.

Among the modern writers Montesquieu proposed a three-fold division: republican, monarchical and despotic governments. Republican government is that in which the people as a body, or even a part of the people, possess the sovereign power. Under a monarchical form of government there is rule by one single person, but he governs only by fixed and established laws. In a despotic government on the other hand, there is a single person who rules, but without any law and conducts everything according to his will and caprice. How long a particular form of government can last? Montesquieu's reply is that it depends upon the "persistence in a given society of that particular spirit which is characteristic of the form."

Rousseau divided governments into monarchies, aristocracies, and democracies. He subdivided aristocracies into three forms—natural, elective, and hereditary. He considered elective aristocracy as the best and hereditary the worst. Rousseau was the great champion of direct democracy. He also admitted the existence of mixed forms of government. Bluntschli gives us another classification. He accepted Aristotle's classification as fundamental, but added to it one form of his own. His division was : monarchies, aristocracies, democracies and theocracies. Theocracy is that form of government where the supreme power is attributed to God, or to a God, or to some other superhuman being, or to an Idea. The men who exercise authority are deputies or vicegerents of God or a God. Theocracy, according to Bluntschili, is a normal form of government, but when it becomes perverted it is known as idolocracy. But such a classification seems quite fallacious. The modern political scientist separates religion from politics and he does not bring God in his division of forms of government. His task is to locate sovereign power and it rests, for all intents and purposes, either in one person or in a number of persons.

There are other writers who classify States on a historical basis. Von Mohl, a German publicist of the nineteenth century, is prominent out of this school. He distinguishes patriarchal, theocratic, despotic, classic, feudal and constitutional States. He gives other types of government as well and subdivides classic States into monarchy aristocracy and democracy. Von Mohl's classification, even on a superficial examination is forthwith rejected. It is based on no single principle and he does not distinguish between the State and government.

Marriot's Classification. Sir J.A.R. Marriot, a political scientist of recent times, classifies States on a three-fold basis. He accepts Aristotle's classification as fundamental, but regards it as inadequate for modern governments. Marriot's first basis of classification is the distribution of powers of government. The governments are, accordingly, divided into *unitary* and *federal*. In a unitary government there is concentration of powers at the centre and the provincial governments enjoy only delegated powers as they are the creation of the central government. In a federal government there are two sets of government and authority is divided between these two—Central and State governments. Both the parts of government have original powers granted to them by the constitution and each is autonomous in its own sphere of jurisdiction.

Marriot's next basis is that of a rigid and a flexible constitution. In the third place, his basis of classification is the relation between the executive and the legislature. When the executive is superior to the legislature, the form of government is *Despotic*. If the executive is co-ordinate in power with the legislature, the type of government is *Presidential*. If the executive is subordinate to the legislature, as in the United Kingdom, the form of government is *Parliamentary* or *Responsible*.

Leacock's classification. Dr. Stephen Leacock's classification is almost similar to the one given by Marriot. He, however, does not attempt to include in his classification all the historical forms which have appeared in the evolution of the State. Leacock confines himself to actually existing types of government. His fundamental division is between despotic and democratic types. In a despotic government the sovereign power is concentrated in the hands of one single person who rules according to his will. In a democracy sovereign power rests in the people or majority of them. Democratic governments are divided into a *limited monarchy* and a *republic*. In a limited monarchy the head of government is the king, but his authority is limited. In a republican government, the executive is elected by the people for a fixed term of office. Each of these types may assume one of the two forms, unitary or federal. A unitary or a federal government may either be parliamentary or non parliamentary. In a parliamentary government the real executive is responsible to the legislature. In a non-parliamentary or presidential type the executive is not responsible to the legislature.

Dr. Leacock's classification can best be explained by the following table borrowed from him:

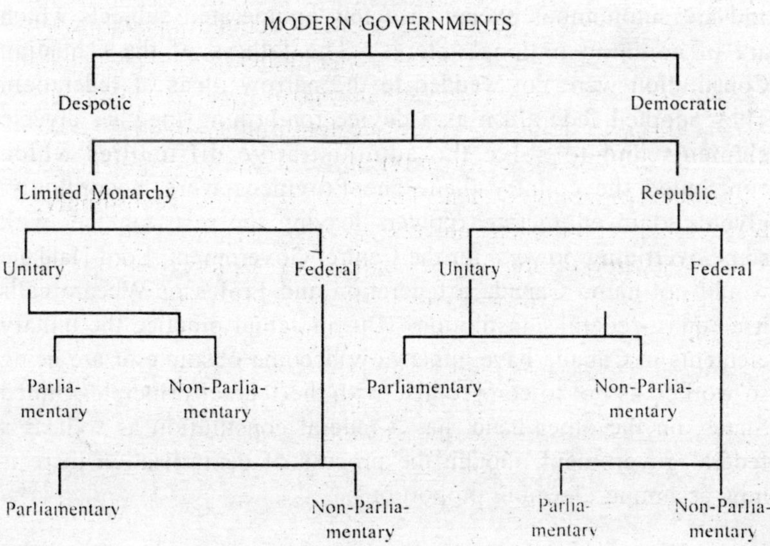

It is, indeed, extremely difficult to have a proper classification of modern governments. The form of government is, in fact, the product of numerous factors, historical, geographical, social, economic, psychological. Some of these factors are comparatively permanent and give a peculiar impress to the institutions in their evolution and functioning. Both England and France, for example, have in common a parliamentary system of government. But the government of England is in ultimate theory an absolute monarchy, in form a limited constitutional monarchy, and in actual practice a democratic republic. Practice outruns theory in England. France, on the other hand, is a country with the form of a republic, the institutions of a monarchy, and the spirit of an empire. There is, in general, a tendency for the French citizen to think of politics in intellectual rather than in practical terms, to attach more importance to symbols than to concrete achievements. The result is, as Siegfried says, "French politics are often both unrealistic and passionately ideological."

The United States of America and Canada, the neighbouring countries, are federations. United States is the classical example of a federal polity which brought into existence the union of the hitherto sovereign States for purposes of national unity. The component States enjoy a juridical status and corporate personality and are autonomous except in a few enumerated subjects which are of common national interest. The fathers of the Canadian Constitution were not wedded to the narrow ideas of federation. They adopted federalism as a device for brining together diverse elements and to solve the administrative difficulties which confronted the country then. The Provinces were, accordingly, given certain enumerated powers leaving the rest, together with some overriding powers, for the Central Government. Lord Haldane would not name Canada a federation and Professor Wheare calls it a "quasi-federal constitution." But in actual practice the unitary elements in Canada have either now become obsolete or are being so worked as not to compromise with the federal principle. United States, on the other hand, has a federal constitution as well as a federal government, though the process of centralisation there is now assuming alarming proportions.

The Indian Constitution is federal in form, but it sets up a highly centralised structure of government. The unitary tendencies found therein nullify to a great extent the broad feature of federalism. And the founding Fathers deliberately did it. Dr. Ambedkar, the principal architect of the Constitution, himself claimed in the Constituent Assembly that India was a federation during times of peace with a unitary system of government during times of war.

It follows, then, that no two forms can be absolutely identical any more than two human beings, whatever likeness there may be. And, like a human being, no government remains the same. Change is at work all the time and more so in the atomic age of our times. The needs of man and his environments have become so numerous and complex that no mechanism of government can claim perfection and consequently finality. The atomic age needs revolutionary changes and a dynamic mechanism of government to suit the purposes to be realised. Could anyone visualise a decade or so before that planning would become a democratic plea for the realisation of the well-being of man within the framework of a capitalistic structure of society?

Need for a new classification. With the emergence of the Welfare State the distinction between States based on 'socialism' and those based on 'private enterprise' is wearing pretty thin. This necessitates revision in the traditional methods of classification. Our approach should not be confined merely to outward forms as they give no clue to the real purpose of the State. Paine wrote 150 years ago: "When it shall be said my poor are happy, neither ignorance nor distress is to be found among them; my jails are empty of prisoners, my streets of beggars; the aged are not in want, the taxes are not oppressive, —when those things are said, then may that country boast of its government." The primary purpose of every State is the same and every government is charged by the community with the double task of maintaining what MacIver calls "an established code of living and of adjusting this order to new conditions and emergency needs." It does not matter what the head of the State is called. We shall assign to a particular government its proper place and label by knowing what it actually does in realising the purpose entrusted to its charge; the well-being of people. Well-being and well-feeding are not synonymous. Well-being really means the expansion in human spirit, and, as such, it is a question of liberty in all its aspects. The responsiveness of government is what it matters and the responsiveness of government depends upon the size and freedom of the electorate and the extent of its influence over the selection and work of the government. The Greek statesman Alcibiades remarked to his uncle Pericles that a law adopted even by the popular assembly was nothing but an arbitrary act when the majority imposed it on the minority without persuading the latter.

MONARCHY

Absolute Monarchy. Monarchy represents that form of government where the source of all political authority is to be found in a supreme ruler. All the organs and officers of government are the agents of this ruler for the purpose of carrying out his will. All acts of government are his acts and derive their validity from his sanction. All laws are his commands, though they may have been formulated by one of his agents. As the bearer of sovereignty, his authority is supreme, unlimited, and self-determined, both as regards the extent to, and the manner in which it shall in fact be exercised.

The institution of monarchy is a product of history and it has grown as a part of the evolution of the State. In the early stages of the development of the State monarchical system was the most beneficial, for it was characterised by singleness of purpose, unity, vigour and strength. The monarch combined in him the functions of the law-maker, the judge and the executive. He was, thus, able to hold together by his own personal force a society which otherwise might have broken up into many elements.

In the beginning the monarch was elected and, then, the institution became hereditary and it is now the normal type. The early Roman kings were elected. The medieval kings were both hereditary and elected. A king may be elected in our own times,

Nadir Shah, the father of the present ruler of Afghanistan, Zahir Shah, was an elected king. But it is not a normal feature and all monarchies are now hereditary. A hereditary king enjoys a life-long tenure and the office passes to his heirs according to the law of primogeniture.

Absolute monarchy has existed both in the East and in the West up to the very recent times. In the East, the leading example of a government of this character was that of Japan. In the eighties of the last century, Japan decided to abolish her old system of government and to establish in its place one corresponding to modern political ideas as represented by existing governments of Europe and America. But even the new constitution established a type of absolute monarchy. Article 1 of the constitution clearly stated that "the Empire of Japan shall be reigned over and governed by a line of Emperors unbroken for ages eternal." Baron Its, in his *Commentaries on the Constitution of the Empire of Japan*, explained the meaning of the phrase "reigned over and governed" and said that "it is meant that the Emperor on his throne combines in himself the sovereignty of the State and the government of the country and of his subjects."

In the West, the two most important examples of governments resting on absolute basis were those of Russia before the Revolution of 1917, and Germany immediately before the adoption of the Weimar Constitution of 1919.

The despotic king always claimed that he got his authority direct from God, that he was God's viceregent on earth, that he ruled by divine right. This belief in the divine right of the kings to rule prevailed in all countries. In China the Emperor was described as the "Son of Heaven" and that he ruled by virtue of the mandate that he had received from Heaven. Referring to Europe and England, Bryce says, "From the fifth to sixteenth century whoever asked what was the source of legal sovereignty and what the moral claim of the sovereign to obedience of subjects would have been answered that God has appointed certain powers to govern the world and that it would be a sin to resist His ordinance." The king was, accordingly, free from all human limitations. He was accountable to God alone and not to his subjects. Some kings, no doubt, took a high view of their duties and governed well and yet they were subject to no restraints except the law of God.

Merits of Absolute Monarchy. Perhaps, there could be no other better form of government than absolute monarchy in disciplining the uncouth and uncivilised people who had emerged out of barbarism. John Stuart Mill has rightly said, "Despotism is a legitimate mode of government for dealing with barbarians, provided the end be their improvement and the means be justified by actually effecting that end." Absolute monarchy possesses the merit of strength, vigour, energy of action, promptness of decision, unity of counsel, continuity and consistency of policy. Undivided counsel, promptness of decisions and a consistent policy are the essential requisites of a good and efficient administration, particularly during periods of national crises and emergencies. Monarchy, therefore, comes as a beneficial antidote to chaos or weak government. History is full of examples when the rule of one has been reimposed as a means of protecting the interests of the people at large from the rapacity of the few. The English supported their strong Tudor king "to be their protection against the lawlessness of the armed nobility."

Moreover, a monarch generally takes a very high view of his duties. He is free to select his officials according to his own pleasure and make them work according to his directions. As the officials can be held to strict accountability, they run the administration to the best of their ability and capacity. The absolute monarchies of the seventeenth and eighteenth centuries, says Bryce, "saw many reforms in European countries, which no force less than that of a strong monarchy could have carried through."

Defects of Absolute Monarchy. But no man is fit enough to exercise absolute power. A bad despot crushes his subjects to the earth and leaves them nothing they can call their own. Even a good despot teaches his subjects to mind their own private interests and to have everything else to the government. Absolute government is a government by one single person and he administers according to his own good sense of what can be good and right for his subjects. And history tells us that the good of the subjects has really meant the interests of the ruler himself. He has never cherished the interests of the subjects. If he does, his despotism disappears. Moreover, a good king, under a system of hereditary monarchy, is a sheer chance or accident. There is no guarantee that an able, capable and benevolent ruler must always succeed to the throne. History tells us that imbeciles and fools have been the rules whereas wise statesmen and sage rulers have been the exceptions. "A hereditary ruler," says Leacock, "seems on the face of things as absurd as the hereditary mathematician or hereditary poet laureate."

Even if it be admitted that absolute monarchy is a good form of government, we, who are brought up in the twentieth century, do not believe in good government unless it is self-government. Good government is no substitute for self-government. "No government which does not rest upon the affections of the people, which does not stimulate among them an interest in public affairs and create an active, intelligent, and alert citizenship, can be called ideal, and, certainly, no government from which the participation of the people in some form is excluded will ever be able to produce such a body of citizens." A despot dare not allow liberty and rights to his subjects. He does not inspire in his people a vigorous political vitality, a patriotic loyalty and social solidarity. If he does, he does not remain a despot. Power is always intoxicating and a despot will like to see that he remains the fountain of all authority and power. To infuse the spirit of awakening among the people and to permit them enjoyment of liberty and rights means the destruction of his authority and most probably his own annihilation.

Limited Monarchy. Limited monarchy is that type of government in which the authority of the monarch is limited either by the prescriptions of a written constitution or by certain fundamental conventions as in the United Kingdom. Limited monarchy is a constitutional government and is, in principle, like the republican form of government. The only difference between the two is that under a system of limited monarchy the chief executive head of the State is a hereditary king whereas in a republic the chief executive, usually called President, is elected for a number of years and after the expiry of his term of office, if not re-elected, he joins the ranks of the ordinary citizens of the State. But both the constitutional king and the President of a republic exercise nominal authority. The real functionaries are the ministers who are elected members of the legislature and belong to the majority party. They remain in office only as long as they retain the confidence of the legislature. They cannot be dismissed by the king at his pleasure. Nor can they be chosen at random. England is a typical example of a constitutional monarchy where the king reigns but does not rule.

Uses of Limited Monarchy. The very fact that the authority of the monarch is limited goes to show that in essence it is a democratic form of government. The king in England as Bagehot remarks, has the right to be consulted, the right to encourage, and the right to warn. He does not exercise any real authority. The actual government is carried on by ministers who represent the majority party in the legislature. Limited monarchy, therefore, gives the people real opportunity to actively participate in public affairs and elect administrators who rule the country according to their behest. It is the people who, in the last resort, are the ultimate sovereigns.

The chief virtue of a limited monarchy is the hereditary nature of the ruler. By virtue of a long and uninterrupted tenure of office the king gains considerably mature administrative experience to guide his ministers who are generally amateurs in the art of administration. He exercises, what Lowel calls, the "unifying, dignifying and stabilising influence". Moreover, the monarch belongs to no party whereas his ministers belong to one. The king, therefore, is an umpire in the midst of rival parties, who has to see that the game of politics is played according to rules.

The days of absolute monarchy are over now. Except for King Ibn Saud, in all other monarchies it has been the tendency to limit the powers of the king, either by the prescriptions of a written constitution or by certain fundamental conventions, as it is in England. The king has, thus, been made the national symbol, outside all controversies and party politics, whose powers are exercised by his ministers in his name. Such a kind of monarchy is called limited or constitutional monarchy and it is now the only way in which the hereditary principle and royal dignity can be preserved in democracies. A limited monarchy is a constitutional form of government and a constitutional government is, according to Woodrow Wilson "one whose powers have been adapted to the interests of the people and to the maintenance of individual liberty...Roughly speaking constitutional government may be said to have had its rise as Runnymede when the barons of England exacted the Magna Charta of John."

ARISTOCRACY

Meaning of Aristocracy. Originally, aristocracy meant that form of government which was conducted by the best men of the community and was prompted by the most virtuous principles. Such a form of government comes down to us from Aristotle. *Aristos*, in Greek, means the best and *Kratos* means power. Aristocracy, therefore, according to Greek philosophers, was a form of government *per excellence*. Its principle was virtue: the moral and intellectual superiority of the ruling class. Aristocracy has, now, come to signify that form of government in which the political power rests in the hands of a small section of the community. But this is not the true test of aristocracy. The character of aristocracy depends on the method of selection of the people who wield power and not on the smallness of the number.

The methods of selection have been devised in accordance with certain leading ideas which have pervaded and still pervade society. First, there is the idea of the importance of birth. In primitive society, families most directly descending from a common ancestor constituted a class by itself in which outsiders were not admitted except perhaps by adoption. In modern society we do not speak of a common ancestor, but we still defer to the notion that some families are better than others and consequently they are best fitted to rule. Secondly selection may be by merit, that is, persons of superior intellect and ability are chosen to govern others. Selection by favour is another method. When a king confers high rank on those who serve him best, the method of selection is by favour. Again, there may be an aristocracy of wealth, when the criterion of selection is only the possession of riches. The poor whatever be their intellect or merit, have no chance to assume public offices and participate in public affairs.

Professor Jellinek has laid emphasis on the social aspect of aristocracy. He maintains that there is always some social class which wields the dominant power in the State. It may be a priestly class or military class or landed aristocracy. But whatever be the type, power will belong to that social class which is more powerful than the rest, and this class enjoys certain special privileges which are denied to other classes. Jellinek, accordingly, concludes that it is an error to define aristocracy merely as a government by the few.

Kinds of Aristocracy. Aristocracy for Aristotle was a normal form of government. Its perverted form was oligarchy, government for the rich by the rich. Rousseau divided aristocracies into natural, elective and hereditary. The general basis of classification had been: of wealth, of birth, of talent and intellect, and of culture and education. Some writers have during recent times used the term aristo-democracy" for aristocracy. Aristo-democracy means that only best types of men wield power. In a sense a democratic government is more or less aristocratic in that a considerable proportion of population takes no part in government and the greater share of governing power is concentrated in the hands of a comparatively small number. Public opinion, upon which democracy thrives, is influenced and determined by the leadership of the few. The masses have neither the knowledge nor the time nor the interest which would enable them to rule. The line between aristocracy and democracy is, therefore, difficult to draw. But aristocracy, it must be remembered, places no confidence in the ability of the masses and believes in government by the select few. Democracy, on the other hand, has faith in the ability of man and accepts man as a man. Its principle is that all persons who are fit to perform the duties of citizens can have a share in the direction of the affairs of the State.

Merits of Aristocracy. One of the great merits of aristocracy is that it emphasises quality. It assumes that some are better fitted to govern than others. They govern as they are the best and the criterion of their being best is the moral and intellectual superiority which they possess over others. "It is the everlasting privilege," says Carlyle, "of the foolish to be governed by the wise." Aristocracy gives to the community a ruling class who can be trusted to administer public affairs with complete integrity and honour, because they possess a great position independent of politics. It can also claim superiority over other forms of government in respect of stability and efficiency. John Stuart Mill says that "the governments which have been remarkable in history for sustained ability and vigour in the conduct of affairs have generally been aristocracies." It is further argued that aristocracy would refrain from unwise and immoderate use of power. Its supporters would even defend hereditary aristocracy, for it provides a body of persons who possess a certain hereditary familiarity with public affairs. Political training runs in their blood and they take naturally to the business of government. They represent standard of perfection, derived from heredity and environment, that all should imitate as well as revere.

Aristocracy, it is claimed, is pre-eminently conservative. Since administration rests in the hands of the wise, talented and experienced administrators who have inherited high traditions of public service, they would naturally avoid rash and radical political experiments. Moreover, stability is one of the foremost requirements of a good government and stability demands a "conservative innovation". Violent changes involving suppression of institutions, which have become venerable with age, agitate popular feelings and, as such, endanger the stability of government. "It is, therefore, of the greatest importance in social and political progress that the principle of progress of liberalism should always be joined to the principle of stability or conservatism." Aristocracy serves best the desired purpose.

In fact, cabinet government is in essence aristocracy. Those who make the ministry are party leaders. According to Laski the essential contribution of the ministers to the cabinet is "their commonsense, their ability to put before their colleagues that judgement about decisions which public opinion, and especially party opinion, will make after they have been published." This is aristocracy tinged with responsibility. Modern governments have preserved the element of aristocracy in the composition of the upper chambers of legislature. For instance, the British House of Lords consists of primary hereditary peers. In countries, where the second chambers are elected, the elections are usually so arranged as to make the second chamber representative of the best minds in the nation. The Council of States, the second chamber in India, consists of two hundred and fifty members of whom twelve members are nominated by the President. The members nominated by the President consist of persons having special knowledge or practical experience in respect of such matters as literature, science, art and social service. This system of representation is aristocratic in the best sense.

Weakness of Aristocracy. But the evil inherent in all kinds of aristocracies is that they form a separate interest which is almost certain to come into conflict with the interests of the community. Privileged persons form a class of vested interests and they look on their privileges as an inheritance which they are bound to transmit unimpaired to their successors. Aristocracy of the best, therefore, soon degenerates into class-rule. The interests of the classes, excluded from a share in the government are likely to be ignored by even the best-intentioned of aristocracies. Flushed with power and authority, they become arrogant and proud. "The ruling aristocracies have often displayed towards the lower classes a harshness and cruelty which have been the more intolerable because accompanied by contempt."

The rule of hereditary succession works evil as well as good. Where it has prevailed for a long time, a considerable number of hereditary dignities descend to persons quite unfit to exercise power or to make a good use of social influence. Division of the people in classes provokes envy and opposition. Moreover, it is not rational to maintain and believe that some are born to rule and others to be ruled. Such a government is undemocratic, for it excludes the masses from finding interest in government and, thus, they become only recipients of orders. Aristocracy, therefore, does not offer the people political training or political consciousness, which is so essential for citizenship. It is a government for passive dumb-driven creatures and not for politically awakened and active citizens. Similarly, property, like birth, should not be the criterion for elevating a person to rule, Governing power cannot be wisely restricted to persons who either by accident of birth are born in rich families or to whom some freak of fortune has brought riches Such fortunate persons when in power devise all means, sane or insane, to perpetuate their own interests reducing the masses to a still more pitiable plight.

A great defect of aristocracy, says Bluntschli, is its excessive rigidity. A government which has reverence for long-established customs and traditions cannot have a dynamic outlook. A good government must keep pace with the economic and social requirements of society. Aristocracy will resist all such changes in order to preserve its power. It is not a dynamic mechanism of government for the fulfilment of the needs of dynamic man. It cannot, therefore, serve the purpose of our time.

DEMOCRACY

Meaning of Democracy. The term democracy is derived form the Greek words *demos* and *kratos*, the former meaning the people and the latter power. Democracy, thus, means *power of the people*. It is now regarded as a form of government in which the people rule themselves either directly or indirectly through their representatives. Definitions of democracy, as a form of government, are various. But like many other definitions in Political Science, they differ in their content and application. The Greeks meant by it the government by many and Aristotle considered it as a perverted form of government. But modern writers do not employ the numerical criterion. They lay emphasis on the principle of democracy that all persons who are fit to perform the duties of citizens should have a share in the direction of the State and their will should ultimately prevail. Professor Seeley means by it "a government in which every one has a share." Dicey defines democracy as that form of government in which the governing body is a comparatively large fraction of the entire nation. Bryce accepts the definition of Herodotus and says that democracy denotes that form of government in which the ruling power of the State is largely vested in the members of the community as a whole. He adds, "This means in communities which act by voting, that rule belongs to the majority, as no other method has been found for determining peaceably and legally what is to be declared the will of the community which is not unanimous."

But a mere consent of the people is not sufficient enough to make a government democratic. The people ought to be, to use the words of Plato, their own "watch-dogs". The consent of the people must be real, active and effective in order to make it a genuine democracy. Eternal vigilance is the very life of democracy, if democracy can really claim, in the words of President Abraham Lincoln, to be a government of the people, by the people, and for the people. Government is, of course, always of the people, but it need not be government by the people. Monarchies and aristocracies are governments of the people and not by the people. A government by the people means that people either directly or through their representatives govern themselves, and their will remains supreme on all questions of social direction and policy of the government.

It is not correct to say, however, that democracy is a government by the representatives of all the people. "The people" has been a varying term, as Bryce points out, and it has come to mean something vastly different from what it meant to Aristotle, or even to Lincoln. It now means the majority of the people. Democracy, according to Bryce, is a form of government "in which the will of the majority of the qualified citizens rules, taking the qualified citizens to constitute the great bulk of the inhabitants..." And it is obvious that democracy allows every qualified citizen to express an opinion on affairs of the State. But it cannot secure that every man's opinion shall influence the actions of the State. All citizens cannot be made to agree on all questions of importance.

Moreover, all citizens cannot have a voice in determining the policy of the government. Even the most ardent democrat will not vote for lunatics, criminals or infants. Whenever, therefore, we speak of government by the people or the will of the people, we mean the will of the majority for the time being.

There are two reasons for the will of the majority to prevail. First, they are on the whole more likely to be right than the minority. Secondly, a majority, in most cases is physically stronger than a minority. Unless the majority grossly abuses its power, it is politic for the minority to submit to its will, lest the majority may resort to coercion. But it must be admitted that "the coercion of dissentient minority constitutes a special difficulty for a government founded on the principle of consent." Democracy can be successful only when minorities feel that they are not subjected to oppression by the majority and that their case has been properly heard. When we admit that under a democratic government there is political equality, we mean thereby that opportunity is provided to all citizens, "to pass judgement freely and frequently on the work of the political engineers whose decisions affect their lives." It is then only that a government can be by the people. A democratic government cannot please everybody any more than a monarchical or an aristocratic government. But the former concedes to every citizen the rights of speech, publication and association. "These rights are integral to democracy because they make possible free discussion and the continuous participation of the people in the government." A government by the people must, accordingly, mean a government by discussion and criticism—discussion of competing ideas, "leading to a compromise in which all the ideas are reconciled and which can be accepted by all because it bears the imprint of all."

The meaning of government for the people can best be explained in the words of Mazzini: "the progrers of all through all under the leading of the best and wisest." The test of government is the welfare of the people, and that form of government is to be preferred which gives to human tendencies the fullest scope of development. The primary functions of a democratic government are similar to those of any other form of government. But, in addition to this, "democracy stimulates to self-education, for participation in governmental activities, opens wider horizons for the individual, and leads to broadened interests." The lessons of democracy are liberty, equality and fraternity. Its principle is that all persons who are fit to perform the duties of citizens should have a share in the direction of the State so that each man may have an identical opportunity to grow and expand to the best of his capacity, and there is no man or group of men who will exploit the weakness of others. Democracy does not differentiate between man and man. It raises the common man high on the pedestal of political and social glory and this is the meaning of a government for the people.

For a democratic government there must be a democratic society. A democratic government aims at justice and happiness justice, because "no man or class or group will be strong enough to wrong others; happiness, because each man judging best what is for his own good, will have every chance of pursuing it. The principles of liberty and equality are justified by the results they yield." Here liberty and equality have a reference to the well-known dictum of Kant: "So act as to treat humanity whether in your person or in that of another, in every case as an end, and never merely as a means." This is the requisite of a democratic society, for it instils in human mind the democratic ideal. It is the worth of man which a democratic society recognises and it is, again, the worth of man which a democratic government maintains and pursues. Both aim at what Bentham has reduced into a beautiful formula: Every one to count for one and no one for more than one. A democratic government, therefore, can exist and thrive when the society is democratic.

Dunning has rightly remarked that "our failure to understand democracy in its wider meaning, as a form of society, is the main reason for its being subjected to severe criticism." "Democracy," writes Sir Stafford Cripps, "is a system of government in which every adult citizen is equally free to express his views and desires upon all subjects in whatever way he wishes, and to influence the majority of his fellow-citizens to decide according to those views, and to influence those desires." It means that uniformity of belief or action is neither necessary nor desirable in democracy. Truth only comes by the clash of opinion with opinion and every citizen has something of value to contribute and he must not be hindered in bringing it forward. Democracy is, thus, rooted in equality and can be found in a democratic society in which all enjoy equal rights and privileges without any barriers of class distinctions.

"A democratic society," says Wolff, "is a society of free, equal, active and intelligent citizens, each man choosing his own way of life for himself and willing that others should choose theirs." The brotherhood of man is the basis of democratic society and all its members stand equal in the common fraternity. Birth, wealth, caste, or creed do not determine the status of man. A society riddled with social and economic inequalities cannot be called a democratic society. Social and economic inequalities bring inequalities of treatment and right. Where a common man is not as good a factor of society as another, true citizenship cannot be secured there and a democratic government is an impossibility.

The Communists give a new meaning to democracy. They deny the need of a democratic government, but emphasise the necessity of a democratic State and a democratic State to them is only a socialist State with the dictatorship of the proletariat. They ridicule the western system of democracy with its economic and social inequalities and regard the toleration of minorities, which is the life-blood of democracy, as a show of hypocrisy, for their existence does not help the abolition of economic privilege. In a socialist State, they claim, there are no exploiters and since all the people are toilers there is no antagonism between them. But the Communists are really not democrats and theirs is not a democratic State. They accept the State only as a temporary institution and "so long as the proletariat needs the State," says Engels, "it needs it not in the interests of freedom, but in order to suppress its opponents and when it becomes possible to speak of freedom, the State as such ceases to exist." The Communists, wherever they have established their system of government, do not permit political conflicts and opposition to a socialist system of society. There can be only one party, the Communist Party, and it carries with it the constitutional sanctity of being the vanguard of the working people in the struggle to strengthen and develop the socialist system. Criticism, from the socialist point of view, is considered detrimental to national solidarity and to the cause of socialism. As there can exist only one party and the party insists on unanimity in order to achieve solidarity for the fulfilment of socialist programme, the people can have no control over political affairs and they exercise no choice in appointing and dismissing a government. This is not democracy. The essence of democracy, as a form of government, lies in the opportunity it affords to every citizen to contribute his judgement to the determination of public policy. As a theory of society it stands for that social order which recognises the inherent worth of every human being and faith in the common man.

DIRECT AND REPRESENTATIVE DEMOCRACY

Democracies are usually classed into types—(1) pure or direct, and (2) representative or indirect.

Direct Democracy. When the people themselves directly express their will on public affairs, the type of government is called direct democracy. The people formulate and express their will in a mass meeting and they assemble for this purpose as often as required. In the small city-States of ancient Greece and Rome all adult male citizens were expected to meet together in the assembly—the Ecclesia of Athens, the Commitia of Rome. Pure democracy has not been confined to the ancient world. Its surviving relics are found today in the Swiss *landsgemeinden*. There were twenty-six *landsgemeinden* in the middle of the eighteenth century; today, there are only five, and one of them has been confined to elective functions. On a Sunday in April or May, the adult male citizens assemble out-of-doors and by a show of hands elect cantonal officers and adopt legislation.

But pure democracy can exist and function only in small States with limited population where people can conveniently meet and deliberate together. In large and complex societies, when the number of the people is too numerous and the area of the State is too extensive, direct democracy is impracticable. Even the Swiss *landsgemeinden* is cantonal and nowhere is it associated with national government. This institution has been commended by some writers with great enthusiasm, but a close acquaintance of its actual working produces a very different effect. "It would be naïve," says Professor Rappard, a Swiss scholar, "to believe that even a small community of a few thousand well-trained citizens could, under the complex conditions of the twentieth century, effectively govern itself by means of such an ephemeral legislative assembly. One might as well expect a football crowd, assembled for a few hours in a stadium, to make itself responsible for the establishment of an academic curriculum or for the drafting of a measure of social insurance."

Direct democracy now assumes the form of the *referendum* and the popular *initiative*, and they have long been familiar in Switzerland and the United States. After the First World War they made an appearance in Germany, Latvia, Estonia, Ireland and even in Soviet Russia. They were deleted from the Irish Constitution in 1928 and were lying dormant for thirteen years in Germany when Hitler struck down the Weimar Constitution. In Russia, the Presidum may submit the proposed legislation for the popular vote and hold referendum, but it has never been held so far. In the United States direct legislation is obtainable only in eleven States, most of them in the west. Popular, or direct legislation, as Sait remarks, "is little more than a fad outside of Switzerland, where unique conditions prevail." In Switzerland direct legislation has a natural growth, or, as Bryce says, it is "racy of the soil. There are institutions which like plants, flourish only on their hillside and under their own sunshine."

Indirect or Representative Democracy. The prevailing system of democracy is indirect or representative. The will of the State is formulated and expressed not directly by the people themselves, but by their representatives. The representatives are periodically elected by the people and are entrusted with the administration of public affairs. John Stuart Mill defines indirect or representative democracy as one in which "the whole people or some numerous portion of them, exercise the governing power through deputies periodically elected by themselves."

Even in a representative democracy the ultimate source of authority remains with the people. The people elect the representatives for a number of years and after the expiry of their term, they report back to their masters, the electors. The electors judge them by their deeds and determine whether or not they should repose their trust in them for the next term. If they feel to discontinue with them, they would do so by electing new representatives. Representative democracy guarantees, in other terms, a general harmony of purpose between government and governed by reconciling effective authority and political freedom.

After the First World War a good deal of dissatisfaction was expressed against the working of indirect democracy, and devices of popular control, the *referendum*, the *initiative* and *recall*, were introduced by some of the States. These devices aimed at transferring from the representatives to the people themselves the right to have the final verdict over legislative and administrative matters and to recall those representatives back from office who did not perform their duties diligently and honestly. But the dominant verdict has, undoubtedly, proved hostile and the representative institutions continue to be instruments of democracy.

Requisites of Democracy. Democracy in its broader sense means faith in the common man. A genuine democracy, therefore, is an active, growing, progressive force responsive to the will of the people and animated by ideals of mutual service and public welfare. It involves the presence of a democratic idea among the people. A democratic idea, according to Ivor Brown, means:

1. An "action of will." The people should not only imbibe the will to have democracy, but the power to retain it as well. They should be fully conscious of their political rights and duties as vigilance is the price of democracy. The citizens should not be silent spectators, simply watching the game of politics. Democracy demands from the common man rational conduct and active participation in government. A democratic government is a government by criticism. The people should have the courage to protest against and criticise the injustice and tyranny of the government. "To be articulate is its very

life; to be dumb its demise." It is only the will of the people to action which can save them from the tyranny of the rulers. The rulers become masters when the citizens are passive. They become their servants so long as the citizens remain masters. The successful working of democracy, accordingly, depends upon the intelligence, interest, public spirit and civic sense of its citizens, the sense of 'public spirit' and 'social consciousness', in brief.

2. Democracy involves fellowship, that is, a feeling of fraternity or what Giddings calls, 'consciousness of kind.' Fellow-feeling aims at realisation of a common end—the welfare of humanity. Fellowship, therefore, appeals to our common humanity. Democracy does not recognise class distinctions. Fellowship knows no limits created by religion, caste, birth or wealth. It is only in a society of equals that harmony can be secured. By equality we mean, of course, equality of opportunity—fair and open field for all. This kind of equality ensures social justice and it is the very life-breath of democracy. But when there exist huge inequalities of wealth, social justice cannot be obtained. A wide gulf between the rich and the poor makes it impossible for the latter to live and exercise their political rights independently and freely. The rich become a class of vested interests and equality in all its meanings disappears. When there is no equality, there can be neither liberty nor fraternity.

3. Democracy demands a spirit of tolerance. This is necessary as democracy involves the rule of the majority and the submission of the minority or minorities to the decisions of the majority. The majority should not be prompted by sectional interests and thereby ruthlessly disregard the interests of the minorities. Nor should the minorities always suspect the integrity of the majority and be at perpetual political animosity with the latter. There should prevail a sense of give-and-take: the habit of tolerance and compromise among the citizens. The more there are cleavages in society and party squabbles, the more difficult it is to work democracy. The differences in majority and minority opinion

prove beneficial only when they are directed towards the common good. Each party should have a full opportunity to express and propagate its opinion, but once the decision has been taken all should scrupulously adhere to it. "This is true resignation. This is true service and this is all that is demanded by a common fellowship in democracy."

4. There should be adequate provision of opportunities for the individual to develop his personality. This can be realised when everyone has free access to knowledge, security against unemployment, a minimum wage, fair conditions of work and leisure, provision against sickness and old age. Democracy here invades the realm of industry. It has now become a common slogan that economic democracy must precede political democracy. A society where wealth is most unevenly distributed and one class of people exploit the rest, democracy cannot succeed. A democratic society is a partnership among equals. A democratic ideal, therefore, cannot be realised until industry is entirely democratised and inequalities in the distribution of national wealth are reduced to the minimum. This may mean to some socialism, but democracy, too, aims at social justice. Justice, as Barker says is a joining or fitting together not only of persons, but also of principles. "It joins and knits together the claims of the principle of liberty with those of the principle of equality, and both with those of the principle of fraternity or co-operation. It adjusts them to one another in a right order of *their* relations."

5. Democracy is participation, it means doing things in common with others, and taking your share of the responsibilities involved. "The democratic problem," says Lindsay, "is the control of the organisation of power by the common man." The citizens must be thinking human beings possessing an independent opinion and intelligent interest in public affairs. The success of democracy depends upon the ability, character, and power of discrimination a common man possesses. Democracy becomes a show affair if citizens exhibit a sheep-like behaviour—a crowd mind—in public affairs.

The active and intelligent participation of citizens in public affairs can be assured if all of them are adequately educated. The government must, therefore, provide a system of free and compulsory education for all. Education produces thinking human beings who know, according to Rousseau, that they are both sovereign and subjects and they must accordingly, fulfil their dual obligations. "A citizen of democracy is not merely to obey; he has also to see if his obedience is rational." Vigilance, wisdom, intellect, common sense and honesty are the virtues which should be possessed by the citizens of a democratic State and all these qualities flow from the gift of education. President Lincoln said: "you can fool part of the people all the time, and all the people part of the time, you cannot fool all the people all the times." If citizens are educated and they have the courage to be critical of the government this befooling business becomes infinitely difficult. Those who follow Bentham's maxim "While I will obey punctually, I will censure freely" are true citizens of a democratic State. They possess the powers of discrimination to obey and to criticise. They do not belong to an uncritical herd. This means that there should be a free and fearless press which serves as a popular forum of educating and expressing public opinion. Press should really be a jealous guardian of the rights and liberties of the people if democracy is to serve its purpose.

Defects of Democracy. But the assumptions of democracy, it is pointed out, are too idealistic and difficult to be realised in practical life. Democracy demands from the people a high degree of civic capacity which involves intelligence, self-control and devotion to a common cause, capacity to subordinate to it private interests and desires. It relies on the spirit of give and take. It also demands time to share in common activities, to study the issues involved. The common man, the critics of democracy maintain, is indolent in politics. He is neither politically intelligent nor sufficiently educated. He does not possess the capacity to understand complex political problems and is incapable of intelligent action. "Democracy is suited," observes Dr. Beni Prasad, "to a State of society in which the people want to exercise power, are capable of sinking differences and co-operating for the general good and have acquired knowledge and judgement enough to elect suitable representatives and to judge as to the propriety of general lines of policy." Lecky, accordingly, characterised democracy as "government of the poorest, the most ignorant, the most incapable, who are necessarily the most numerous." The average citizen has not the time, inclination and ability to inform himself on the affairs of the State. The apathy of the voters in most of the democratic countries is proverbial. A voter has to be cajoled and dragged out from his place of work in order to cast his vote. The obvious result is that power passes into the hands of a professional politician, a demagogue, who is ever ready to exploit the masses.

It is further maintained that democracy is inefficient as a form of government. Democracy, its critics urge, is based on the assumption that all men are equal and that one man is as good as another, whatever his real worth. He votes and is eligible for office on a level with them all. But this is an irrational and impracticable dogma. The critics of democracy assert that men are manifestly not equal. Physically and mentally they differ widely from one another. Votes are, then, counted and not weighed. Counting of votes determines a majority and the decisions will have to be those of the majority no matter what the margin of majority may be and howsoever superior wisdom and better judgement the minority may claim. Faguet considers democracy as a hopeless rule of ignorance. He makes democracy synonymous with incompetence, as it is a government by amateurs. The representatives assume responsibility of governing the State not because they are able and possess specialised knowledge in administration, but only as they command a majority. "A youth must pass," says Sir Sydney Low, "an examination in Arithmetic before he can hold a second class clerkship in the Treasury but a Chancellor of the Exchequer may be a middle-aged man of the world who has forgotten what little he ever learnt about figures at Eton or Oxford and is innocently anxious to know the meaning of those little dots." The inefficiency of a democratic government is essentially reflected in its policies, especially relating to defence and foreign policy, which are weak and vacillating. A government which depends for its existence upon the uncertain passions of unthinking people and is never sure of its life cannot afford to undertake sound and long-term policy.

Party system is indispensable for democracy. But the manner in which party system actually works in modern democracies deprives countries of the services of some of their best citizens. Political parties encourage hollowness and insincerity, create cleavages in the life of the nation, debase normal standards and distribute the "spoils". Election propaganda misguides and mis-educates people. Moral considerations are subordinated in order to secure the largest number of votes. People vote for the party and not for the candidate. The representative owes responsibility to the party on whose ticket he contested the election and he must say and do what he is told to do. Rigid party discipline makes representatives cowards and subservient as they lose honesty, courage and independence. Under such a system of representation popular control, which is the essence of indirect democracy, becomes illusory. Then, the system works mechanically. There is no option for the individual voter who intends to exercise his independent judgement. "He has to choose between two or more candidates who may be either knaves or fools and for none of whom he cares, and decides between two or three issues, none of which meets his approval." When voting becomes so mechanical democracy loses its educational value.

Again, democracy is criticised because it has encouraged growth of class struggle. Candidates who offer themselves for election are generally moneyed men, who can foot election bills and contribute liberally to the party funds. This propertied oligarchy will make laws to the advantage of its own class rather than to the interests of the community as a whole. The obvious result will be the prosperity of the few at the cost of the many, creating thereby a class with vested interests. This privileged class will struggle at the costs to perpetuate its interests. Modern democracy, its critics further assert, is capitalistic and a capitalistic society cannot be truly democratic, for there is neither social nor economic equality. Economic democracy, it is emphasised, must precede political democracy.

Then, it is said that democracy is a highly expensive form of government. Its governmental machinery is complex and its functions involve much waste of time and money. At many stages the process of administration is just a duplication. Take, for instance, the system of bicameralism. Whatever be its political utility, bicameralism is a heavy toll on the exchequer. Elections, which are so frequent in democracy, have become inconceivably expensive. Even in a poor country like India it may cost a candidate near about Rs.50,000, and it is really a very conservative estimate. In the U.S.A. a Senator is reported to have spent half a million dollars over his election. This is surely a waste, not only of money, but also of time and is inconsistent with the spirit of democracy.

The ethical value of democracy is also seriously questioned. Its critics assert that it discounts honesty—honesty is the sense of reasoned conviction, refined habits and integrity of character. There is much falsification and vilification. Election campaigns and party meetings convened for purposes of "nursing the constituency" are very often mud-slinging campaigns where issues are "vulgarised and popularised" before they can make an appeal to the people. Questions are not discussed dispassionately. They are discussed in such a manner as to catch votes. And catching of votes is a nefarious device because it strangulates thought and chokes reason. The voter is not given an opportunity to pause and think. A man who does not think is not serving the purpose of his creation. The result is that he can be easily led astray. The politician does his own job. He would not even hesitate to corrupt the voters. Votes are actually purchased. Bryce who devotes a separate Chapter to "Money Power in Politics" shows that electors, members of legislatures, administrative officials and even judicial officers frequently succumb to the lure of money.

Bryce on defects of Democracy. Lord Bryce, a fervent exponent of democracy, points out the following defects. His conclusions are based upon his personal observations of the six major democracies of the world.

1. "The power of money to pervert administration or legislation."

2. "The tendency to make politics a gainful profession."

3. "Extravagance in administration."

4. "The abuse of the doctrine of equality and failure to appreciate the value of administrative skill."
5. "The undue power of party organisation."
6. "The tendency of legislators and political officials to play for votes in the passing of laws and in tolerating breaches of order."

Merits of Democracy. Bryce, nevertheless, points out that the first three defects are common to all forms of government and are not inherent only in democracy. The last three are associated more closely with democracy, but are not insurmountable evils. "Democracy," as Dunning says, 'has closed some of the old channels of evil; it has opened some new ones, but it has not increased the stream." Democracy must face self-interest and irresponsibility of power, both of which underlie its major problems. But it has two powerful weapons to fight against these evils: law and opinion. The latter cannot be realised in any other form of government except democracy. While admitting that democracy has defects, Dr. Finer says, but the political, social and economic gifts of democracy endow mankind-with vast riches. He observes that under a democratic government, "we have the assurance that the sphere of our private life—our family, our diversions, our worship, our work—will not be invaded except by due process of law in which we have an equal say with any. We rest tranquil that officials and judges will not abuse us, and that they themselves will have to answer for discrimination and bias and unauthorised invasions of our private and public life to a public tribunal in which we, as of right sit as judge and jury."

In spite of the unsparing attacks to which democracy has been subjected, it still tends to spread, conferring more and more power on the people. The Second World War was fought on the basis of democracy vs. dictatorship. It was a victory for democracy as people had not lost their faith in it. The problem of democracy, thus, centres on the point whether or not man is increasing in wisdom. The answer is in the affirmative, for while no government gives so much to the citizen as does democracy, at the same time, no other form of government demands so much from him. All the rights and duties which democracy confers upon its citizens make him a thinking human being. After all what is the difference between a man and an animal? The former can think and reason; the latter cannot; he does what he is made to do. Dictation is not the way of democracy. Democracy will never perish as long as there is hope in the rational nature of man; as long as it produces thinking human beings. Thinkers are doers and a citizen of a democratic State is an active participant in its affairs.

Democracy, as said previously, is more than a form of government. It is a form of society as well, even an ideal or spirit, a doctrine of human optimism. Democracies, says Dr. Finer, "admit the pragmatic nature of their search for perfection, and recognise that of perfection there is no single exclusive principle. Yet they surmise that if such there should be, it is one yet to be discovered in a process of evolution, and if the unfolding is to arrive at unsoundness it must be founded on the unfettered expression and interply of all opinion." Democratic societies recognise and welcome change. They must evolve with the development of new points of view, new techniques, new possibilities for human life. With the extension of the concept of democracy old egalitarian doctrines have been discarded. By equality we do not now mean that all men are alike. There are physical, intellectual and moral differences between one man and another Granting all these obvious variations, the term equality is interpreted to mean equality of opportunity. Democracy is that form of society in which every man has a chance and knows he has it. Democracy, therefore, has the merit of ensuring the twin principles of liberty and equality. Under it there is no class of persons possessing special privileges.

The test of governments is the welfare of the people, and that form of government is to be preferred which gives full scope to the development of human capacities. Democracy makes authority a trust. Those who exercise authority are chosen by their fellow-citizens for short terms of office and are responsible to them for the exercise of their trust. It implies a recognition of the duties of the government and the rights of the people. Democracy is superior to other forms of government, as John Stuart Mill points out, for two reasons: First, the rights and interests of the individual can be safeguarded only when he is able to "stand up" for them himself. Secondly, there is a greater degree of general prosperity which is more widely diffused as the energies and interests of all the people are stimulated and enlisted in its support. Indirect democracy does not mean actual rule by the people, "for the people rather determine the ends towards which their government shall aim, and watch over those into whose hands they have placed the actual power of administration." In short, it is claimed that popular election, popular control, and popular responsibility are more likely to ensure a greater degree of efficiency than any other system of government. There is, thus, no justification for the claim of Sir Henry Maine that aristocracy is the mother of all progress, that popular government is characterised by great fragility, and that since its appearance, all forms of government have become more insecure than they were before."

But the merit of democracy does not lie in its efficiency as a form of government. Nobody has ever defended democracy on the grounds of efficiency, but only on the grounds that, as for freedom, its denial involves the denial of certain personal values more important than efficiency. A good government therefore, is no substitute for self-government. Democracy is a government by the people for their welfare. It stimulates them to self-education. The supreme test of excellence in government is not the well feeding of the people nor is it to be found in the rigidity of order the State maintains. "It is the character a polity tends to create," as President Lowell remarks, "in the citizens by whom it must be sustained. The best government in the long run is one that nurtures a people strong in moral fibre, in integrity, industry, self-reliance, and courage." Democracy elevates the character and develops the political intelligence of the masses. It is an active, growing, progressive force inspired by ideals of service to mankind. Self-government is not a mere form of institution to be had when desired. It demands from an average man a certain degree of intelligence, honesty, public spirit and discipline. These virtues give a people, as Woodrow Wilson points out, "self-possession, self-mastery, the habit of order and peace and common counsel and reverence for law which will not fail when they themselves become the makers of law; the steadiness and self-control of political maturity". Democracy, therefore, develops the potential intellectual and spiritual qualities of man. It promotes a better and higher form of national character, because the citizens feel that they are a part and parcel of government.

Democracy is inseparable from a belief in methods of peaceful persuasion, in the ultimate reasonableness of man, and his response to rational argument. A democratic society is not susceptible to revolutions. The people know and feel that they are both sovereign and subjects. If they have any grievances the redress is easy and can be had by peaceful and constitutional means, because the political life of the community is based on a complete freedom of discussion out of which emerges the public opinion which is the ultimate source of authority. "Since the law will be made and the administration be given momentum and controlled by us, voters," writes Finer, "and since our power can be successfully exerted by association and persuasion, the impulse of the system is to foster fellowship and a common conscience among all men"; the spirit of self-help, self-reliance, self-respect and co-operation and a sense of responsibility in the individual.

Future of Democracy. Democracy, no doubt has its own defects, but "no form of government", as Lowell maintains, "is a panacea for all human ills." Democracy may not have created a sense of fellow-feeling; it may not have drafted the best trained mind to State service, or dignified and purified politics, but in comparison with governments of the past it has justified itself. "Things may be bad today, but they were worse yesterday." The world tried unlimited monarchy, aristocracy and oligarchy at various times and there is no desire to go back to them. Burns has strikingly said, "No one denies that existing representative assemblies are defective, but even if an automobile does not work well, it is foolish to go back into a farm cart, however romantic." We experimented with dictatorship lately and gave it up as a hopeless form of government, since dictatorship is the negation of individual liberty and initiative and is antagonistic to the development of human personality. It is, accordingly, mischievous to search for another form of government instead of improving what we have. The essence of democracy, in the words of Mazzini, is "the progress of all through all under the leading of the best and wisest" Its supreme value is ethical and educational. As a form of government democracy can flourish and decline in proportion to the moral and intellectual progress of mankind.

But democratic institutions require urgent readjustment consistent with changing conditions. Political democracy cannot be divorced from a social and economic programme. Moreover, democracy must be progressive, adaptable, and flexible. Capitalistic democracy, which is the traditional democratic theory, is now out of date, for it does not respond to the needs of the people. The demands of democracy are the speedy responsiveness to public opinion and the social needs. Capitalist society cannot fulfil the demands of democracy, because where it is tempted to be active in defence is just where democracy is tempted to be active in offence. Capitalistic democracy, accordingly, requires to be abolished root and branch, if democracy can have an appeal. Old values are being questioned and the foundations of our social, economic and political order have become shaky. Unless democracy finds the means of equalising opportunity and wipes out existing economic disparities, its future appeal seems to be doubtful. Our social and economic needs are prior to political needs. Political needs arise for the sake of good life. If democracy, as a form of government, fails to provide for good life, it may be substituted by a Stateless society in which there will be neither social nor economic disparity. How far such a society is feasible, no one can foresee. But no one can deny, at the same time, that the traditional concept of democracy is a menace to democracy unless the former reforms itself.

References

Barker, E.: *Reflections on Government,* Chaps. III, VI.

Bryce, J.: *Modern Democracies,* Vol. I, Part II; Vol. II, Part III.

Burns, C. D.: *The Challenge to Democracy.*

Burns, C.D.: *Democracy: Its Defects and Advantages.*

Dealey, J.Q.: *The State and Government,* Chaps. X-XI.

Faguet, E.: *The Cult of Incompetence.*

Finer, H.: *The Theory and Practice of Modern Government* (1954), pp. 937-54.

Follet. M.P.: *The New State,* Chaps. XVI, XXI.

Garner, J.W.: *Introduction to Political Science,* Chaps. VI-VII.

Garner, J.W.: *Political Science and Government,* Chaps. XIII-XVI.

Bearnshaw, F.J.C.: *Democracy at the Crossways.*

Lindsay, A.D.: *Essentials of Democracy.*

Lindsay, A.D.: *The Modern Democratic State.*

Maciver, R.M.: *The Modern State,* Chaps. XI-XII.

Maine, H.: *Popular Government*, Chap. II (1885).

Maritain, Jacques, : *Man and the State*, Chap. V.

Mill, J.S.: *Representative Government* (1890).

Sait, E.M.: *Democracy* (1929).

Sfeley, J.R.: *Introduction to Political Science,* Lectures II, VI-VII.

Sidgwick, H: *Elements of Politics,* Chaps, XXII, XXX.

Wallas, G.: *Human Nature in Politics.*

Wells, H.G.: *Democracy under Revision.*

4

Forms of Government Unitary and Federal Governments

The Unity of Government. In our consideration of the nature of the State, we have shown how unity constitutes one of its most essential attributes. A like quality attaches to its government as well. It is rather unfortunate that the term "government" is employed to designate the Several sub-divisions of the machinery made use of by the State for the conduct of its affairs, as, for instance, the government of a province, the government of a city, etc.

It would appear from such a use of the term as if there could exist within a State a number of governments at the same time. But it is not so. In a real sense there can be no governments within a government. What seem to be separate governments for the administration of public affairs for the country as a whole and such subdivisions as provinces, cities and the like are, in reality, but parts of one governmental system.

They all form parts of one integrated scheme of governmental organisation. This point is important to grasp, if we are to properly appreciate the problem of the distribution of governmental powers among its various parts and the character of the governmental system resulting thereform.

The necessity for the distribution of government powers. Though a State can have but one government yet such is the extent of territory over which many modern States exercise jurisdiction and so numerous and varied are their functions that it is impossible for any single authority to do its work from one single centre. Then it is not only the problem of doing the work. It must be done effectively and efficiently if the purpose of the State is to be truly realised. It is, therefore, imperative that the sum total of government powers should be split up and distributed among different organs and authorities and, together, they all constitute one harmonious scheme for the administration of public affairs.

Territorial and functional division of powers. There are two methods of dividing governmental powers, territorial and functional. The territorial division of powers seeks to divide the territory of the State into a number of distinct divisions and sub-divisions each of which is charged with the performance of certain governmental functions within its boundaries and it provided with a governmental organisation for that purpose. The result of such territorial division and sub-divisions is the national government and a series of local governments. The functional method is that where the distribution to particular organs or authorities is made in accordance with the character of the functions to be performed. Those two are not alternate methods. Both are employed in the organisation of all modern governments, but differently. This leads to different characters of the resulting governmental systems.

Division of powers on territorial basis. The desirability of distribution of governmental powers among territorial units results not only from the extent of territory of modern states, but also from the fact that many functions of government affect exclusively, or primarily, the interests of particular localities rather than the country as a whole. It does not, however, mean that one single central authority cannot perform these functions. But if it does, the burden of work and responsibility would be too great for effective and efficient administration. It would also result in intolerable expense and delay. Moreover, it is politic to entrust the smaller communities with the affairs that concern themselves alone, because of the presumption that the people belonging to a particular locality can best know and appreciate their needs. Besides, it gives to a larger number of persons an interest and share in political action. "We cannot realize the full benefit of democratic government," says Professor Laski," unless we begin by the admission that all problems are not central problems, and the results of problems not central in their incidence require decision at the place, and by the persons, where and by whom the incidence is most deeply felt."

The system of territorial sub-division is essentially similar in all modern States. First, for certain purposes which are vital to the life of the nation the entire country is treated as one political unit and the organisation managing all such affairs is called the Central or National government. Next, the country is divided into a relatively small number of important divisions variously designated as constituent States, Provinces, Cantons, Departments, etc, each with a complete governmental organisation. These grand divisions are, in their turn, further sub-divided into smaller areas known as Districts, Countries, Townships, Communes etc. each also having its political organisation. Further sub-divisions, if there are usually of a purely administrative character. In addition, all States recognize that urban and rural present different problems of government and consequently grant to them distinct political organisations for the performance of the governmental duties specially affecting their peculiar interests.

Analysis of the Problem. But the real problem is that of determining how the sum total of governmental powers shall be distributed territorially. If we analyze this problem, it will be found that in it are involved four distinct questions: (1) What authority shall decide, the distribution of powers? (2) what shall be the geographical system of division into different political units? (3) What shall be the powers of government of each territorial unit? (4) What shall be the type of governmental organisation in each territorial unit?

For a student of Political Science the first of these four questions, *viz.* what authority has the legal right to determine the distribution of governmental power among the different territorial units, is much the most important, for its decision determines the character of the resulting governmental system.

Two types of Government—Unitary and Federal. Two systems are found in modern States with two types of resulting governments, *unitary* and *federal*. A unitary government is a single integrated system of government for the exercise of all powers. The legal sovereign confers all the powers of government in the first instance upon a single central government. The central government may exercise all these powers by itself or crate political sub-divisions and delegate to them such powers as it deems wise. The central government is competent to change their boundaries as well as powers at its pleasure by ordinary legislature enactment. A federal government, on the other hand, is a system of government in which powers are divided and distributed between a central government and governments of political divisions. Both set of governments exercise powers granted to them by the constitution and are each, within a sphere, co-ordinate and independent, that is, both are free and autonomous within the spheres assigned to them by the constitution and none is helplessly dependent on the other for its existence and proper functioning. It means equality of status between the two sets of government, the one is not simply the creation of the other. Both the national government, and the regional governments, enjoy a juridical status and corporate personality.

We can sum up the difference between a unitary and a federal government and say:

> In a unitary government the political sub-division are integral parts of the single central government. They are created, their powers defined and their form of organisation determined by that government. In a federation the powers of the central government and regional governments are defined by the constitution and both sets of governments are co-ordinate. Only by constitutional amendment can any readjustment be made.

Unitary Governments. England, France, Italy, Belgium, Japan, Afghanistan, Iran, and many other countries has unitary governments. There is one integrated system of government and the supreme power belongs to the central government. For administrative convenience and other considerations the country may be divided into political divisions of different categories, but all authority emanates from the central government. These sub-divisions have no original existence of their own. They are the creation of the central government and may be altered at its will. The power exercised by them is only a delegated and subordinate authority which can be increased, diminished or withdrawn at the discretion of the central government. The sub-divisions are, therefore the agents of the central government and whatever autonomy or governmental competence may have been conceded to them exists by sufferance rather than by constitutional guarantee.

The real point to know is the authority by which such areas are established and their powers and governmental organisation determined. England allows maximum autonomy to her local areas, but they are the creatures of Parliament and their powers are determined and derived from the Acts of Parliament and all such powers can be enlarged or restricted at the will of the government at London. Whitehall also exercises considerable administrative control over all such areas and as Ogg sums up : "All told, however, control is both wide and deep; not only so, but it is steadily penetrating to new phases and levels."

France is divided into administrative units called "Departments" which are divided into cantons, *arrondissements,* and communes, each having its organs for local administration. But general opinion is that it is almost misleading to talk about local government in France. Centralisation is the essence of French local government—"Centralisation raised to a raised to a superlative degree. All authority converges inward and upward." The local organs area merely agents of the central government. From the Communes to the Ministry of the Interior the administration is linked up with one chain. The Minister of the Interior just "presses a button—the prefects, sub-prefects and mayors do the rest. All the wires run to Paris." Ogg gives a matter of fact summing up of the nature of local government in France. He says, "Not only are there no constitutionally separate spheres of governmental authority, there is really one government, functioning equally through Ministers and Parliament at Paris and prefects and councils throughout the country at large. Local areas have only such governing organs, local bodies only such powers as are given to them by national law. All of the threads are gathered ultimately in the hands of the central government at Paris. More then this the entire mechanism of departments, *arrondissements* and communes, heads up at a single ministry at the capital, *i.e.* Interior."

The Government of India, too, was unitary in character under the Act of 1919. Although the provinces were given a partial responsible government, called *diarchy*, and the central and provincial subjects were demarcated normally allowing the provinces to legislate on provincial subjects, yet the Government of India was supreme in all affairs of provincial government, executive and legislative. The Act of 1919 had vested the superintendence, direction and control of the civil and military government of India in the Governor-General-in-Council who was required to pay due obedience to all such orders as he might receive from the Secretary of State for India. The Governor-General had wide powers of assenting to, vetoing, or of reserving for the signification, and of returning for further consideration bills passed by the Central Legislature. He could exercise similar powers in relation to bills passed by the provincial legislatures. The Indian Legislature was competent to make laws for all persons and all things within British India, except that the previous sanction of the Governor-General was necessary for the introduction of any measure regulating any provincial subjects as classified according to the Act of 1919. Similarly, the Central Legislature had the power to repeal or amend any laws in force in any part of British India, except that the previous sanction of the Governor-General was necessary for introducing a bill, repealing or amending any Act of a provincial legislature.

Merits of Unitary Government. The unitary type of government represent the most effective type of governmental organisation. The whole problem of the organisation of government is enormously simplified and the system possesses the merit of flexibility. One of the essential features of a good governmental system should be its ability to modify and adjust its organisation, and the manner in which its powers are exercised, as new needs and conditions demand such change. In a unitary government territorial division of powers is a matter for the government itself to determine; it has accordingly full powers to modify its scheme of internal organisation and distribution of powers and when need arises.

The outstanding feature of the unitary government is, as the name implies unity. All powers of government are concentrated in the hands of a single set of authorities and all organs of government constitute integral parts of one piece of administrative mechanism, There is uniformity of laws, policy, and administration. "All the organs of government can thus be brought to bear directly upon the problem of administration to be solved. There can be no conflict of authority, no conflict or confusion regarding responsibility for work to be performed, no overlapping of jurisdictions, no duplication of work, plant, or organisation which cannot be immediately adjusted." In the fields of foreign policy and national defence the strength of the centralised government is especially manifest. It exhibits promptness of decision and firmness of action. Unified administration checks centrifugal forces and saves administration from disruption. Finally, a unitary government being simple in organisation, it is less expensive. There is no duplication of political institutions.

Defect of Unitary Government. The only defect which can be ascribed to a unitary government is, as Professor Garner puts it that it "tends to repress local initiative, Discourages rather than stimulates interest in public affairs, impairs the vitality of local governments and facilitates the development of centralised bureaucracy." The present-day central governments, it is further maintained, have to tackle so many complex problems, national and international, that they have neither the initiative nor the time to devote to local affairs. Local areas cannot, accordingly, progress. But such a criticism will not hold valid once we distinguish between a centralisation of authority and a centralisation of the use of this authority. A really centralised government is one in which the central government, instead of making used of agencies to which large powers of discretion are granted, attempts itself directly to administer local affairs. It is in this sense that France, in comparison with other countries, has a highly centralised government, and not because it has adopted a unitary form of government. There is nothing in the unitary form of government which does not permit decentralisation in the actual exercise of governmental powers, or the conferring of autonomy or powers of self-government upon political sub-divisions. All the same, unitary government is best suited for small countries which have a geographical unity and which are racially and culturally homogeneous. It does not suit a country with big territory and huge population of diverse races and cultures. Only a federation can bring unity out of this diversity.

FEDERAL GOVERNMENT

What is a Federation? The term federation is derived from the Latin word *foedus* meaning treaty or agreement. A federal government comes into existence either as a result of centripetal or centrifugal forces. When hitherto sovereign and independent States, either because they are too weak to resist individually foreign aggression, or because they remain economically backward by standing, alone, voluntarily agree to unite, as in union there lies strength, they form a federal union. Such a union comes into operation as a result of centripetal forces. The instrument by which a federation is brought about is of the nature of a treaty or agreement between the independent States and the new unit of government, national or central, which they agree to create. A new State is, thus, created to which the hitherto sovereign States surrender their sovereignty and agree to become its component parts, known by different names—States in the United States, Australia and India, Provinces in Canada, Cantons in Switzerland—in different federal States.

The central or national government, which comes into existence, as a result of such a union, is entrusted with powers of general character, which concern the nation as a whole. Other subjects, which are of local interest, or in which variety of practice can be permitted, are left within the jurisdiction of the regional governments. States, Provinces or Cantons whatever be their name. The powers so distributed between the sets of government central and regional, are protected by the constitution and neither of the two can encroach upon the jurisdiction of the other or destroy its existence. Alterations can be made by amending the constitution alone. Sovereignty lies neither in the central government nor in the regional governments. Neither can it be divided between the two, as many writers have held. It resides in the State alone and it is exercised by the authority which has the power to amend the constitution. In a federation, therefore, "the separate States disappear, their sovereignty being destroyed and their citizens having divested themselves of the old allegiance, create, on the basis of a national unity, a federal State."

A federation may also come into existence when a unitary State with a large area, which needs unit out of its diversity, divides its powers into two sets of government and grants constitutional independence to its units. The new apparatus of government comes to be like this: the central government retains only those subjects which are of national importance and transfers the rest to the jurisdiction of the units. In this case centrifugal forces operate and bring about a federal form of government. For example, and Government of India Act, 1935, envisaged a federation consisting of all the eleven Provinces and those princely States which were to express their provinces and those princely States which were to express their desire to accede to federation after signing the Instrument of Accession.

Whatever be the method of its coming into existence and whatever be the system of division of powers a federal government is a dual government in which powers are divided and distributed by the constitution between a central government and regional governments. Unlike the unitary government, powers of the units in a federation are *original* and not *derived*. They are not the grant of the central government, but the gift of the constitution and the are constitutionally protected. Both the central and regional governments are co-ordinate, independent authorities within their allotted spheres of jurisdiction. None can encroach upon the powers of the other. If any change is desired to be made in the distribution of powers, it cannot be done by any one of the two sets of government. It must be done by amending the constitution as prescribed by law. This means equality of status and this is the essence of federalism, although equality of status does not necessarily imply absolute equality of powers. This is an impossible task and not within the reach of practical politics. The distribution of powers between the central government and regional governments, depend upon various factors and every country has its own peculiar problems. The balance of powers is, accordingly, differently tilted in different federations; in some it is in favour of the central government and in others it is in favour of regional governments. But it does not deprive the government of its federal character so long as the one is not rendered thereby helplessly dependent on the other for its existence or proper functioning. By the federal principle, observes Professor Wheare, "I mean the method of dividing powers so that the general and regional governments are each within a sphere, co-ordinate and independent." The existence of sphere of activities for each government—central and regional—where they are co-ordinate and independent is the essential quality of federalism. Prof. Dicey defines federation as a "political contrivance intended to reconcile national unity with the maintenance of State rights", *i.e.* the desire for national unity and determination of each individual unit to maintain its identity and independence.

What a federation is, may, thus, be summed up:

1. A federation is born out of the desire for *union* rather than *unity*. Unity is the essence of a unitary system of government. Federation allows the federating units to preserve their identity by retaining their independent jurisdiction expect in matters which are deemed to be of common national interest.

2. The State willing to federate lose their sovereign character as soon as a federation is formed. A new State emerges as a result of this union and it, accordingly, becomes sovereign.

3. The mechanism of a federal government consists of two parts, national or central government, and the regional governments

called States in America and India, Provinces in Canada and Cantons in Switzerland.

4. The powers of government are divided and distributed into these two parts. The central government is given jurisdiction over subjects of a general nature, which are common to all and among other those promoting the union. The regional governments are given power over matters of local importance and utility, which do not require uniformity.

5. A federation is made, it does not grow. It is made deliberately with a view to having the benefits of union. And since the union establishes a system of dual government in which powers are divided and distributed, a written constitution is the logical necessity of a federal government.

6. It also involves rigidity of the constitution so that neither the central government nor the regional governments may be in a position to deprive the other of its powers. If any change is desired to be brought about, it must be done by amending the constitution.

7. The process of constitutional amendment is prescribed in the constitution. This establishes the supremacy of the constitution. The supreme constitution is essential if government is to be federal.

8. Federation is a permanent union in contrast to various other kinds of unions and alliances between States.

Federation and Confederation. Sometimes the terms federation and confederation are used interchangeably as if they are one and carry the same meaning and set up a similar form of government. For example, the Swiss constitution of 1874 is titled as Swiss Confederation and the used of the term is continued in the Preamble and various Articles of the Constitution. Even a modern authority like Dicey uses the terms interchangeably in a single sentence. A federation and on confederation resemble one another inasmuch as that both the words come from the same root, otherwise there is a fundamental difference between the two. "A confederation," says Hall, "is a union strictly of independent States which consent to forego permanently a part of their liberty of action of certain specific objects, and they are not so combined under a common government that the latter appears to their exclusion as the international entity."

Confederation is an association of sovereign States formed for the purpose of promoting or achieving certain specific objects. They unite on a basis of equality and the most obvious motive for such a union is to gain security and strength in foreign relations. A central organisation is set up usually consisting of a congress of delegates who represent the governments of the States composing the confederation. The delegates usually vote by States and under instructions from the governments that they represent. The member States retain their sovereignty and they do not create a new state. The instrument which creates the Confederation and defines the powers of the central organisation so crated is of the nature of a compact or treaty among the sovereign States. Any member of a Confederation may withdraw therefrom. To sum up, a confederacy, in the words of Oppenheim, consists of "a number of full sovereign States linked together for the maintenance of their external and internal independence by a recognised international treaty into a union with organs of its own, which are vested with a certain power over the member 'States', but not over the citizens of these States."

Confederations have been numerous in the historical development of the States. More recent examples were the old German Confederation from 1815 to 1866, the Swiss Confederacy from 1815 to 1840, and the union of the Thirteen American States under the Articles of Confederation from 1781 to 1789.

A confederation is similar to a federation in two respects. Both in a confederation and a federation different States associate with one another for certain specific purposes, and in both cases a central authority is established for the realisation of common objects. Beyond this the similarity does not go and the differences between the two appear fundamental. The most important distinction between the two is that the States entering a confederacy preserve their full independence or sovereignty and that States entering a federation lost it. According to the expressive German term, the former is *staatenbund* or league of States, and the latter is ***bundesstaat*** or a united State. Through federation on State appears in the place of several; through confederation no such change occurs. Confederation does not bring a new State into being, it only creates a new relationship between existing States.

A federation is created on a constitution which is legally a law, and which depends upon the consent of the people. A confederation on the other hand, is created by an agreement or a compact which is of the nature of an international treaty concluded by the confederating States and, accordingly, it rests upon the consent of the member States. A federation is a permanent union and it is illegal for the units composing it to secede or withdraw there from. But the confederating States may withdraw from the union whenever they desire and when they do so their action is not illegal, though it may be deemed a violation of international good faith. If there is armed conflict between the various units of a federation, as there was one between the Northern and Southern States of America on the question of slavery, it is a civil war. If hostilities break out between two or more confederating units, then, it is an international war and not a civil war.

The national or central government in a federation is created by the Constitution and its powers are defined therein. The federating units can neither destroy the central government nor modify its powers on their own initiative. It can only be done by amending the Constitution and according to the prescribed method. But in Confederation the member-States create the central authority, Sometimes called even government, which they can destroy, or widen or narrow its powers. Control of such an authority or a government over the member-States in a Confederation may be of a shadowy sort. Under the Articles of Confederation, the Congress in the United States could requisition the States for soldiers and money upon a fixed system of quotas and make treaties with foreign countries. But while the States were bound by the agreement to honour the requisition and comply with the treaties, there were no means of compelling them to do so; the power was a power of recommendation. Finally, a federation deals with the citizens of a federal State; in a Confederation the common organ of authority deals with the governments of the member-States; it is a union of States and not of the people. A Confederation has no citizens or subjects to whom its commands can be directly addressed.

Pre-requisites of a federation. Federal government exists, as said before, when the powers of government are divided according to the principle that there is a single independent authority for the whole country in respect of some matters which are national importance and concern the interest of the community as a whole, and that there are independent regional authorities for other matters, and each set of authorities co-ordinate with and not subordinate to the other within its own prescribed sphere. Such a system of government demands the presence of certain condition which should exist before the federal principle is adopted. According to Dicey there should be, in the first place, a strong desire to have to a union. The will to have a union and to be under a single independent government for some purpose is really the basis of a federation. It means that the federating units must be inspired and bound together by a sense of oneness with a desire to objectify it politically. Unless they become a community of interests their cohesion into a new State is extremely difficult. The second requisite condition for a federation, according to Dicey, is that the federating States must desire union rather than unity, that is , while there should be a desire on the part of the federating States for national unity and to be under a single independent government, they must, desire, at the same time, to maintain their individuality and autonomous existence by establishing independent regional governments in some matters at least. The aim of federalism is to give effect to both these sentiments. It is in this context that Dicey defined a federation as a political contrivance intended to reconcile national unity and power with the maintenance of State rights or, to put it in the words of Professor Wheare, the group of States or communities "must desire to be united but not to be unitary."

But this is not all. Something more is needed. There should not be only the desire to have a federation, but the power or ability to operate it as well. The States or communities desiring to have a federation, says Professor Wheare, "must have the capacities to work the system they desire. Federal government is not appropriate unless the communities concerned have the capacity as well as the desire to form an independent general government and to form independent regional governments." The factors which determine their desires or aspirations as well as their capacities to make them operative ideals are the following and may be called the pre-requisites of a federation. It may, however, by remembered that it is unlikely that all these factors will be present in States desiring union, but it is necessary that most of them must be present if the federation can really, be a federation and prove an enduring contrivance.

1. One of the main incentives to closer association is a feeling of homogeneity, what Mill calls mutual sympathies among the population. "The sympathies available for the purpose," he says, "are those of race, language, religion, and above all of political institutions as conducing most to a feeling of identity of political interest." In his earlier enumeration of the factors making for nationalism. Mill included geographical unity and common memories, that is, a common historical tradition. Obviously both should appear here. They help to create at the same time a sense of oneness. But Mill observes that, even without these cohesive factors, peoples may bind themselves together in resistance to oppression. The Swiss did so and they continued to co-operate in spite of the diversity of language and religion at a time "when religion was the grand source of irreconciliable political enmity throughout Europe." Exposed frontiers and the danger of aggression from avaricious neighbours dictate union for the purposes of defence. The greater the menace, the closer will the union be. In Canada the desire to unite arose in spite of difference of languages and race. And the union of South Africa occurred in spite of similar difference between Dutch and English.

It will thus, be clear that strong as the force of language. race, religion and nationality are in producing a desire for union.

such a desire can nonetheless be produce among people who differ in all these particulars, but possess a sentiment of union, *i.e.* a common sentiment of union, that in union lies strength and this strength can be achieved by a political cohesion. "The sentiment of unity," says Gilchrist, "is the index of a common mind A great deal, therefore, depends upon the political leadership or statesmanship at the right time which helps to combat the forces of racial, religious and linguistic differences and instill in the people instead a desire to unite itself. The desire for union in Canada was made effective by the leadership of men like John Macdonald, Alexander Galt and George Etienne. In America, the people had a community of language, race and religion and similarity of political institutions, but these factors had failed to produce anything beyond a confederation. It was under the leadership of Washington, Hamilton, Madison, Jay, Benjamin Franklin and James Wilson that the delegates at the Philadelphia Convention of 1787, "with a manly confidence" in their country threw the Articles of Confederation aside and designed to bring unity into the diversity of the new nation. But it happened the other way in India. The Muslim League, under the inspiration of the late Mr. M. A. Jinnah, had all through relied upon the theory of a separate Muslim nation and the creation of a separate homeland for them If the separatist tendencies had not been fostered so assiduously by the Muslim leadership, the result would have been a united Indian federation rather than the division of the country into two part, India and Pakistan. "This factor or leadership, of skill in negotiation and propaganda, can make," observes professor Wheare, "all the difference between stagnation and an inactive desire for union."

2. The areas having the desire to federate should be geographically contiguous, that is to say, the States desiring to federate should not be separated from one another by distant spaces of land and water. They must exist in the vicinity of one another, for neighbourhood makes them a community, of interests and the desire for union is prompted by the needs of common defence, common economic advantages, and similarity of institutions. Geographical contiguity also helps to produce a capacity to work federal

union. A federal government demands units to run their own administration as well as to participate in the federal government. "Distance leads to carelessness or callousness," says Gilchrist, "says Gilchrist, "on the part of both central and local governments. National unity is difficult to attain where the people are too far apart." The benefits of common defence and the economic advantages from union cannot be adequately secured. One of the causes of success of federalism in America is the contiguity of all the States. So are the Cantons of Switzerland, the Provinces of Canada and the States of Australia. The Indian federation also commands contiguity of its component States. But there is no contiguity of area between the two parts of Pakistan. West Pakistan is separated from its eastern counterpart by a wide stretch of land. Eastern Pakistan, as a matter of fact, is landlocked by Indian territory. Federation is, thus, not a convenient mechanism of government for Pakistan.

3. Of all the factors which produce the desire for union, similarity of social institutions and particularly political institutions is the one which is very important, because it produces best the capacity for union. Professor Wheare remarks that the desire for union has practically never been aroused unless similarity of political institutions "was present actually or potentially among those who envisaged the union." Similarity of institutions helps the States to work together and its importance can be reslised from the fact that statesmen in framing federal constitutions have even insisted that all the unit should adopt the same of government. The constitutions of the United States and Switzerland both require that their respective unit must have a republican form of government. In Canada, Australia and India parliamentary system of government had been explicitly established in all units.

4. Not only is it desirable that there should be similarity of political institutions in the federating units, but it is also essential that these institutions should not be autocratic or dictatorial. "For autocracy or dictatorship, either in the general

> governments or in the regional governments, seems certain, sooner or later, to destroy that equality of status and that independence which these governments, must enjoy, each in its own sphere, if federal government is to exist at all." Federalism demands forms of government which have the characteristics usually associated with democracy or free government and whatever be the variety of a democratic government, it must ensure free elections and a party system and the existence of the Opposition. There can be no free elections wherever there is autocracy and the representatives in the government are the nominees of the autocrats in the regions. Dictatorship is a one party government and it does not permit existence of Opposition. Elections are just a routine affair wherever dictatorship has existed. This is negation of free elections and, as such, incompatible with the working of the federal principle.

It would have been difficult to operate a union between the Provinces and Princely States as envisaged in the Government of India, Act, 1935. The proposed federation would have been, indeed, a combination of strange bed-fellows. The Provinces were given, under the Act of 1935, provincial autonomy with representative in situations and responsible form of government whereas the State were to continue under the personal rule of the Princes. As such, the representatives of the Indian States in the central legislature would have been nominees of their rulers and not elected representatives of the people of the States. The British Government, in the words of Sir Samuel Hoare, the then Secretary of State for India, had really intended to counterpoise democracy with aristocracy. Before inaugurating the new Constitution of India, in 1950, which declares India the union of States, all the Princely States were liquidated and homogeneous political institutions established in all the component States of the Union. The States Reorganisation Act, 1956 abolished the distinction between Part A, B and C States, which the constitution in 1950 had established. The States Reorganisation commission aptly remarked that the "only rational approach to the problem, in our opinion, will be that the Indian Union should have primary constituent units having equal status and a uniform relationship with the centre, except where, for any strategic security or other compelling reasons, it is not practicable to integrate any small area with the territories of a full-fledged unit."

Similarly there should be similarity of social institutions generally. It is true that the desire for union can be created in spite of dissimilarities of social institutions, as it happened in the United States and Canada "but such differences," says Wheare, "do make a government more difficult, and there is a limit to the degree of dissimilarity which can be permitted. The capacity to work together cannot survive an extreme divergence." The capacity of States to form and work a federal union, he adds "Depends upon some agreement to differ but not to differ too much."

5. The capacity of States to work a federal union is also greatly influenced by their size. It is desirable that there should be as far as possible, equality among the component part of a federation in their size and population. If there are wide differences in size and population, the federating States are not equal partners in a union. Units larger in size and population and more powerful in resources than the others may be too proud and domineering for smaller ones. They may even overrule the other and bend the will of the central government to themselves. The idea of dominance by some creates suspicion and lack of confidence in others. Confidence is the essence of the will to federate and the capacity to work in federal government. The essential of a federation is, as John Stuart Mill says, "There should not be any one state so much more powerful than the rest as to be capable of vying in strength with many of them combined. If there be such a one, and only one, it will insist on being master of the joint deliberations; if there be two, they will be irresistible when they agree and whenever they differ everything will be decided by a struggle for ascendancy between the rivals."

It is true, that some divergence in size between the units must necessarily be present before a federal union is desired, and this is an important factor in the making and maintenance of federal systems today. But "there must be", succinctly observes Wheare, "some sort of reasonable balance which will insure that all the units can maintain their independence within the sphere allotted to them and that no one can dominate the others. It must be the task of those who frame and work a federal government to see that no unit shall be too large, and, equally important, none too small."

6. Finally, the federating states must possess adequate economic resources to support both an independent national government and independent regional governments. A federal government establishes a new national government and it must be given sufficient independent economic resources if it is to perform its duties well. But this is not enough. It is also essential for a federation that the regional governments must also be left with adequate economic resources to run their governments and perform functions assigned to them. If the resources left are no sufficient to support independent regional governments, "then no matter how much states desire a federal union no matter whether a federal constitution is drawn up, in practice federal government will not be possible. Soon the regional governments will be unable to perform their function or they will be able to perform them only at the price of financial dependence upon the general government, that is, at the price of financial unification." One of the reasons for which the leaders in South Africa rejected a federal union was that the country would be unduly taxed if they were required to support both a central government as well as independent regional governments. A federation is really an expensive mechanism and it should be adopted only when the units can pay the price for the independence they retain.

American federalism, the start of an invention. Federalism is of extreme modernity. Its theory and practice in the modern State are not older than the American federation, which came into existence in 1787. Prior to 1776, the thirteen colonies were severally and separately bound to Britain. In no way were they connected together. The Declaration of Independence announced the colonies States, each independent of the Crown and politically independent of each other. But to declare independence, to fight and win war against British Imperialism and to build a new nation, required union and the result was a confederation, a "firm league of friendship" under the name of the United States. The declared purpose of the Confederation was to provide for the common defence of the States, the security of their liberties, and their mutual and general welfare.

The war against the British ended and the Treaty of 1783 acknowledged the independence, freedom and sovereignty to the thirteen colonies. But the Confederation became a league of disgruntled independents which revealed the powerlessness of the Congress created under the Articles of Confederation. It lacked the authority to weld the States into a unity, to mitigate their commercial rivalries, to establish a sound currency, to remove the causes of domestic disorders, and to foster American interests abroad. Washington, Hamilton, Madison and many others, who had laboured to bring together the States in bonds of union, were convinced that the government of the confederation must either be revised or superseded entirely by a new system. Washington wrote, "I do not conceive that we can exist long as a nation without having lodged somewhere a power which will pervade the whole nation in as energetic a manner as the authority of the State Governments extends over the several States." They all experienced the feeling that all America should be one, a feeling which cements the bonds of oneness giving birth to a new nation. "We are now a new nation," said Rush, "...the more a man aims at serving America, the more he serves his colony. We have been too free with the word—independence; we are dependent on each other, not totally independent States... when I entered that door I considered myself a citizen of America."

Here are the germs of a union which now carries the nomenclature of a federal government. The delegates to the Philadelphia Convention of 1784, who were sent by the States for the purpose of preparing a revision of the Articles of Confederation, went beyond their instructions and drafted a new constitution without knowing that they were devising an entirely novel and ingenious scheme of government, and it would become a distinctive and influential contribution of America to the art of government.

The Founding Fathers sought to remove the two principal defects of the Articles of the Confederation: (1) to remove the predominance of the parts over the whole and to reconcile two different powers, the power of the States and the power of the central government; and (2) to remove the dependence of the government at the centre upon the governments of the States that acted as intermediaries between it and the individual. They adopted the principle that the functions and powers of the national government being new, general and inclusive had to be carefully *defined* and *stated*, while all other functions and powers were to belong to the States. To make the powers of the central government real, they accepted the fact that it be empowered, among other things, to coin money, to regulate commerce, to declare war, to make peace, and to levy taxes. The central government was endowed with a Congress, to make laws on subjects assigned to its jurisdiction; an executive, with adequate means of enforcement; and a judiciary with authority to preserve an, equilibrium between the whole and parts and to uphold the supremacy of the Constitution. Above all, the national government was to derive its support and mandate from the people as voters and to carry its services directly to them as individuals.

Adoption of federal type of government by other countries. Once the example of the United States had demonstrated that a federal union could work successfully, a precedent and established that others whose situations were similar could follow. The first to do it was Switzerland. In 1847, the Swiss Confederation was convulsed by an attempt of seven Catholic cantons to secede. The Protestant majority crushed the secessionists, who had formed a separate league called the *Sonderbund.* The defeat of the seven Catholic cantons, was, in fact, the triumph for the movement of national unity. Next year, the Swiss Diet approved a new constitution which created a federal union closely patterned on that of the United States.

The next to adopt was Canada in 1867, although the Canadian federation was produced by a different combination of factors. The direct cause of the federation movement was the racial conflict between the British and French "national groups", "Two nations warring within the bosom of a single State" as the Durham Report had lamented, which rendered the unitary government unworkable. Economic problems also plagued a divided Canada. Nor was defence unimportant. In 1864, a coalition government took office pledging unification. The final outcome was the North America Act, 1867 and the Dominion of Canada was established. The scheme of distribution of powers between the Centre and the Provinces was just the reverse of the American model and it was essentially due to the lessons of America' s civil war of 1860. The Provinces were given exclusive legislative control over a list of enumerated subjects reserving the rest for the Dominion. The Dominion government was also given the power to disallow any Act passed by a provincial legislature, to appoint the Lieutenant-Governor of a Province and to instruct him to withhold his assent from provincial bills and to reserve them for consideration of the Governor-General, and he might refuse assent to such reserved bills. Finally, appointments to all the important judicial posts were placed in the hands of the Dominion executive.

In the formation of the Australian federation the need for common defence was probably the strongest, though economic issues were also involved. The Commonwealth came into existence on January 1, 1901. The Constitution enumerated substantial powers for the federal government, the residue remaining in the hands of the States. The main taxation powers were given to the federal government, with three-quarters of the revenues to be returned to the States during the first ten years.

The Soviet Union adopted the federal form of government as a concession to the various nationalities and tribes inhabiting Russia with a view to building a strong and powerful State. Lenin Characterised federalism as a step towards "the most solid unification of the different nationalities into a single, democratic, centralised Soviet State". The Constitution of 1936 gives certain specified powers to the Union government and leaves the residuary powers with the constituent republics and each republic exercises its authority independently of the central government. The

Constitution also gives to the constituent republics the right to secede.

When India became independent, the Government of India Act, 1935 provided a working machine in the Provinces, and, as Dr. Jennings correctly points out, "it was not possible to start afresh when Provinces became States." The scheme of federation under the Constitution of 1950 is fundamentally the same as under the Act of 1935. There are three lists of subjects, the Union List, the State List and the Concurrent List, exhaustively enumerated in the Constitution, and the residuary powers rest in Parliament. The Constitution empowers the Union Government to give directions to the States and failure to comply with such directions entitles the President of India to supersede the State government for the time being and thereby bring it under the unitary rule of the Union. The State Governors are appointed by the President and the State government can be superseded on a report from the Governor. The Governor may reserve a bill passed by the State legislature for the consideration of the President. The Upper House of the Union Parliament may, by resolution passed by two-thirds majority, declare a particular subject or subjects in the State List to be of national importance and interest empowering Parliament to make laws there to. Then, there are the Emergency Powers of the President. When the Proclamation of Emergency is in operation, Parliament is empowered to make laws for the whole or any part of the territory of India with respect to any matter contained in the State List. Finally, the Union Parliament is also empowered to pass legislation implementing any treaty, agreement or convention with another country.

Methods of distribution of powers. These variations as the federal theme show that two methods have been adopted in the distribution of powers between the central government and the regional governments. The systems of the United States, Switzerland and Australia are that their central governments have been given enumerated powers whereas the residuary powers are left with their State governments. For United States, this point is covered by the Tenth Amendment which provides that " the powers not delegated to the United States by the Constitution nor prohibited by it to the States, are reserved to the States respectively, or to the people. The Swiss Constitution expressly declares that the cantons "are sovereign in so far as their sovereignty ins not limited by the Federal Constitution, and, as such, they exercise all rights which are not transferred to the Federal power." The reasons for the adoption of this system are largely historical. The federal union was in each case formed by the union of previously independent sovereign states. At the time of the union, the latter desired to retain to themselves all governmental powers except such as was plain necessary to confer upon the central government in order that an effective union might be established.

In Canada the method adopted was just the reverse of the United States and Switzerland. Here too, the historical event determined the course. "All Constitution," as Jennings remarks, "are the heirs of the past as well as the testators of the future." The persistent racial conflict between the British and the French and the failure of the unitary government coupled with the cool relations with the United States enforced the argument for unification and for national authority. Federal government seemed the obvious solution. But the experience of the "near-dissolution of the American Union" in the Civil war led British and Canadian Statesmen to the conclusion that the Central government must possess more powers than belonged to its counterpart in the United States. The Canadian Constitution—the British North America Act, 1867—accordingly divides the powers between the Provincial and Dominion government in such a way that the Provinces have exclusive control over a list of enumerated subjects, and the Dominion has exclusive control over the rest, which "for greater clarity" were enumerated also, though not exhaustively. The legislatures of Dominion and Provinces are distinct from other; neither has the power to alter the Constitution so far as the distribution of powers is concerned. In Canada, therefore, enumerated powers are given to the Provinces and residuary powers are left to the Dominion government.

The Constitution of India contains three lists of subjects, the Union List, the State List and the Concurrent List, and the residuary powers rest in Parliament. The total number of subjects exclusively given to the Central government are ninety-seven as compared with sixty-six which are under the actual exclusive control of the States. Concurrent List contains forty-seven subjects upon which both Union and State legislatures makes laws. Here is an enumeration more than anything attempted in any other federation. The provision which deal with a conflict between the Union and State laws are interesting. In general, they require that State laws on concurrent subjects must give way to the laws of the Union government to the extent of their repugnancy to such laws. As previously said, Union legislate has also been empowered to legislative on any matter in the State List if the Council of States (Rajya Sabha) passes a resolution by a two thirds majority declaring a particular subject or subjects of national importance or interest. When an Emergency is in operation, Parliament makes laws for the whole or any part of the territory of India with respect to any matter enumerated in the State List. Article 253 further empowers Parliament to pass legislation implementing any treaty, agreement or convention with any other country. This last phrase is remarkably vague as Jennings remarks because under this provision the Union Parliament can acquire jurisdiction on any subject, as for example, even over university education "by the simple process of a decision of the Inter-university Board of India which is an international body because it contains representatives of universities in Burma and Ceylon."

Dr. Ambedkar, the Law Minister in the Government of India and the principal architect of the Constitution, admitted in the Constituent Assembly that "the constitution has not been set in a tight-mould of federalism." The federal principle has, indeed, been so much modified by unitary elements in the form of control by the Central government over the State government and the intervention in the conduct of affairs of the State governments has become so proverbial that the Indian Constitution cannot claim to establish a federal union. And the Constitution nowhere uses the word federation. The omission seems to be deliberate and it shows the intentions of the authors of the Constitution. It is true that the federal principle has been introduced into the terms of the

Constitution to some extent and Professor Wheare deems it "justifiable to describe it as a quasi-federal constitution," but a system of government in which one partner can unmake another cannot claim to have even the semblance of a federation. The Indian Constitution may have the form of a federation but to have federal form does not make a federation. A federation is a partnership among equals, oneness of the State with the separateness of the units is its formula, although equality of status does not mean absolute equality of powers.

There are some students of federalism who hold that the federal principle consists in the division of powers in such a way that the powers to be exercised by the central government are enumerated in the Constitution and the residue is left to the regional governments. It is not enough for federalism, they assert, that the central and regional governments should each be independent in its own sphere. That sphere must be marked in a particular way, that is, the residuary powers must lie with the regional governments. Applying this criterion, a government is not federal if the powers of the regional governments are specified and the residue is life to the central government. The Constitutions of the United States, Switzerland and Australia embody the federal principle because they distinctly enumerate subjects over which their central legislatures exercise control and they further provide that powers not so given to the central governments remain with their states and cantons.

But such a test of federalism, in the opinion of Professor Wheare, concentrates on a relatively superficial characteristic. "The essential point," he says, "is not that the division of powers is made in such a way that the regional governments are the residuary legatees under the constitution, but that the division is made in such a way that, whoever has the residue, neither general nor regional government is subordinate to the other." It is, no doubt, true that the question of residuary power is important as it affects the balance of power in a federation, but this question itself does not make a government federal. The fundamental point in a federal principle is whether the powers of government are divided between co-ordinate, independent authorities or not. It is immaterial what the system of distribution of powers is and where the residuary power rests. Circumstances of each country decide which method is adopted.

What distinguishes a federal from a unitary government is that the regional governments are not subordinate to the central government; the one is not simply the creation of the other. Both enjoy a juridical and corporate personality, no matter whether division of powers is made by enumerating the powers of the central government and leaving the rest for the regional governments, or the division is made by enumerating the powers of both the central and regional governments and leaving the residue to the former. What makes the Canadian constitution "quasi-federal" are the matters in which the Provincial governments are subordinate to the Central government, and not co-ordinate with it. These matters are: the power of the Dominion executive to disallow any Act passed by a Provincial legislature even if it falls within its sphere of jurisdiction, the Dominion executive appoints the Lieutenant-Governor of a Province and it can instruct the Lieutenant-Governor to withhold his assent from Provincial bills and to reserve them for consideration by the Dominion executive, and it may refuse assent to such reserved bills if it thinks fit.

These are all unitary elements in an otherwise strictly federal form of constitution. But the law of the constitution is one thing; the practice is another, thus, signifying the difference between a federal constitution and a federal government. Professor Wheare places particular emphasis on this difference and says, "A country may have a federal constitution, but in practice it may work that constitution in such a way that its government is not federal. Or a country with a non-federal constitution may work it in such a way that it provides the example of federal government." In actual practice the unitary elements in Canada have either now become obsolete or are being so worked as not to compromise with the federal principle. If Canada, therefore, as Professor Wheare concludes "has not a federal constitution, it has a federal government." The United States, Switzerland and Australia have federal constitutions as well as federal governments, though the process of centralisation in all these countries is assuming alarming proportions. If this tendency is allowed to work unchecked, their governments may be transformed in the very near future into quasi federal governments.

A concurrent jurisdiction in found in all modern federal governments and with it a provision that when the laws of the central government upon matters in the concurrent field conflict with the laws of the regional governments in that field, then, the regional laws must give way to the central laws to the extent of their repugnancy. The extent of the concurrent jurisdiction varies greatly. In Canada it consists of only two subjects whereas in the United States and Australia the concurrent field is extensive. In Switzerland it is smaller than in the United States and Australia, though wider than in Canada. A concurrent jurisdiction is not incompatible with the federal principle. There are indeed many good reasons for providing a concurrent jurisdiction. Professor Wheare is of the opinion that "it is better always, if possible, to admit concurrent jurisdiction, if only perhaps as transitional measure. In most cases it will be unavoidable. But what is likely to work best is a short exclusive list and a rather longer Concurrent List."

ESSENTIALS OF FEDERAL GOVERNMENT

The division of powers between central and regional governments, which is the essence of federalism, involves three consequences. First the arrangement must be embodied in a written constitution, secondly, the constitution must be rigid, and finally, the presence of a Supreme Court.

1. A Written Constitution. For a federal government the constitution must almost necessarily be a written constitution. "To base an arrangement of this kind," writes I icey, "upon understandings or conventions would be certain to generate misunderstandings and disagreements." The articles of the treaty, or in other words, of the constitution, must, therefore, be reduced to writing; the constitution must be a written document, Professor Wheare says that if the government is

to be federal, its constitution must be supreme. By the supremacy of the constitution he means that "the terms of the agreement which establishes the general and regional governments and which distributes power between them must be binding upon these general and regional governments. This is a logical necessity from the definition of federal government itself." If the central government and the regional governments are to co-ordinate with each other, neither must be in a position to override the provision of the constitution regarding their powers and status which each is to enjoy. Definiteness of constitutional status and powers stimulates the will to federate and creates confidence in the federating unit that the sanctity of their spheres of jurisdiction will be religiously maintained.

2. A Rigid Constitution. The natural corollary from the supremacy of the constitution, and it being a written constitution, is that it should not be alterable either by the central legislature or by regional legislatures under their ordinary law-making procedure. "The law of the constitutions," says Dicey, must either be immutable, or else capable of being changed only by some authority above and beyond the ordinary legislative bodies whether federal or State legislatures existing under the constitution." It is essential for a federal government, says Professor Wheare, that the power of amending the constitution, "so far at least as concerns those provisions of the constitution which regulate the status and powers of the general and regional governments, should not be confided exclusively either to the general government or to the regional governments." If it is confided exclusively to one set of the government, it does not give equality of status to both and it is also probable that one which possesses this powers may in ordinary process of legislation make an invasion on the powers of jurisdiction of the other.

It does not matter logically where the power of amending the constitution is placed, but "there can be no doubt," as Professor Wheare suggests, "that practically it is wise to associate both the general government and the regions, either their governments or their peoples, in the process." In the United States amendments of the constitution may be proposed by a majority of two-thirds of both Houses of Congress or by a convention summoned by Congress on the application of the legislatures of two-thirds of states. The proposed amendments become effective when ratified by the Legislatures of three-fourths of the states or by conventions in three-fourths of the states according as one or other method of ratification may be proposed by Congress. No alterations in the boundaries of the existing states, the constitution further prescribes, can be made without the consent of the legislatures of the states concerned as well as of congress. In Australia the Constitution can be amended on the proposal by an absolute majority of the two Houses of Parliament of the Commonwealth—or in certain circumstances one House—and its ratification at a referendum of the people. If at this referendum a majority of all the electors voting approve the proposed law, and if, in a majority of the states, a majority of the electors voting also approve the proposed amendment, then, it is submitted for the royal assent. It is further provided, that amendments relating to changes in the representation of the states in either House of Parliament or any alterations in the boundaries of the states must be approved by the majority of the electors in the states concerned.

In Canada, the power of amending the North America Act, 1867 rests with the Parliament of England. No authority in Canada has power to alter the division of powers between Dominion and Provincial governments. The convention as it is, Parliament in England would amend the Canadian Constitution on a request from Canada. But there is no settled convention whether the request for amendment should come from the Dominion Parliament and government alone, or from the Provincial Legislatures and governments alone or through some co-operation of the two. "In seven out of the ten amendments passed up to 1947, action was taken by the United Kingdom Parliament on requests from the Dominion government or Parliament, alone; there was no consultation with all the provinces nor was their consent asked. The amendment of 1871, 1886, 1915, 1943, 1946 and 1949 affected the provinces, but none was consulted. The amendment of 1930 affected some provinces, and these alone were consulted and their consent obtained. In once case where all the provinces were consulted and asked for their consent—that of —1907—the amendment was passed by the United Kingdom parliament at the request of the Dominion parliament in spite of the fact that one of the provinces concerned, British Columbia, did not give its consent to the proposed amendment." Such a position, Professor Wheare views with alarm, although the legal position, he says, "would still be in conformity with federalism for neither Dominion Parliament alone nor provincial parliaments alone could alter the constitution." The question of an appropriate method of amending the constitution by purely Canadian agencies is under discussion in Canada. "It is recognised by Canadians that they must devise some method of making amendments which will be in conformity with federalism, since they wish to preserve the federal element in their constitution, and that meanwhile the United Kingdom Parliament should be careful not to permit itself to become the agent of the Dominion alone or of the Provinces alone."

The Constitution of India, like the Union of South Africa Act of 1909, makes no pretence of making a federation. Since Prof. Wheare says that the "new Constitution of India... established, in deed, a system of government which is at most quasi-federal, almost devolutionary in character; a unitary state with subsidiary federal features rather than federal state unitary features", it will be interesting to note the process of constitutional amendment. The Constitution prescribes three different methods of amending the Constitution. Some parts of the constitution can be amended by a simple majority in both Houses of Parliament and new states may be created or the existing states reconstituted, and upper chambers may be created or abolished in the states by this process. Then, certain specified subjects, as amendments affecting the method of electing the President, the extent of the executive and legislative powers of the Union or the states, the provisions regarding the Supreme Court, the representation of the states in Parliament, and the method of amending the constitution, require a majority of the total membership in each House of Parliament, a majority of two-thirds of the members present and voting in each House of Parliament and ratification by the legislatures of one-half on the states. Finally, for the remaining provisions there must be a majority of total membership in each House of Parliament and a majority of not less than two-thirds of the members present and voting in each House of Parliament.

3. Presence of the Supreme Court. In a federation the necessity of a supreme or federal court with an authority to interpret the constitution is an established fact. The federal judiciary performs two important functions: (1) it decides disputes of jurisdiction arising between the central governments and the regional governments or between one regional government and another; and (2) it keeps different government within their limits so that none may encroach upon the sphere of jurisdiction of the other. If the federal principle is to really work, it is necessary that there should be an umpire independent of both the central and regional governments which should ever be vigilant to prevent either set of government from disturbing the balance between the centrifugal and centripetal forces. Happy balancing between the two forces is the essence of federalism and there can be no other authority than an independent and impartial judiciary which can act as the guardian of the constitution and there by protect the constitutional distribution of powers. The need for the federal judiciary has been expressed by Mill in his characteristic way and his words have often been quoted or paraphrased. "It is evidently necessary," he say, "not only that the constitutional limits of authority of each (central and regional governments alike) should be precisely and clearly defined, but that the power to decide between them in any case of dispute should not reside in either of the governments, or in any functionary subject to it, but in an umpire independent of both. There must be a Supreme Court of Justice, and a system of co-ordinate courts in every State of the Union, before whom such questions shall be carried, and whose judgement on them in the last stage or appeal, shall be final." Sidgwick says that the more stability is given to

the constitution by making the process of changing it difficult, the greater becomes the importance of this judicial function of interpreting its clauses.

Advantages and drawbacks of a Federal Government. Federalism is a device which has rendered immense service in the past and may still render in knitting together under a common government peoples whose political interests are alike. Many regard it as a panacea for so many economic and political ills from which the world suffer today and envisage the scheme of a World Federation. Without going into the realm of political speculation regarding the feasibility of World Federation and accepting federalism as it is, it can be said that small independent States cannot exist in midst of modern competing states and they find a good substitute in a federal system of government which brings them the advantages of union while maintaining their political autonomy at the same time.

Federalism has, as a principle, the combination of unit and diversity. Such a need exists particularly in countries of great territorial expansion or deep-seated racial, cultural, religious or linguistic differences. For the solution of such problems, a federal government is probably the only possible answer. It harmonizes local autonomy with national unity and thereby provides an equilibrium between the centripetal and centrifugal forces. The central government is assigned functions which are of national importance and general concern. Other matters of local interest that differ in different sections of the country are left to the people of those areas for their solution. In this way a federal government presents a happy blending of centralisation and decentralisation.

A federal government prevents rise of a single despotism, checks the growth of bureaucratic authority and conserves the political liberty of the people. Abuse of power by the central authority is more easily checked by vigorous federalism than by any other form of government. Federalism, observes Bryce, allows experiments in local legislation and administration that might be dangerous if applied to the entire country. Territorial division of functions also relieves the central government of many burdensome functions and relieves congestion of legislative and administrative work at the centre. It adds to the efficiency in administration as well because the division of powers is related to the actual needs of life.

Federal governments also afford excellent schools for political education as they are founded on the democratic principles of free election, free criticism and representative institutions. Each citizen has a full-fledged miniature government relatively near his abode on which he can make far more easily than on national administration. He is encouraged to take greater interest and initiative in public affairs. His needs and aspirations also are better satisfied.

It cannot be denied that federalism has its disadvantages. The constitution framing body of a federal government has to bear the burden not merely of providing for two sets of government, but also of determining the manner in which the total of government power shall be distributed among them. This is a task of such difficulty that a satisfactory performance of it at time is impossible, as it is tantamount to compartmentalizing the life of a nation. What might formerly have been safely left to the separate units may with the lapse of time and under changed conditions demand a national regulation and decision. This leads to bitter contests regarding the jurisdiction of the two governments and the political history of the United States and other federal countries are marked by such controversies. "The proper adjustment of central to local governments thus becomes," writes Gettel, 'a constant source of difficulty, and the danger of rebellion or the formation of sectional factions is always present."

Then, the pre-requisite of a federal government is the supremacy of the constitution which implies a written and rigid constitution. Supremacy of the constitution means that the terms of the agreement, which establishes the central the regional governments and which distributes powers between them, must be binding upon them. If any change is desired to be brought about, it must be done by amending the constitution as prescribed by law and not by the unilateral action of any of the two sets of government. But the process of amending the constitution being difficult and circuitous, it is not possible to get the desired result as and when the needs of the people and the country demand. It is also possible that the capricious policy of a number of regional governments may crate unnecessary difficulties in the passage of the amendment. All constitutional amendments in the United States require ratification by three-fourths of the States after having been passed by two-thirds majority of Congress. There is no prescribed time-limit for ratification unless specifically determined by a resolution of Congress. Absence of such a prescription makes the issue a plaything of the States and indefinite delay takes away the purpose underlying the amendment. For example, the child labour amendment was proposed by Congress in 1924 without specifying the time-limit for ratification. So far only twenty-eight states have ratified it, the last one being Kansas in 1937. The American system of constitutional amendment also makes it possible for thirteen small States to pool together and hold up an overwhelming majority of the remaining States in their efforts of make a much wanted constitutional change.

The powers of government in a federation are divided among as many sets of officials as there are major political divisions plus, of course, the central government. The organs of government, instead of being parts of one highly integrated pieces of administrative machinery, are parts of as many different administrative systems. Being co-ordinate, as regards their status, uniform for a common good can only be secured by a voluntary agreement among all to co-operate. This is something which it is often difficult if not impossible to secure. The particular interests of all the component units of a federation are not always identical and each units likely to pursue a policy which seems to be conducive to its own interests over those of the State as a whole. More serious still, this difference of interests many bring the several units into sharp conflict with each other or collectively into conflict with the central government. Even when there is no conflict of interest, great loss often results when a given work is not under a single direction.

In the conduct of foreign affairs, the critics of federal government maintain, it exhibits inherent, weakness and inconsistency. "The experience of the United States in particular has shown that in individual members of the federal union, by virtue of their reserved powers over the rights of person and property, may embarrass the national government in enforcing its treaty obligations in respect to aliens residing in the United States." When internal differences are carried into foreign relations, the national government loses its international prestige. A fluctuating foreign policy leads to manifold troubles. Federation becomes a weak government both internally and externally. Similarly, in times of war federal government may sometimes be found lacking in promptness of decision and firmness of action, which national emergency of this kind demands.

A federal government is financially expensive since there is much duplication of administrative machinery and procedure. It is wasteful of time and energy, in that it much depends on negotiation, political and administrative , to secure uniformity of law and proper administrative fulfilment thereof.

Universal tendency to increase the powers of the Central Government. Theory and practice of federalism has under one a radical change and the fact of the matter is that in all those States which have adopted system of government, there has been a steady movement to counteract the disadvantages resulting form a constitutional distribution of powers by progressively increasing the powers of the Central Government. In the United States it has been accomplished partially by constitutional amendment, but, chiefly by giving to the clauses of the Constitution defining the powers of the Central Government a broadness of interpretation that certainly was not in the contemplation of the framers of the Constitution. The doctrines of implied powers, of inherent powers, of the sanctity of contracts and many other decisions of the Supreme Court stand conspicuous in extending the influence or control of the national government over functions which formerly were considered under State jurisdiction. In Australia, likewise a centralizing process has been sanctioned by the High Court. "The

Australian States," says W.K. Hancock, "have learned in bitterness that it is not always the residuary legatee who comes off best under a will. Sometimes the specific legatee takes but bulk of the estate and leaving him nothing but debts."

In Switzerland four important factors have contributed to the process of centralisation: war, economic depression, the demand for ever increasing services, and the mechanical and technical revolution in transport and industry. These factors are not peculiar to Switzerland. They are as much in the Swiss as in other federations. "Intensive government," says Sait, "is the reaction against intensive pressure" and the pressure may be internal as well as external. War is always a greater. It increases the control of the States over society, since protection and security become the nation's paramount concerns and these are pre-eminently the primary functions of the State. War demands, in order to win it, unified command, coordinated plans and prompt action. It also means mobilising the necessary activity and powers of all institutions of government, central and regional. The obvious result is that the constitutional checks which tend to check the jurisdiction of the various parts of government become unworkable. It is, of course, true of a world that is scared by past wars and scared of new ones. And no country can afford to wait for defence until war is declared. It must always be prepared to ward off the probabilities of war and to win, if it actually comes. It means the ability to man the industrial resources of the country and to apply nation's scientific knowledge to the task of defence. Everything from the physics courses taught in the schools to the conservation of natural resources and the maintenance of economy affects the war-making potential.

New deal legislation of President Roosevelt and the Supreme Court's attitude thereto is clearly indicative of the rapid development of centralisation. The New Deal was devised as the new means of combating a new national emergency, the depression. The world today is as much scared of depressions as it is scared of war and this emphasizes the recognition of the need for reallocation of powers in a new balance, not excluding strong local organs of government." Since the New Deal," says Lipson, "the situation has changed almost beyond recognition. Federal-state relations have become ampler and closer. Federal-local relations have been established. Federal-State-local co-operation is new frequent." Much of this is due to the more generous use of the device of the conditional grant-in-aid. A Committee of the Council of State Government, appointed in the United States, defined federal grant-in-aid as "payments made by the national government to State and Local governments, subject to certain conditions for the support of activities administered by the States and their political sub-divisions". As these grants are conditional, it is a matter of common experience that one who gives money must see the fulfilment of those conditions. The conditions that the central government imposes are in respect of the purposes and principle of service in question the structure and procedure of administration, the recruitment and management of the personnel, the furnishing of reports, and submission to inspection. The grant-in-aid, accordingly, offers a middle ground between direct federal assumption of certain state and local functions and their continuation under exclusive state and local financing, with haphazard coverage and diverse standards. It makes possible the achievement of national minimum standards, yet retains most of the benefits of administration close to the people."

All federal countries are moving towards a unified economic and social system co-extensive with its whole territory. No single problem can be isolated and looked at from a local point of view or local solution may be found for local problems. "As population grows more dense and industry is highly developed, the mechanism of life become so complicated, its parts so closely entwined, the activities in various areas so intimately bound together that local regulation will no longer suffice." I business corporations and trade unions become big, developing into nation-wide organisations and producing goods that will move across state lines, it is evident that relations can no longer remain within the exclusive jurisdiction of the states. If vagaries of nature are to be counteracted by harnessing nature, then, agriculture can no longer remain a state subject. The authority that is wider and wealthier can only sponsor huge irrigational schemes, like the Damodar Valley Project and Bhakra-Nangal schemes.

But the great centralizing factor has been the contrast in the attitude of the people towards the central government and the governments of their states in former times and at the present day. At the time of the making of the United States, of Switzerland, and of Canada there were differences of nationality, but as time went on a common nationality came to impose itself upon the differences. Citizens of these federal states come to feel that their primary interests and allegiance was in and to the nation as a whole rather to their particular states. Thus, there is not only the constantly increasing tendency to look to the central government for action in meeting their problems as they arise, but the growing conviction that only by the action of the central government their problems can be satisfactorily solved. A good part of President Roosevelt's New Deal sought to permanently regulate matters that had hitherto rested with the states. But many Americans justified that "usurpation" on the ground that the pressure of economic and social problems could be borne effectively only by the Federal Government. The old school of states rights, therefore, is steadily losing its hold upon the people, and in its place is arising the tendency to look to the central government for the solution of the more important political, economic and social problems. This makes a fundamental change in the theory and practice of a federal government.

Future of Federalism. The result is obvious. There is one general tendency in all federal governments that the central government have increased in importance and strength at the expense of the regional governments. Some students have concluded from this tendency that federal government represents but an intermediary stage in the political development of the modern State. "States move forward," says Sait, "from alliance to confederacy, from confederacy to federation, from federation to complete union, that is from lower to higher forms. These successive forms, therefore, may be regarded as a biological series." W.F. Willoughby maintains, "This step taken (the formation of a federation), there immediately develops a steady growth of the spirit of nationalism and, in response to needs actually felt, a progressive development, both absolutely and relatively, of the powers of the central government as opposed to those of the states. So marked is this that it may almost be said that from the moment the system of multiple government is adopted, the tendency is for efforts to be made to get away from the consequences of the decision that has been made." To Lipson it seems an unavoidable conclusion that "older patterns of decentralisation—whether in the form of local autonomy under a unitary system or of states' rights in a federal union—were doomed to dissolve in the corrosive acids of twentieth century politics economics and technology: Virtually all the great driving forces in modern society combine in a centralist directions." The critics of federalism further assert that integral economic planning and true federalism are incompatible. A planned economy, it is maintained is national in character and it is an expression of unity, while federalism is based on division and diversity.

Professor Wheare does not accept the point of view that federal government is really no more than a stage towards unitary government. He says, "This is a prophecy, not an historical judgement, for, so far, no federal government—as I define it—has become a unitary government." He admits that war and economic depression are the enemies of federal government and if they secure frequently, " will almost certainly turn federal governments into unitary governments." So far as the growth of social services is concerned, he does say, that they will tend towards the same end. But he also says that the growth in the powers of the central governments is only one tendency. "One other tendency at least must be noticed. It has not been the general governments alone which have grown in strength. The regional governments have also expanded. In all the federations the regions now perform function which at the establishment of the federations, they performed either not at all or to a much less degree than now." This is one element in a tendency, he adds "which may be broadly stated by saying that there has been a strong increase in the sense of importance, in the self-consciousness and self-assertiveness of the regional governments. This has gone on side by side with the growth in importance of the general governments and it has obviously been stimulated by it." It has led to a sense of grievance in the regional governments that their position is being imperiled by this tendency of centralisation. "And in some cases they have felt so unjustly treated by the general governments that they have talked of resigning from the federation. The secession movement in the State of Western Australia was one example." Professor Wheare emphasizes that the reasons which originally prompted the independent States—oneness of the State with the separateness of the units —to form the federal union and not a unitary union have not ceased to operate. True it is, he further says, that every region in a federal system does not feel the desire for independence to the same degree. "But in every federation a few regions feel it so intensely that no attempt could be made to impose uniformity without bringing into view the possibility of breaking the union in Pieces." Keeping these considerations in mind Professor Wheare concludes "that prospect of federal government is not so short as is suggest by those who concentrate entirely on the tendency of the general government to increase at the expense of the regions. Federal government is still desired by some regions in all the federations. There is no conclusive evidence that federal government is to be no more than a stage in the process towards unitary government."

Professor Kennedy, who takes a more liberal view of the minimum requirements of a federal constitution observes, "The real questions to decide, shorn of all theories are these: Are the national and provincial governments related to one another as Principal and delegate? What is the real and precise nature of authority which they exercise within their spheres ? ...." The regional governments have a juridical status and a corporate personality. They are clothed with plenary powers, legislative and executive. The provisions of the constitution relating to the scheme of distribution of powers cannot be unilaterally altered. Finally, in every federal country is the provision of an independent tribunal in the Supreme Court to give interpretations to the Constitution with finality. This is the crux of the whole problem.

People and countries have not lost faith in federalism so far. While federal States have shown signs of closer unification, States are adopting federal constitutions and many writers predict a further unification of States, at present independent, on federal basis. It has happened very recently in the case of Egypt and Syria with the consequent emergence of a federation named the United Arab Republic. Nationalist leaders from many parts of Africa met from December 5 to 12, 1958 to attend the All-African People's Conference with a view to getting rid of the remaining colonial regimes on their continent, and to begin the first steps toward federation of their existing States. Federalism, in fact, has made an important contribution to the solution of world politics. By reconciling the claims of local autonomy with those of national unity, federalism paves the way for the adjustment of inter-state disputes. Even a great admirer of unitary government Professor W.F. Willoughby admits that we should not "close our eyes to the immense service which the development of the idea of multiple government has rendered in the past and may still render in knitting together under a common government peoples whose political interest are largely identical but which for sentimental reasons are unwilling wholly to surrender their political autonomy." Federal government, as Professor Wheare says, does not stand for multiplicity alone. "It stands for multiplicity in unity. It can provide unity where unity is needed, but can ensure also that there is variety and independence in matters Where unity and uniformity is not essential." This exercise in self-governments, he further says, "is sufficiently valuable to be worth the cost it entails, and federalism marches towards triumph."

References

Beard, C. : *American Government and Politics.*

Bryce. J. : *The American Commonwealth*, Rev. ed. 2 Vols.

Dicey, A. V. : *Introduction to the Study of the Law of the Constitution.*

Finer, H. : *The Theory and Practice of Modern Government* (1954), Chaps. X, XI.

Garner, J. W. : *Political Science and Government*, pp. 346-356, 412-422.

Goodnow, F. J. : *Social Reform and the Constitution.*

Kennedy, W. P. M. : *The Constitution of Canada.*

Lipson, L. : *The Great Issues of Politics.*

Lowell, A. L. : *Government of England*, Vol. II, Part III.

Machiver, R. M. : *The Modern State*, Chap. XII.

Mogi, S. : *The Problem of Federalism*, 2 Vols.

Satt, E.M. : *Political Institutions, A Preface*, Chap. XVII.

Sharma, B.M. : *Federal Polity.*

Sidgwick, H. : *Elements of Politics*, Chap. XXVI.

Wheare, K. C. : *Federal Government.*

Willoughby, W. F. : *The Government of Modern States*, Chap. X.

5

Forms of Government
Cabinet and Presidential Governments and Dictatorship

Modern democratic governments are further divided into cabinet and presidential governments. The former also carries the name of parliamentary or responsible government and the latter is called non-parliamentary or non-responsible or congressional government. This classification is made on the basis of the principles governing the relations between the executive and the legislature. If both these departments are unified and coordinated under the control of the same persons, so that they must work in harmony, such a system of government is called cabinet, or parliamentary. It is responsible, because the cabinet is responsible to the legislature for its political politics and acts and it remains in office so long as it retains the confidence of the legislature. If the executive and legislative departments are largely independent of one another, but each possessing checks on the powers of the other in order to make the power limited, controlled and diffused, the system of government is Presidential. Here the head of the executive is constitutionally independent of the legislature in respect of the duration of his tenure and is not responsible to it for his political policies; hence it is non-parliamentary or non-responsible.

Cabinet or Responsible Government. In a cabinet form of government a clear distinction is made between the *nominal* and the *real* executive. The chief executive head of the State, whether he be a hereditary king, as in England, or one like and president of India, who is elected for a fixed number of years, Possesses only nominal powers. He is the *chief* executive, but not *the executive*. He is just a titular head of the State although his authority is *de jure*. Legally, he possesses all those powers and privileges which the Constitution may confer upon him, but in practice he exercises none of them. One may say that the legal powers of the executive head of the state, under a system of cabinet government, have fallen into disuse.

The real executive power rests with the Cabinet. The Cabinet ministers are the real functionaries who run the government. It is immaterial whether the existence of the cabinet is *de jure* or *de facto*. In England, the cabinet is the child of chance. Although unknown to law, yet it is the pivot around which the whole political machinery revolves. It is the supreme directing authority; the magnet of policy, as Barker calls it, which co-ordinates and controls the whole of the executive government, and integrates and guides the work of the legislature.

There is a sharp distinction between a Cabinet and a Ministry or the Council of Ministers. The Cabinet, wherever parliamentary system of government exists, has an extra constitutional growth and consists of about twenty or less Ministers, who are the most influential and most important of the Council of Ministers or the Ministry. These members of the Cabinet meet collectively, under the chairmanship of the Prime Minister, generally once a week, decide upon policy and in general 'head up' the government, whereas the Council of Ministers or the Ministry includes some sixty or more Ministers of different categories—Cabinet Ministers, Ministers of the Cabinet rank, Deputy Ministers and Parliamentary Secretaries. The Council of Ministries or the Ministry has no collective functions. It never meets as a whole and it never deliberates on matters of policy The duties of a Minster, unless he is a Cabinet Minister, are individual duties relating to the administrative department or departments of which he hold the charge. The Cabinet is, thus, the supreme directing authority; the motive power of all political action or, as Sri John Marriot describes it, "the pivot round which the whole political machinery revolves." Such a system of government is named the Cabinet government, as it is the Cabinet which is the master of the government.

The Council of Ministers is headed by the Prime Minister. He is the captain of the team which plays the game of politics in accordance with the mandate, which the majority party in the legislature and of which the Prime Minister is a duly accredited leader, had received at the general elections. The Prime Minister performs four important functions: (1) he is the head of the Ministry, that is the government of his country; (2) he is also the leader of the parliament of the country—the one whose intervention in the debates have the greatest weight, who states and interprets government policy, who is responsible to get the approval of Parliament for the policy of his government; (3) he is the person through whom the head of the state, King or President, normally communicates with the cabinet, with parliament, and ultimately, with the country; (4) he is the head of his party and responsible for the maintaining of harmony between the party and the majority that returned it to power.

The Constitution of France specifically provided for the Council of Ministers (*Consel de ministers*). It further provided that each of the acts of the President must be countersigned by the President of the Council of Ministers (the Prime Minister) and by a minister. This reduced the authority of the President to that of political impotence. The ministers being responsible to the legislature it was naturally their right to determine when the President should exercise his authority. The Constitution of India vests the executive power of the Union in the President, but subject to the qualification that it may be exercised by him in accordance with the constitution and the law. The Constitution and the law provide that there shall be a Council of Ministers with the Prime Minister as the head to aid and advise the President in the exercise of his functions, and that the Council of Ministers shall be collectively responsible to the House of the People.

Mechanism of the Cabinet Government. The Ministry or the Council of Ministers will, according to the party system of the country, be made up either entirely of members of the same political faith (single-party system) or of members of somewhat differing affiliations, yet able to agree on a programme of immediate action (multiple-party-system). In any case the ministry is formed by the person who seems to the head of the State best able to form a term in conformity with the existing parliamentary majority. Under the single-party system the choice of the head of the State is obvious and he summons the leader of the majority party to form the government. He is the only possible Prime Minister and there is no discretion. But when the party has not elected its leader or when there is not one single party having a legislative majority, as it is usually under the multiple-party system, the head of the State has a real choice. The Ministers are by law or by binding convention members of the legislature. Sometimes a Minister may not be an elected member of the legislature, for example, Ramsay MacDonald and Malcolm MacDonald were both members of the Cabinet in England, from November 1935 until early in 1936, though they were not members of Parliament. But the House of Commons is extremely critical of such exceptions and Ministers remain out of Parliament only while they are trying to find seats. If they cannot get in, and are unwilling to be created peers, they resign from their offices. The Constitution of India provides that a Minister may not be a member of either House of Parliament for a period of six consecutive months. But such Minister ceases to be a minister at the expiration of that period unless he is duly elected. In England no one may speak in either House of Parliament unless he belongs to that House. In India a Minister enjoys the privilege of occupying a seat in either House of the legislature, of being heard, and of participating in its deliberations, but with the right to vote in a House of which he is a member.

A cabinet government works on the well-accepted principle that Ministers are responsible to the legislature for all their official acts and they remain in office so long as they retain its confidence. This is called ministerial responsibility and it is this responsibility that gives to the cabinet government the name of a responsible government as well. In England, legally Ministers hold office during the pleasure of the King. But a legal truth there is a political untruth and the pleasure of the King really means the pleasure of Parliament. The Constitution of India also provides that Ministers hold office during the pleasure of the President. But the pleasure of the President vanishes when the Constitution simultaneously prescribes that the Council of Ministers is collectively responsible to the House of People (Lok Sabha). Ministerial responsibility is the essence of cabinet system of government. Responsibility to the legislature means that so long as the policies and official conduct of the Ministers command support of the majority of the members of the legislature, they continue to hold the reins of office and govern the country. But as soon as the majority is reduced into a minority and the ministry loses the confidence of the representative House, House of Commons in England, and the House of People (Lok Sabha) in India, it must resign office and give an opportunity to the Opposition to assume office, or the legislature may be dissolved on the advice of the defeated Prime Minister and new elections held in order to ascertain the opinion of the electorate. The party returned in majority to the legislature as a result of general elections then forms the ministry. The second alternative is more common and is generally resorted to. The legislature reveals its disapproval of the acts of the ministry either by an adverse vote on an important measure, or by a specific vote of no-confidence.

"The ministerial office," says Dr. Garner, "is not incompatible with legislative mandate. It means that the executive and legislative functions are "inextricably co-mingled" and there is no such separation between the executive and legislative powers as that which forms the distinguishing mark of the American Constitution. On the contrary there is a close and intimate interdependence of both the executive and the legislative departments. Professor Dicey emphasised that the cabinet system is founded on a fusion of the executive and legislative powers and, at the same time, upon the maintenance of harmonious relations between them. Bagehot defines cabinet as a "hyphen that joins, the buckle that binds the executive and legislative department together." The members of the cabinet are members of the legislature as well as heads of the executive departments of the government. They are responsible for defining the broader lines of national policy, collectively constituting the government and running the administration. They resolve, initiate and pilot in parliament legislation which they deem essential for carrying out their policy. The Ministers must always be prepared to answer questions put to them while the legislature is in session; impart all information which members consider necessary to elicit from the government, and defend their polices whenever questioned, criticised, or when called upon to give an account of their official conduct. The cabinet, therefore, is a committee of the legislature sharing in both the creation and administration of law and responsible to an subject to the control of the legislature. I cannot successfully function independently of the legislature. Such a form of government may also be designated as parliamentary type of government.

Cabinet government is a party government. It come into office as a unit and goes out of office as a unit. It means that the essence of the Cabinet government is its solidarity, a common front and it becomes binding on every member of the Cabinet, and, of course, on every Minister outside the Cabinet, to pursuer an agreed policy for which all accept responsibility and on which they stand and fall together. It is, therefore important that Ministers must essentially belong to one single political party. Collective responsibility, which is the *sine qua non* of the stability of government, can be obtained only when Ministers come in as a team and go out as a team. When Ministry is composed of heterogeneous parliamentary groups, it is most unstable, for compromise when brings the various groups together, is sure to break down at the slightest pretext. In a composite cabinet there is no homogeneity in the ranks of Ministers and there is no team spirit which can ensure oneness of purpose.

Pre-requisites of a Cabinet Government. Cabinet government is the system to which most countries aspire. The whole system of this type of government is based upon the fact that the government is carried on in the name of the king or President by ministers who are the members of the majority party in Parliament and are responsible to Parliament for all their public acts both individually and collectively. There are, however, certain pre-requisites without which cabinet government easily turns into something quite different.

1. The first pre-requisite is the presence of a titular executive head of the State who is not the directing and deciding factor responsible before the nation for the measures taken. The whole of the political and executive power of the government is exercised in his name by political men who belong to the majority party in Parliament. Legally, the government is vested in the head of the State, the officers of the State are appointed in his name and dismissed by him. The Ministers are his Ministers and they remain in office during his pleasure. He summons, dissolves and prorogues parliament, laws made by parliament cannot be enforced without his assent and if he wishes he may withhold his assent thereto. But all this remains in theory and the chief executive head of the State, does nothing by doing everything. Mr. Asquith, Prime Minister of England, wrote in 1913, a Memorandum on the rights and obligations of the King. He said, the King "is entitled and bound to give his ministers all relevant information which comes to him; to point out objections which seem to him valid against the course they advise ; to suggest (if he thinks fit) an alternative policy. Such intimations are always received by ministers with the utmost respect and considered with more respect and deference than if they proceeded from any other quarter." Beyond this he must not go. In the oft-quoted phrase of Bagehot, the King has three rights—the right to be consulted, the right to encourage, the right to warn. "A king of great sense and sagacity," he adds "would want no others." This is the classical exposition of the powers of the head of the State in a cabinet system of government.

2. It is necessary that there must be a clear and stable majority in parliament. Cabinet government means party government. Party, therefore, provides the machinery to secure a stable government under a unified command of the politically homogeneous and disciplined leaders. The fall of the ministry is the fall of the party and the strength of the party in the

legislature determines the solidarity and stability of the government. This is best achieved when there is a two-party system. But fairly good results can also be obtained where there are fairly solid blocs, each consisting of parties who habitually work together and who have enough in common to permit them to evolve a definite political programme. The classical example of a two party system is England. England, in fact, hates a coalition government, because it contradicts the fundamental principle that cabinet represents a party united in principle. England's example has been admirably followed in the Dominion countries, although in Australia and New Zealand the anti-labourite groups formed a partnership in order to defeat their Labourite opponents, which they did in 1949. In France and other Continental countries multiple-party system sexists and coalition government is the only possibility there. The result is that the government is a combination of strange bed-fellows who have nothing in common, no leader to follow, no definite programme to pursue and discipline to observe. All this leads to a precarious tenure of the government. For example, during the twenty-three years from the end of the First World War to the French collapse in the Second War. France had forty-two governments, while England had eleven, averaging six months, and twenty-five months respectively. When the life of government is precarious and short it is hesitant and unable to take a long view of policy. Its work is largely limited to matters of daily administration and its chief purpose is to remain in office instead of really governing. Moreover, when no party can definitely be made responsible because of coalitions, the government can neither be responsive nor really representative. Irresponsible government coupled with incoherent public opinion is always a sectional government which encourages corruption jobbery, nepotism, toadying, and various other accompanying evils. The final result is the failure of the parliamentary system of government as it has happened in France.

3. Another essential feature of a successful cabinet government is a certain degree of moderation among political parties Cabinet government is a democratic mechanism and

democracy is inseparable from a belief in methods of peaceful persuasion in the ultimate reasonableness of man, and his response to rational argument. It is, accordingly, necessary that both the majority party and Opposition should understand and observe the rules of the game. The public duty of the Opposition is the oppose the policy of the government, to attack upon the government and upon individual Ministers. The majority party must govern openly and honestly and it should meet criticism not by suppressing Opposition but by rational argument. It means that there should prevail a sense of give and take; the habit of tolerance and compromise. When political parties become intolerant of one another and virulent in their opposition and attacks, orderly government cannot exist. "Every trick, every method of obstruction and filibuster, is used to effect a certain political result, and if everything else fails, force may eventually be applied......when that occurs orderly government often comes to an end and emergency decree takens the place of legislative act. From there it is only a step to dictatorship."

4. Experience has shown that the right of dissolution is vital to the smooth working of a parliamentary system. If judiciously used, it is the solution to any possible deadlock. If cabinet and Parliament disagree the electorate will decide between them. The appeal to the people, as the ultimate source of political authority, is the only logical manner of settling any serious dispute between rival agencies of the State. Lack of it means parliamentary absolutism. Being safe from dissolution and confident that its tenure goes by calendar, the legislature can overthrow cabinets with impunity. This is what happened in France in the Third and the Fourth Republic and it made infinitely worse the tendency towards cabinet instability already created by the multiple party system.

Merits of Cabinet Government. The great virtue of a cabinet government is that it ensures harmony between the legislative and the executive departments. Ministers are heads of the executive departments, and, at the same time, they are members of the majority party in the legislature. In that capacity they lead the legislature and provide parliament with the policy upon which decisions are to be made. There is no working at cross purposes between the executive and legislative departments as may be found in the United States when the President belongs to one party and the majority in Congress to another. On the contrary, under a system of cabinet government, "from first to last there is full and harmonious collaboration between the law-making and money-granting authorities. On the one hand, and the law-enforcing and money-spending authorities on the other." The members of the legislature can also call to the attention of the government any grievance of the people and secure quick redress.

Cabinet government is the best specimen of representative democracy, for it recognizes the ultimate sovereignty of the people. Ministerial responsibility is, of course, immediately to the legislature, but no majority dare ride rough-shod over public opinion. The ultimate appeal rests with the people, and it must remember those to whom it will have to account in the future. "Government with us," says Jennings, "is government by opinion and that is the only kind of 'self-government' that is possible." The government is ever under scrutiny and the system of parliamentary government provides for daily and periodic assessment of what the rulers do.

Cabinet government is in the real sense a government by criticism. The majority party form the government. The minority constitutes the Opposition. The Opposition must oppose and criticize the government. There is a saying in England that the Prime Minister knows the leader of Opposition more than his wife. It explains how far the Ministry is alive to the opinion of the Opposition and apprehensive of its criticism. A government which neglects the Opposition does so at its peril. The lapses of the government are its opportunities and the Opposition uses then to appeal to the public opinion. "The House is its platform, the news papers are its microphones and the people is its audience.

Another merit claimed for the cabinet government is its flexibility and elasticity. Bagehot highly eulogised this aspect and pointed out that people can, under this system of government "choose a ruler for the occasion" who may be especially qualified to successfully pilot the ship of the State through a national crisis. Churchill replaced Chamberlain as Prime Minister, because national emergency demanded it and this change was brought about without any political upheaval in the country. But such a smooth change is not possible under a Presidential type of government. The office of the President goes by calendar. "The American Government," says Bagehot, "calls itself a government of the supreme people; but at a quick crisis, the time when the sovereign power is most needed, you can not find the supreme people...all the arrangements are for stated times. There is no elastic element; everything is rigid, specified and stated. Come what may, you can quicken nothing and can retard nothing. You have bespoken your government in advance, and whether it suit you or not, whether it works well or works ill, whether it is what you want or not, by law you must keep it.

Moreover, cabinet government can claim high educative value. It cannot function without well-organised political parties. The object of every political party is to win elections and capture government. To win elections mean that the party should be in a position to secure the majority of votes and the electorate should approve its programme. It is like placing one's cards on the table and acquainting the nation with its political programme. It is for the people to judge one party or the other on its merits. If an issue of national important arises subsequently, on which the verdict of the people had not been obtained by the party in power, the legislature may be dissolved and appeal made to the electorate. All this makes the people politically conscious. They are always vigilant of their rights and vigilance is the true price of democracy.

Finally, cabinet government has succeeded in democratizing governmental machinery in all civilised countries, particularly where exists the institution of hereditary monarchy. If England is called the citadel of democracy it is because there is constitutional monarchy and the King does not actively govern. He reigns but does not rule. The latter is the function of his responsible ministers.

Defects of Cabinet Government. In spite of the many practical advantages of the cabinet system some objections have been urged against it. It is maintained that it violates the theory of the separation of powers, and as such cannot commend itself. Combination of executive and legislative functions in the same set of individuals, it is argued, leads to tyranny. Sidgwick, while admitting the undeniable gain of harmony between these two chief organs of government, maintains that it is "to be purchased by serious draw backs. Ministers, he says, "are liable to be distracted from their executive duties by the work of preparing legislative measures and carrying them through Parliament while Parliament is tempted away from legislative problems by interesting questions of current administration in which, especially in foreign affairs, it is liable to interfere to an excessive extent. The advantages of the division of government into different departments are, thus, "lost in the fusion or confusion of legislative and executive functions." This criticism however, does not seem to be valid. Practical experience tells us that collaboration between the executive and legislative power is essential to the well-being of the State. These departments cannot be divided into water-tight compartments. Theory of the separation of powers in its rigid form is inconceivable.

It is further pointed out that cabinet government is unstable. The government has no fixed life. It remains in office only so long as it can retain parliamentary majority which is subject to the vagaries of the representatives, particularly "if the dominant majority in the representative chamber is either small or wanting in cohesion; and in the latter case it is also liable to be upset by a new combination of parties in the chamber—aided perhaps by personal intrigues—if the opportunity for the combination is skillfully chosen, so that the newly-formed majority is not reversed on an appeal to the country. The uncertainty the tenure of office, the critics of cabinet government maintain, does not prompt the party in power to adopt a far sighted and consistent policy. A new ministry which assumes office is sure to reverse the policy of the defeated ministry, for it comes in with its own definite policy and programme. It may, however, be said that much of the above criticism is true only in countries with multiple political parties where the lease of the life of the cabinet is short and precarious . Countries, like Great Britain, having dual party system, do not demonstrate such a state of affairs and dual party system is really the true basis of parliamentary democracy.

It is sometimes deplored that the cabinet system of government divides the country into a set of men who strive their utmost to get things done and another set who do their utmost to obstruct. The Opposition under the cabinet government must oppose tooth and nail all measures sponsored by the government irrespective of their practical utility. Sometimes governmental policy is subjected to such a scathing criticism that it proves detrimental to national solidarity and prestige. When the Opposition indiscriminately opposes what the government may say or propose, it retards the progress of the country and, also, amounts to national wastage both of money and time.

But the fact is otherwise. The essential feature of parliamentary government is a certain degree of moderation among the political parties or what may be described as political forbearance. The minority agrees that the majority should govern and the majority agrees that the minority must criticize. The Opposition is the prospective government and it understands and observes the rules of game as the majority does. The government so arranges the parliamentary programme so as to give due opportunity to the Opposition to discuss and criticize its actions. The government even becomes wiser by the criticism and arrives at a compromise. This is the essence of discussion and parliamentary government is *par excellence* in this respect. The situation of ruthless opposition prevails only when extremist and anti-democratic forces gain a substantial membership in the legislature which they proceed to terrorize and ridicule. But this is not the way of parliamentary system of government. "Whatever be the form of government," says Guerin, "a regime is democratic when the will to social co-operation of its members is stronger and more spontaneous than its anarchical impulses." Parliamentary government recognizes and welcomes difference and it provides the machinery for is expression. But these differences must not go so far as to make impossible the work of government.

Again, cabinet government is said to be inefficient because it is a government by amateurs. The headship of different departments of the executive is entrusted to persons who may not be familiar even with the rudiments of administration. "A youth must pass," says Sir Sydney Low, "an examination in Arithmetic before he can hold a second class clerkship in the Treasury; but a Chancellor of the Exchequer may be a middle-aged man of the world who has forgotten what little he ever learnt about figures at Eton or Oxford, and is innocently anxious to know the meaning of those little first dots when confronted with Treasury accounts worked out in decimals. Disraeli, while forming a ministry, offered the Board of Trade to a man who wanted instead the Local Government Board." It does not matter," said Disraeli, "I suppose you know as much about trade as—the first Lord of the Admiralty knows about ships." Dr. Gopi Chand Bhargava is the Finance Minster in the Punjab Government, but with everything to learn about public finance; for the whole of his life Dr. Bhargava has belonged to the medical profession. The Prime Minister is not concerned in the choice of ministers with their aptitudes and knowledge of the departments they have to boss. His choice is seriously limited by political considerations, the foremost of which is preservation of stable parliamentary majority. Hence the amateur who obtains offices is not always a gifted amateur, "weak men, incompetents, are sometimes appointed to office or to inappropriate departments, out of such considerations of popularity, sometimes gained or faded a decade or more ago, or through the personal esteem or friendship of the prime minister." And once in office, major part of their time is devoted in parliament and cabinet meetings social and other political activities and in nursing their constituencies. Nor does the brief and precarious tenure of their office leave any stimulus for them to learn the departmental technicalities. The result is, the critics of cabinet government point out, that it is a government by the inefficient who are more tools in the hands of their permanent civil servants.

But this is not a correct appreciation of parliamentary government. The essence of cabinet government is the responsibility of the ministers to the legislature. It is, no doubt, always preferable to appoint a minister who is well informed about the working of the department he is to preside, but it does not mean that he should be an expert. The business of the minister is not to do the work of the department. He is only to see that it works properly and consistent with the declared policy of the government. In fact, there are many advantages if the head of the department is an amateur. A layman sees the department as a whole and his appraisal is entirely different from that of an expert. "The cabinet," according to Ramsay MacDonald, "is the bridge linking up the people with the expert, joining principle to practice. Its function is to transform the message sent along sensory nerves. It does not keep the departments going; it keeps them going in certain direction."

Another serious difficulty of the parliamentary system of government is the ever-growing size of the cabinet in every country. In fact, cabinets have grown everywhere too large for prompt and effective discussion and decision. The huge amount of work to be done by the cabinet and the tremendous burden on each minister—departmentally, parliamentarily, electorally and socially—leave very little margin for serious thought on any subject beyond the immediate task. Then, participation in international conferences impose on several ministers, particularly on the Prime Minister, the Foreign Minister, and the Finance Minister, rather long occasional absences from current duties of administration at home. All taken together, the period of office of ministers, as Dr. Finer observes, "is a period of practical work, not of reconsideration and survey." The obvious result is, as the critics point out, a deep continued reliance on the administrative services. Bureaucracy under the circumstances, according to Ramsay Muir, "thrives under the cloak of ministerial responsibility." Whatever be the justification of the criticism there is no denying the fact, that the necessity of reducing the size of the cabinet is being felt in every country and in England it was reduced in 1947 to sixteen members only, and so was the size of Mr. Churchill's Cabinet in 1951. Anthony Eden continued with the practice when he formed his government in May 1955 and Macmillan followed Eden after the latter's resignation. Mr. Amery Suggested that no cabinet should exceed six to seven ministers.

Cabinet system, its critics maintain, has degenerated into a party government in which political power is monopolised by the majority party. So long as parliamentary majority is assured it assumes dictatorial powers. The minority party is completely left out of active participation in the government and the nation is deprived of the services of the talented persons who might be belonging to the minority party. Ramsay Muir is of the opinion that dictatorship of the cabinet in the last resort means the dictatorship of the Prime Minister who is the leader of the majority party. He says the cabinet government is "a dictatorship of one man or of a small group of men exercised through a subservient party majority of more or less tired members." But it must not be forgotten that the Prime Minster's position is bound up with the party. His prestige no doubt, is one of the elements that make for the success of the party. He is also responsible for party cohesion. But without his party the Prime Minister is nothing. Whatever he is and whatever he can claim to be is due to what the party has made him. Once the party disowns him, he meets the fate of Ramsay MacDonald. Within the cabinet he cannot do all what he wishes to do. He must listen to and respect the opinion of his colleagues. It is essential for the Prime Minster to retain the loyalties of his political friends who owe him a personal as well as party allegiance. Laski beautifully sums up the whole position when he says, "The parliamentary system is conducted on the vital hypothesis that no man is indispensable; and its daily operation is a constant and salutary reminder to the Prime Minister that his fortune depends upon the recognition of this truth."

Finally, cabinet government is charged with lack of promptness in deciding and taking immediate action in times of national crisis or emergency. In emergency promptness and vigour of initiative are essential for success. But a cabinet consists of a large number of ministers which need minds to be consulted. A quick and decisive opinion cannot, accordingly, be secured. Moreover, a cabinet under a parliamentary system with its divided responsibility, open discussions, and shifting majorities can hardly be expected to take prompt, united and vigorous decisions. These objections are also not borne by facts. The Second World War has fully demonstrated how cabinet governments withstood the test of time. In India, too, we have the cabinet governments both at the Centre and in the States. How successfully the Central and the State Governments grappled with the 'refugee and other post-partition problems is a matter of contemporary history.

PRESIDENTIAL GOVERNMENT

Nature of the Presidential system of government. Presidential government should be clearly distinguished from cabinet governments. Both Cabinet and Presidential governments are representative in their character, but responsibility of the executive to the legislature is the *sine qua non* of the former whereas the latter is constitutionally independent of the legislature. Under the Presidential system the legislative and the executive are two distinct departments of government. There is a more or less divorce between the two and the executive is neither responsible to the legislature for their public acts nor do they depend on it for remaining in office.

In fact, it is a misnomer to designate them ministers who constitute the presidential cabinet. The members of the President's cabinet are not members of the legislature and they do not belong to the parliamentary majority. They have no access to the legislature. They neither take part in its debates nor do they go there to initiate and pilot legislation or to defend the policy of government or stand in need of seeking its confidence. Nor have they any power to dissolve the legislature and appeal to the electorate, if the legislature does not approve their policy. They have, indeed, no policy of their own. The policy of the government is that of the *head* of the State, who appoints them and retains them in office as long as it pleases him. They are responsible to him alone and to no one else. The cabinet under a Presidential system of government, in brief, is the tool of the *head* of the State. He can override the opinions of its members or he may not seek it or even if he does seek, it is for him to decide whether to consult them individually or collectively. And as for its members. "breath unmakes them as a breath has made."

The chief executive in a Presidential system of government, therefore, has a status independent of, and co-ordinate with the legislature, and it is no subject to the direction or control of the latter either for his continuance in office or in respect to the manner in which he exercises his powers. The duties of the chief executive and his administrative officers (members of the cabinet) lie wholly in the executive and administrative filed and that they have no responsibility in respect to the legislative functions, except as it may be their duty to make known to the legislature the need for the legislation in orde1 that their executive and administrative functions may be more effectively performed.

To sum up, following are the chief characteristics of the Presidential form of government:

1. The head of the State, who is called the President, is not merely the chief executive, but he *the* executive. His powers are real both in law and fact.
2. The chief executive head of the State is the elected representative of the people. His method of election and the term of office are provided for in the constitution. His powers are the direct grant from the constituent authority effected through express provisions of the constitution.
3. The office of the President goes by calendar. He cannot be removed from office expect by impeachment.
4. The executive is not the creature of the legislature nor does it depend on its confidence for remaining in office.
5. The chief executive has, thus, a status independent of, and co-ordinate with the legislative branch, and is not subject to the direction and control of the latter either for his continuance in office or with regard to the exercise of his powers.

6. The fact that the president is *the* executive makes all 'ministers' his subordinates. Under the parliamentary government the ministers are always the most important leader of the majority or parties, but under the Presidential system the powerful leaders, with the exception of the President, are usually in Congress and sometimes elsewhere, but rarely in the 'cabinet'.

The 'ministers' are really the secretaries of the President. They are appointed by him, are responsible to him, and remain in office so long as he wishes them to be. They are neither the ministers nor do they constitute a cabinet as it is popularly known. In fact, it is a misnomer to designate them as such. They can appropriately be called the President's family.

7. The duties of the chief executive and his ministers are executive and administrative only. They have nothing to do with legislation except to make it known to the legislature the need for legislation in order to perform effectively their executive their executive and administrative functions. They have no berth in the legislature and law making is the exclusive concern of the members of Congress.

8. The legislature cannot be dissolved. It runs its own lease of life.

9. The Presidential system, thus, assumes separation between executive, legislative and judicial functions.

Presidential Government in the United States. The Presidential type of government started its career in the United States and is now confined to certain republican forms of government which are exclusively in the Western Hemisphere, as well as the three other countries, the Philippines, Southern Korea, and Liberia. It is instructive to know the factors which contributed towards its emergence in the United States and the shape of the governmental machinery which it assumed. There were two factors which influenced the framers of the American Constitution against the cabinet form of government. In the first place, Montesquieu's theory of the separation of powers had a great appeal for the

Americans. The theory of limited government, which is the natural corollary of the doctrine of popular sovereignty, had convinced the authors of the Constitution of the necessity of separating the three branches of government as it prevented tyranny and absolutism. Liberty if it could last, they argued, then political direction of authority should not concentrate in any one of the branches of government. Secondly, they knew that cabinet government could function only when the life of the nation was divided into distinct political parties, each with its separate programme and platform. Political parties, the framers of the constitution believed, weaken national solidarity by creating sharp cleavages and the need of the time was unity out of the diversity of the new nation. They accordingly, created an executive department independent of and co-ordinate with the legislative department; an "energetic yet dignified" executive capable of enforcing national laws firmly and one which should lend a note of stability to the new government.

The Presidency of the United States is one of the greatest political offices of the world. Its occupant has become,—with the exception of the Central European dictators,—the most powerful head of a government known to our day. He is absolutely free, with respect to the exercise of his powers and tenure of office, except that all appointments made and treaties concluded by him are ratified by the Senate. As his term of office goes by calendar, his responsibility to the electorate is unenforceable. He can only be impeached by the Senate. His conviction by the Senate cannot carry a greater penalty than removal from office and disqualification to hold and enjoy and office of honour, trust, or profit in the United states.

In the Exercise of his executive duties, the President is assisted by his Secretaries who are the heads of different departments and are now ten in number. The Secretaries of the President are merely his personal assistants. They are appointed by him and are responsible to him. None of them is a member of Congress nor is he responsible to it. Though popular usage collectively gives to the departmental head the name of cabinet, yet it is a misnomer to designate them as such. The President cannot shift his responsibility to this body or any officer of it. He cannot make them individually or collectively accountable to the legislature or the country for the policies and action of the federal government over which he presides. Their responsibility is to the president alone. Cabinet in the United States is a mere creation of the President's will. It is an extra-statutory and extra-constitutional body. It exists only by custom and if the President desires to dispense with it, he can do so. The procedure, as it stands today, is that cabinet meets ordinarily once a week and the President submits to it questions upon which he thinks he needs their advice and the members bring to the cabinet such matters in their respective departments as they deem appropriate for cabinet conference and general discussion. Votes are seldom takes as they are of no importance beyond securing a mere expression of opinion. And even if ever they are taken, they have no value. Cabinet members have no corporate rights as it is in England. This is well illustrated by two anecdotes, one relating to America and the other to England. "Seven nays, one aye, the ayes have it," announced President Lincoln following a cabinet consultation in which he found every member against him. This attitude is so often contrasted with Lord Melbourne's putting a question on corn laws to the vote in the cabinet and saying "it does not matter what we will say, as long as we all say the same thing." Cabinet, in the United States, has been aptly described as the President's family.

The executive in the United States has no initiative in legislation except that the President may send messages from time to time to Congress recommending enactment of particular laws. It is true that the Presidential messages are favourably received by Congress and greatly influence legislation, yet the executive in America lacks all initiative and guidance which is so conspicuous a feature of the parliamentary government. Nor has the President the right to summon, except for extraordinary sessions, and dissolve Congress. Congress in the United States assembles *ipso facto* and its duration is fixed. No doubt, the President can veto laws passed by Congress but it is only a suspensive veto. He may refuse assent to a bill passed by Congress within ten days after the bill has been submitted to him. If the bill so vetoed is again passed by a two-thirds majority of each House, the President has no option, but to give his assent to it and promulgate it forthwith.

According to Dr. Finer the American Presidency has six outstanding characteristics.

It is a "made executive" but it has grown;

It is a "solitary" not a "collective" executive;

It is popularly elected, in practice directly;

It is more than an executive;

It is separated from Congress;

It may be tinkered with, but cannot be reformed."

Merits of Presidential Government. The chief merit of Presidential form of government is that without, being responsible it retains a representative character. The President is an elected representative of the people, but his tenure does not depend upon the fluctuating will of the legislature. A fixed tenure of office accounts for a greater continuity of policy and firmness in administration. The policy of the government can be successfully carried out without any fear of break. The principle virtue of Presidential government, therefore, is the fact that is creates a stable executive within the framework of a democratic order. This means promptness, vigour and initiative in administration. All executive authority is vested in one centre and the head of the State is *a* executive as well as *the* executive. He is, in a word, the generalissimo of administration and as such, there can be no question of divided policy. His ministers follow the policy initiated by him.

Unity of control, quickness in decision, and concerted policy which emergency of any kind demands, can best be obtained in a Presidential system of government. The head of the State is a chief foreign policy maker and a Commander-in-Chief of the armed forces of the country. As Commander-in-chief he may even take, in case of war, the command of military operations and effectively control matter of vital importance in domestic and foreign affairs, just as Woodrow Wilson and Franklin Roosevelt did in the United States in the two World Wars. What President Roosevelt did, during the economic crisis of the thirties of the present century, is a matter of contemporary history. All this is not possible under a cabinet system of government. Even Winston Churchill, who attained new heights of power and authority has not the personal powers of the President of the United States. To illustrate the difference in the position and powers of the President of the Unites States and the Prime Minister of England, Jennings writes that "the President pledged the United States in the realisation of the objectives of the Atlantic Charter while the War Cabinet, not the Prime Minister, pledged the United Kingdom.

The Presidential system also makes possible the appointment of experts to head the departments and without consideration of Party affinities. The President may even appoint persons not belonging to his own party. Cleveland appointed Walter G. Gresham as Secretary of State and he had been thought of a Republican candidate for the presidency. Theodore Roosevelt and Taft each appointed a Democrat Secretary of War and Hoover made a Democrat Attorney-General. Roosevelt's choice of Henry L. Stimson as Secretary of War and of Frank Knox as Secretary of Navy in 1940 both prominent Republicans, are two more notable examples. A Prime Minister in a parliamentary system of government cannot normally do this. If the Cabinet is to work as a team it must consist of persons who think alike and belong to the same party. Again, a Prime Minister has a choice in selecting his colleagues, yet the Party expect certain men to be in the Cabinet and the country, too, expects them to be there. Then, the allotment of various departments to ministers is a matter of political consideration and expediency rather than the aptitude for the work they are expected to perform. There is no political expediency which may weigh with the President and there is no party crisis of which he may be afraid of.

The advocates of Presidential form of government argue that such a system is best suited for countries inhabited by different communities with diverse interests. Homogeneous dual party system which is so essential for the success of cabinet government cannot be secured under these conditions. Multiple party system is the general outcome when the people are divided both horizontally and vertically. But a government formed out of heterogeneous elements is a weak and unstable government. Under the Presidential system of government it is a "solitary" executive. The President is the unmistakable focus of responsibility.

Defects of Presidential Government. The critics of the Presidential system are numerous and they urge that it divides government into water-tight compartments as it is based on separation of powers. In actual practice there can be no rigid division between the executive and legislative departments, yet to divide them into independent and co-ordinate departments is to create friction between them which is highly injurious to good and efficient government. By establishing the Presidential system of government the fathers of the American Constitution, Dr. Finer says, "separated the executive sources of knowledge from the legislative centre of their application; severed their connection between those who ask for supplies and those who have the power to grant them; introduced the continuous possibility of contest between two legislative branches; crated in each the necessity for separate leadership in their separate business; and made this leadership independent of the existence and functions of the executive. With powers divided between the executive and legislative departments without any means of proper co-ordination, there is always inordinate delay to arrive at an agreement even on pressing matters which demand expeditious disposal. One branch of government may be operating on one policy whereas the other two may be following quite a different one, particularly when the executive belongs to one Party and the legislative majority to another.

Lack of direct initiative in legislation on the part of the executive is really a very serious defect in the Presidential system of government. Legislation is the main function of the executive and the legislature does not act under its instructions. There can, accordingly, be no cohesiveness and the party ties, which bind the executive and the legislature, are too flimsy for an integrated policy.

The result is that the legislative procedure is different essentially from the one in a country having a parliamentary system of government; financial procedure is worlds apart; there is no co-ordination of political energy or responsibility; but each branch has its own derivation of authority and its morsel of responsibility. And in order to remove the possibilities of concentration of authority at one single end, a system of checks and balances may be introduced as in the American Constitution. The system of checks and balances is not only the negation of the theory of separation of powers, but it is also highly injurious to administrative efficiency. Somewhat ironically, Prof. Beard remarks, referring to the checks and balances in the United States "designed to promote over-all equilibrium, often operate rather to aggravate than to ameliorate the ill effects of separation, as for example in the case of the Presidential veto and senatorial assent to treaties".

Again, the Presidential form of government is characterised to be "autocratic, irresponsible and dangerous." Once the President has been elected the nation must continue with him whether they like and approve of his policy or not. He may become autocratic and even degenerate into a dictator, subject to the provisions of the constitution. Since his office goes by calendar, he cannot be removed. The legislature has no constitutional power to withdraw the mandate which the electorate gave him at the time of election. This has been well explained by Bagehot. He says, "You have bespoken your government in advance and whether it suits you or not whether it works well or ill, whether it is what you want or not by law you must keep it." Moreover, Presidential system of government is criticised for its rigidity, for the constitutional provisions must always be adhered to both in times of peace and war. During World War II Presidential elections in America were held twice whereas general elections were postponed in England by an Act of Parliament. In America there could not be any postponement without amending the constitution which is a difficult and lengthy process. The rigidity of the constitution does not take cognizance of the needs of the hour. It must take its own course, though it may at times prove harmful to the interests of the nation.

Finally, the Presidential system has frequently been criticised for being unequal to the task of conducting a vigorous foreign policy. It is asserted that the President's dependence on the co-operation of frequently recaleitrant Congress makes United States' foreign policy slow moving and uncertain affair. No one, including friends and foes, can guess about the degree to which executive action or commitments will be sustained or repudiated by Congress. In the United States of America the Presidential system, in spite of its limitations, has worked vigorously well. Whenever basic unity was required in an exceptional crisis, statesmanship and patriotism has always provided it. By effective appeals to the voters through the spoken word, press, radio, and lately television the President have succeeded to dramatize their programmes and compel consideration of their views. But however successful the Presidential system be in the United States, the results of its working have been unfortunate in Latin American countries, Philippines and Southern Korea.

BUREAUCRATIC GOVERNMENT

Bureaucracy represents that type of government the administration of which is entrusted to the permanent functionaries. They constitute the permanent civil service and are specially recruited to the services as a result of competitive examination or by nomination. The enjoy permanency of tenure and remain in office during good behaviour or till they retire on pension. Their promotion in service depends partly upon seniority and partly upon merit. In such a system of government service is a profession and offers a career to those who enter it. Bureaucratic government is neither representative nor responsible and, accordingly, it is not responsive to public opinion. The most familiar example of bureaucratic government was the British Government of India before 1919.

Merits of Bureaucracy. Its chief merit is that the key posts are entrusted to the charge of officers who are men of high skill and ability and possess expert knowledge. They acquire special training in the art of government and observe a rigid code of traditions. Mill points out that bureaucracy "accumulates experience, acquires well-tried and well-considered traditional maxims, and makes provisions for appropriate practical knowledge in those who have the actual conduct of affairs." It is, accordingly, more efficient than popular government. Usually, there develops among the administrative functionaries and *esprit de corps* and a spirit of discipline similar to those found in a regular army. Bureaucracy, therefore, represents an orderly administration entirely different from what is generally found in a democratic government.

Demerits of Bureaucratic Government. The chief defects of the bureaucratic government are centralisation of control and supervision, red-tapism, strong attachment to routine work, secrecy and undue safeguards for service. Such a government can neither be responsible nor responsive. Those who exercise authority are wedded to official customs and precedents without any regard to the needs of the people. They are conservative in their outlook and, as such, have neither the means to feel the pulse of the people nor an inclination to adjust their policy according to the popular demand. They are primarily concerned with form rather than with substance and according to Mill, "the disease which afflicts bureaucratic government and of which they die, is routine." Urgency has no place in bureaucracy. Every detail of administration must mechanically move through the rut of 'proper channel' till it reaches the head of the department and decision is taken. Years pass before even trifling matters are finally disposed of. All this entails unnecessary waste of time and public money.

Bureaucracy may mean an efficient governments, but efficiency is not the sole test of a good government. A good government always tries to stimulate in the people self-reliance, patriotism, loyalty, and interest in the government. It aims at political education of the citizens. The rulers consider themselves as trustees of public opinion and in their public actions they are guided and influenced by the needs and requirements of the people. Bureaucracy is a denial of all this and so we may conclude that whatever its merits, it is no substitute for self-government.

DICTATORSHIP

Dictatorship Old and New. Dictatorship as a form of government is not new. It was a recognised institution in republican

Rome where normally the authority of government was vested in two presidents called Consuls. In times of emergency the Romans used to appoint a Dictator to supersede the Consuls, granting him supreme powers to meet the crisis. But Roman dictatorship was a temporary expedient to meet a crisis and discarded when the crisis was past. Moreover, the dictator was selected by a legal process with the obligation to submit his use of power to the scrutiny of the permanent authority.

This nature of dictatorship does not apply to the modern dictators of Russia, Italy, Germany and some other countries. Modern dictators are not selected by a legal process for a limited period of time in order to steer the State through a national emergency. They come into power as a result of *coup de' etat.* Force is the criterion of their political authority and they remain in power as long as force can retain them. They are responsible to no other authority except to themselves. In fact, the whole authority of the State is vested in one individual person and he personifies the State. Some writers are of the opinion that the Russian dictatorship is the dictatorship of a party while in Germany and Italy it was the dictatorship of individuals. But Nazism and Fascism were also the rule of a party, though they remained all through overshadowed by a single personality just as Bolshevism was in the days of Lenin and Stalin. Now Khrushchev's personality looms large on the political horizon. In fact, no government, as Maclver has shown, is ever actually in the hands of a single individuals. "if there is a single seemingly supreme ruler, he inevitable rests his power on the active support of an associated class. He rules in its interests no less than with its cooperation. He nearly always has a council of advisers who represent the class." Hitler and Mussolini were leaders of the Nazi and Fascist parties. They selected their ministers from the ranks of their own parties in order to pursue the ends of their respective parties. There is, accordingly, no difference between the Russian type of dictatorship and that of Central European countries. If there is any, it is only of degree rather than of kind.

Rise of Modern Dictatorship. World War I was claimed to be a fight of democracy against autocracy and it was fought to make the world safe for democracy. The Treaty of Versailles was also formed on broad democratic principles. It recognised the principle of self-determination of nations and built new States on the ruins of earlier monarchies. The defeated Germany presented to the world the best specimen of a parliamentary government through the Weimar Constitution. It was hoped that the new States as well as the old would gradually come round to parliamentary democracy. But surprising as it may seem, in close wake of the War nearly three-quarters of the people of Europe found democratic governments either destroyed or in danger of destruction. Italy came under the heels of Mussolini and his Fascist party in 1922 after his famous march on Rome. Primo di Rivero was declared the father of Spain in 1923. Weimar constitution of 1918 was replaced by a dictatorship under Hitler and his Nazi party. In Poland the lingering shadow of parliamentary government was lost in 1929 when Pilsudski sent a body of soldiers into the lobby of the chamber to remind the representatives of their limitations. In Yugoslavia, King Alexander dismissed parliament and suspended the constitution. In Rumania, King Carol made a similar attempt at royal dictatorship in 1931. Besides these countries, Bulgaria, Portugal, Hungary, Austria and Turkey also came under the sway of the dictators. In Greece, John Me taxes established himself in power on August 4, 1939, and began to regiment the life of the country on the pattern of Germany and Italy.

In all these countries it was a dictatorship of the Right. But in Russia it was a dictatorship of Left. The former means the dictatorship of the capitalist and the latter is the dictatorship of the proletariat which is a transitional phase between the destruction of the capitalist society and the emergence of the communistic society when the State withers away. Both these brands of dictatorships are fundamentally, opposed to one another in their ideology, but they operate on roughly the same principles. Their common feature is that both rule by a single group and do not tolerate the existence of any other party. They begin with the community, not with the individual, and consider that the claims of the State, as representing the community, must always have precedence. They deny that the power of the State should be limited by appeal either to individual rights or to fundamental laws; law is the will of the State and there is nothing higher than the State. They deny that any part or aspect of human life can be outside the normal and continuous control of the State; the State is charged with authority over the whole, the totality of what goes within its territories—political, economic, religious, cultural. Government is identified with the State and it is not responsible to anything or anybody. The non-accountability of government is, in fact, one of the fundamental concepts of dictatorship. The dictatorship of all types has, therefore, in common the negation of the fundamental principles on which democracy rests.

Causes of the rise of Dictatorship. World War I had shaken people's faith in democracy. They had always thought that democracy and peace were synonymous, but the events of August 1914 destroyed their illusion. After the War people had expected a better and happier world, but their hopes were also belied. When the war-weary soldiers returned home they found unemployment, budget deficits, new taxes to liquidate war debts, and a host of other problems facing them. They came to the conclusion that the parliamentarians were war-mongers who had safely sat away from the theatres of War in their comfortable homes and accumulated profits. Those who had actually fought the War and had sacrificed their kith and kin to win it, had to bear the brunt even after the War by torturing unemployment and crippling new taxes. They openly contended: democracy had had its way, let us now pass on. The new states, created after the War on the principle of self-determination, did not provide a satisfactory climate for parliamentary institutions. None of these countries had a tradition for democracy. They had no popular training and democracy could not be retained there for long. Even in countries, which had been considered the citadels of democracy, civil liberty, was considerably curtailed and powers of the executive strengthened during the period of War. This tendency endured after the War.

There were economic and financial problems of still more greater magnitude which haunted the world as a whole. The policy of economic self-sufficiency resorted to by the big and small States alike on the plea of nationalism created new peculiar conditions.

As a matter of fact, the movement became "aggressively" national and free international trade was impeded everywhere. Instead of international amity, distrust and suspicion ranged high and all the States became more nationally self-conscious. The slogan of greater Germany and repudiation of the Treaty of Versailles so enamoured the Germans that they fell in line with Hitler. Hunger for more land and to compensate herself from the losses suffered during the War prompted Italy to follow an aggressive policy under the leadership of Mussolini. The world economic depression and the willful policy of the United states of America and France in sterilizing gold with their Reserve Banks further deteriorated the world position. It required, under the circumstances, manning the resources of every country and a bid for more and new world markets. In every country special measures had to be taken to meet the two-fold emergency of postwar dislocation and economic depression.

The aggressive policy adopted by Japan and followed, by Germany and Italy further worsened the international situation. The League of Nations had lost its prestige. The disarmament conferences had failed. Instead of disarming themselves all countries speeded up militarisation and equipment with modern methods of warfare. War preparedness on the part of bigger powers created international suspicions. Particularly in the smaller States. Every nation required sometime at sure their national integrity on nature at what cost. The States were, thus, faced with military dictatorships. Then, there was the bogey of Bolshevism. In reality Communism was made a scapegoat, for in "times of depression and distress it is perhaps natural that every nation should look round for a scapegoat, as it were, and should then make relentless war upon what it regards as the cause of the trouble. even though its diagnosis may quite easily be wrong".

Two broad factors are, therefore, responsible for the rise of modern dictatorships. First, in countries where democracies had appeared, it had been a plant with no deep roots as it was alien to the soil. Conditions there were not favourble for the successful functioning of democracy. Secondly, in every case dictatorship was born of disillusion and despair; war and its spoils, breakdown of old traditions, apparent lack of any decent alternatives and above all economic crisis. This coincided with the existence of a man or group of men with a definite and clear plan of action.

Some of the critics of democracy argue that dictatorship in some form or other was a necessary phase in the progress from monarchy to democracy. Historical examples were cited in support of this contention, for example, the rule of Cromwell in England and that of Napoleon in France. It was maintained that history of Germany and Italy showed the same sequence of events and before the establishment of true democratic systems of government in those countries they had to pass through the phase of dictatorships. But this argument cannot be applied to the conditions of Russia, for after the dictatorship of the proletariat, the state, in the words of Karl Marx, must 'wither away". After capitalism is destroyed the State becomes unnecessary and gives place to a free society of voluntary associations.

Features of Modern Dictatorship: Modern dictatorship gave birth to a totalitarian State as opposed to a democratic State. The Greek City-State was also totalitarian in the sense that the Greeks did not differentiate between the State and society. The State and society were practically synonymous for them and the Greek-City-State was omnicompetent; it was the church, the school, and the State all combined. But the modern dictator's totalitarian State is not one like the Greek City-State.

Two important principles of modern dictatorship are: (1) to make a sharp distinction between rulers and subjects; and (2) to blur the distinction between government, and the state. In order that his authority may not be challenged, the ruler not only monopolises the actual power but denies to others the right to power. An effective means to this ends is to obliterate the difference between government and the State. The ruler becomes the State; "L'etat c'est moi" (I am the State) of Louis XIV. The State and for that matter government becomes omnicompetent. There is no sphere of life which the modern dictator's State will not cover. For Hitler and Mussolini there was noting above the

State, nothing beyond it, and nothing beside it. The State embraced all activities of the individuals and subordinated them to national ends. It was omni competent and infallible State. Mussolini's motto to the people of Italy was: "All within the State, none outside the State, none against the State." This was tantamount to the worship of the State. The worship of the State was cultivated in schools, at the play ground, in clubs, associations and in fact everywhere. The life of every individual did not belong to him, but to the State and State alone. Thus, "Narrow nationalism, chauvinism, aggressive warfare and imperialistic expansion are some of the essential features of Fascism and Nazism. Russian Communism is fast becoming nationalistic and militaristic, although it is not yet aggressively imperialistic, despite what she has done to Finland and the small Baltic States".

When the nation is glorified the obvious result is war. Hitler and Mussolini openly preached war. Hitler extolled force and violence and he had all praise for the man of action. He believed in the power of the victorious sword. According to Mussolini, peace "is an act of cowardice in the face of sacrifice." Italy and Germany pursued a policy of colonial expansion for procuring raw materials for the sale of their manufactured goods and for the realisation of their will to power. Mussolini said, "Imperialism is the eternal and immutable law of life." Italy, he declared, "must expand or perish."

Dictatorship means one-man or one-party political rule. It is therefore, the very antithesis of democracy. Democracy, according to the dictators and their apologists, is a decaying corpse, because it is "stupid, corrupt and slow-moving." Parliaments, it is maintained, are mere talking shops, "incapable of accomplishing results; at times of emergency they are absolutely helpless." Since modern dictatorship is one-man or one-party rule, it permits no political opposition and is hostile to individual liberty. Individual liberty, according to communism, is a *bourgeois* conception and Fascism and Nazism regarded it as a fetish of the Past. The individual, it is said, has no life apart from the State, and so he must be completely subordinated to it. The totalitarian State, thus, does not give to its subjects the right to speech, the right to press, the right to assembly and all those rights which characterize individuals' life in a democratic State. The ideal of Nazism and Fascism was "one reich, one people, one leader." The Fascist oath read: "In the name of God and Italy, I swear to execute without discussion the orders of the duce and to serve with all my strength and if necessary with my blood the cause of the Fascist revolution." Mussolini's motto to the youth organisation of Italy was: "To believe, to obey, to fight." Hitler put it: duty discipline and sacrifice. This is regimentation of human life, pure and simple. The whole nation must think in one way, talk in one way, and act in one way. Free discussion and criticism of government are ruthlessly suppressed.

Again, the totalitarian State is exclusive. This means two things. In the first place, it advocates the purity of race, the purity of language and the purity of literature. According to the teachings of Nazism, "There are to be no more human being in Germany, but only Germans." It the second place, the exclusiveness of the State means the policy of economic self-sufficiency. Finally, the totalitarian State is hostile to religion. Communism and Religion are incompatible. Fascism and Nazism made religion a tool of the Totalitarian State. Nazism enjoined on the People "to give unto Caesar that which belongs to God".

Merits of Dictatorship. There has been widespread praise for dictatorships. They have been claimed as regimes of "Strong men who get thing done." There seems to be some justification in this claim. In majority of the European countries and politicians miserably failed to solve the post-war problems. Their unsettled economic and political condition and extreme economic distress demanded stable government with vigour of will and action. But owing to the presence of multiple parties, divided and debased by their factiousness, they could not forge a united front. So the people were ready to yield to the authority of any power who could give them sufficient to eat and a stable and efficient government respected at home and abroad. The dictators succeeded admirably in fostering national unity and established confidence in the people by demonstrating to them that they could act more promptly and vigorously and arrive at quicker decisions. Their firmness and determination stood in sharp contrast with the weak and vacillating policies of democratic rulers. When Hitler was asked about the programme of the Nazi party he replied that Germany had enough of programmes; she now needed action. Americans had praised particularly the Italian dictatorship, characterizing it as a system which they intended "to run, to function, to do, to accomplish".

The dictator has either no one to consult or the persons whom he consults are his own men who always dutifully submit to his will. He can, therefore, be quick and prompt in his decisions and consequently able to meet emergencies efficiently. The recent history of Russia, Germany, Italy, Turkey and Spain is the history of marvels which a determined dictator can bring about in the national life of his country. Let us take the achievements of the Spanish dictator Rivera as a typical example. Jackson, in his book, *Europe Since the War,* writes: "For the First time in their history the Spanish trains ran punctually. New railways were laid down, and a system of fine motor roads took the place of traditional mule tracks of Spain. The commerce and industry prospered under the dictator...Agriculture flourished. Labour unrest was mitigated." Poverty and unemployment did no longer exist—indeed a remarkable achievement when it remembered that the dictators began their careers at a time when the economic and political conditions of nearly all the Continental countries were in complete chaos. They began in an atmosphere of national revival, and placed the high ideals of patriotism, comradeship and sacrifice constantly before their countrymen, thus, infusing in them the virtue of service. A dictator alone can brush aside ruthlessly all elements of disorder and opposition in order to rehabilitate a nation's political, economic and social life.

Demerits of Dictatorship. Dictatorship may have given to the people well-feeding. But well-feeding is not the end of human life. To regimen human life and to subordinate it to the State is to dwarf intelligence and initiative. "At best a dictatorship is run as an elaborately organised house of correction, in which inmate is assigned his task and vigilantly inspected as to the manner in which he discharges it." This is good enough for the delinquent and defective members of society, but not for normal men or men towering above other in character and ability. A centralised and coercive direction of public life destroys the possibility of the development of human personality, learning, literature and art. According to Mussolini, the Fascist doctrine did not recognise the individual, except "in so far as his interests coincide with those of the State." Totalitarianism, therefore, "has meant the crushing of individual liberty and the suppression of human personality, violence at home and unashamed aggression abroad, the brutalizing of human nature and the militarisation of a whole people." Moreover, the administrative efficiency, which dictatorship secures, in suicidal to the very spirit of the people. The dictator dictates and everyone else is expected to do his duty. It is tantamount to killing the initiative and enterprise of the individual.

Force and fear are natural foundations of authority for they who regard national power and glory as ends in themselves. But indiscriminate use of force involves dangers. The lessons of history are, says Benedetto Croce, "that....regimes of force can survive only among decadent peoples; that they can figure only as temporary expedients in nations that are growing and in the ascendant and that repressions only produced more violent explosions of the forces they would restrain". What is created by force is destroyed by force. Force, therefore, is not the stabilizing basis of the State. Consent of the governed is its real and enduring basis. As dictatorship does not derive its authority from the consenting people the dictator can never be sure of his position. He adopts violence and coercive measures to suppress even the slightest opposition. "Such a policy spells disaster for the future, for to eliminate all differences is to eliminate all that keeps the community mentally and spiritually alive."

Glorification of the national power fosters international intimidation. The ideal of totalitarian State is a national State "well-ordered internally but aggressive, and bent on expansion." It is, accordingly, opposed to international amity and is, thus, the bankruptcy of human reason and intelligence. Can we, under the circumstances, regard dictatorship as a suitable alternative to democracy! Dictatorship, according to a modern writer, is a tyrants' paradise, "the totalitarian State is a prison and its subjects are closed in by walls, none the less real because they are invisible." The dictatorial rule and its methods are repugnant to the finer feelings of man and are disastrous to the promotion of higher values in life.

But whatever we may think of dictatorship ideally, it cannot be denied that it has proved an effective form of government. So far only war and defeat has brought it to an end; after eleven years in Germany and after twenty-two years in Italy. In Russia it is now forty-four years old and in the construction of the socialist society stupendous and incredible results have been achieved.

References

Anupchand Kapur : *Two Constitutions.*

Asirvatham, E.: *Political Theory. Chap XV.*

Bagehot, W. : *The English Constitution* (1867), Chap. II.

Barker, E. : *Reflections on Government*, Chaps, VII-X.

Brogan, D. W. : *The American Political System*, (1933).

Bryce, J. : *The American Commonwealth*, (1888).

Finer, H. : *The Theory and Practice of Modern Government.* (1954), Chaps. XXIII, XXVI, pp. 90-94, 951-54.

Finer, H. : *Mussolini's Italy.*

Ford. H. J. : *Representative Government* (1924), Chap. XI.

Garner, J. W. : *Introduction to Political Science* (1910), pp. 179-91, 197-200.

Garner. J. W. : *Political Science and Government*, pp. 322-44, 423-38.

Hoover, C.B. : *Dictatorship and Democracies* (1937).

Hitler., A. : *Mein Kampf.*

Jennings, W. I. : *Cabinet Government* (1951).

Laski, H. J. : *Parliamentary Government in England* (1938).

Lowell, A. L. : *Government of England*, Vol. I, Chaps. II, III, XVII-XVIII.

Mussolini, B. : *The Political and Social Doctrines of Socialism.*

Row, E. F. : *How States are Governed.*

Sidgwick, H. : *Elements of Politics*, Chaps. XIX-XX.

Wilson, W. : *Congressional Government* (1894).

6

Types of Democratic Government

The forms which popular government have taken are many, and the future may see the emergence of others, though mankind shows singularly little inventiveness in this field of action compared to the resourceful ingenuity it evinces in adapting the forces of nature to its service.

This chapter may be confined to representative Frames of Government, since the direct rule of popular assemblies, universal in the ancient world, but applicable only to very small communities, has disappeared except in the Swiss Forest Cantons, while the direct action of the people by voting in large areas has been dealt with already.

Among representative Governments three specially deserve to be studied—the Parliamentary and Cabinet System of Britain, which, reproduced in the British self-governing Dominions and France, has been more or less imitated in other. European countries; the Presidential system of the United States, adopted in many of the other American republics, and the Executive Council system of Switzerland. As each of these has been described in this chapter is intended only to compare each with the others in respect of characteristic merits and defects. All these Frames have in common certain features, viz.:

1. They can exist (in essentials) either under a Republic or a (Nominal) monarchy, for the form of Monarchy which exists in such countries as Britain and the British self-governing Dominions, in Italy, Holland, Belgium, Sweden, Norway, and Spain, resembles the ornamental facade of a large public

building behind which the work of the office is carried on in a number of rooms, the arrangement of which has nothing to do with the design of the facade.

2. They can exist either under a Rigid Constitution embodied in a single Fundamental Instrument (as in the United States, Switzerland, and Australia) or under a Flexible Constitution, where all laws can be made and repealed by the same authority at any moment (as in Britain and New Zealand) or where there are only two or three Fundamental Laws easily changed (as in France).

3. They are all based on the doctrine of Popular Sovereignty, recognizing the people as the ultimate and only source of Power, to whomsoever it may delegate that power.

4. As a consequence of this feature, the right of raising revenue and appropriation it to the several services of the State belongs in all these systems to the representatives of the people.

5. They are all worked by political parties, this being what the old logicians called an Inseparable Accident, a quality not essential, but in fact always present.

6. The distinctive features of each of these systems or Frames of Government may be concisely stated as follows:

I. The Cabinet or Parliamentary system has for its organs of government:

(a) A (titular) Executive Head of the State, either elected for a term of years (as in France, Germany, Finland, Czechoslovakia, Poland, Esthonia, Portugal) or hereditary (as in Italy, Britain, Holland, Belgium, Greece, Norway), who is not responsible to the Legislature nor removable by it.

(b) A group of Ministers, virtually, if not formally, selected and dismissible by the representative Legislature, and responsible to it. This group, constituting the working executive, is called the

Cabinet, and its members must, everywhere by custom and in some countries by law, be members of the Legislature.

(c) A Legislature, of one or two Chambers, elected by the citizens for a prescribed term of years by (in some counties) liable to be dissolved by the Executive Head, which means in practice the Cabinet.

II. The Presidential System consists of:

(a) An Executive head of the State, elected by the people for a term of years, removable (in many countries) by impeachment for grave offences, but otherwise irresponsible to the legislature, not a member of the Legislature but entitled to address it, empowered to appoint and dismiss the chief officials and to conduct the external affairs of the country, though in these two functions the Legislature, or one branch of it, may be associated with him.

(b) A group of Ministers, called the Cabinet, appointed and dismissible by the President, acting under his orders and responsible to him but not to the Legislature and incapable of sitting therein.

(c) A Legislature, usually consisting of two chambers, elected by the citizens for a term of years, and not dissoluble by the President. Their power of passing resolutions or statutes is subject (in the U.S. and some other countries) to a veto by the President, but (in the United State) any enactment so vetoed can be repassed and so become law by a majority of two-thirds in each Chamber.

III. The Executive Council System, which for brevity's sake I shall call the Swiss, consists of:

(a) A small Administrative Council chosen by the Legislature for a short term of year to carry on the executive business of the State under its direction. its members not sitting in the Legislature though allowed to address it.

(b) A Legislature, consisting in Switzerland of two Chambers, elected for short terms, and not subject to dissolutions.

(c) The people, *i.e.* the whole body of citizens, who can, when any constitutional amendment or law or resolution is submitted to them in pursuance of a demand proceeding from a prescribed number of citizens, approve or reject by their votes such enactment (Referendum), and who have also the power of enacting any proposal for a constitutional amendment, the submission of which has been demanded by a prescribed number of citizens (Initiative).The People are thus a second directly legislative authority, placed above the representative Legislature.

In all these equally democratic forms of government the sovereign power of the people is delegated, being in the Parliamentary form delegated to the Legislature, in the Presidential form delegated partly to the (elected) Executive and partly reserved to the people when they act by amending the Constitution, while in the Swiss form it is divided between the Legislature and the People acting on the occasions when they are summoned to vote by Initiative or Referendum.

In comparing the aforesaid types three points have to be regarded:

(a) Which of them succeeds best in giving prompt and full effect to the Will of the People.

(b) Which is best calculated to guard against errors into which the people may be betrayed by ignorance, haste, or passion.

(c) Which secures the highest efficiency in administration.

The Parliamentary Type concentrates the plenitude of popular power in one body, the Legislature, giving to its majority that absolute control of the Executive which enables the latter, when supported by the Legislature, to carry out the wishes of the majority with the maximum of vigour and promptness. The only power which the Executive has against the Legislature is that of appealing to their common master the People at a general election; and in France the consent of the Senate is required for this purpose. The essence of the scheme is that the Executive and the Majority in the Legislature work together, each influencing the other; the Cabinet being in fact an Executive Committee of the Legislature. The working of the scheme presupposes not only the existence of parties, but a sentiment of party unity strong enough to induce the majority in the Legislature to entrust a large discretion to the Cabinet, and to support it, except now and then in very grave matters, with a trustful loyalty which assumes its action to have been right till proved to have been wrong. The Cabinet on its side is bound to adhere it the principles which are dear to the party as a whole and to keep the majority in the Legislature in good humour, straining its loyalty no further than is absolutely necessary, and taking from time to time into its own body members of the majority who have won their way to the front.

The presence of Ministers in a Legislature has two other advantages. Being in constant contact with members of the Opposition Party as well as in still closer contact with those of their own, they have opportunities of feeling the pulse of the Assembly, and through it the pulse of public opinion, and can obtain useful criticism, given privately in a friendly way, of their measures, while the members can by their right of questioning Ministers call attention to any grievances felt by their constituents and can obtain information on current public questions. Like other things, the right to interrogate is frequently abused, but any one who has been a Minster in the British House of Commons values the means it gives him of correcting or contradicting erroneous statements, of refuting calumnies, of explaining the reasons for this administrative acts without being obliged to seek the aid of the newspapers.

This system is therefore calculated to secure swiftness in decision and vigour in action, and enables the Cabinet to press through such legislation as it thinks needed, and to conduct both domestic administration and foreign policy with the confidence that its majority will support it against the attacks of the Opposition. To these merits there is to be added the concentration of Responsibility. For any faults committed the Legislature can blame the Cabinet, and the people can blame both the Cabinet and the majority. In the long run the enforcement of Responsibility depends on the activity and sanity of public opinion in each party and the strength of its outside party. This Parliamentary system renders an incidental service in bringing able men to the front, giving them a position from which they can catch the ear of the nation and show themselves qualified for office. Power of speech is what first attracts notice, but if to that they add solid qualities of character—good sense, industry, loyalty, honesty—their colleagues in the Legislature come to respect them, and to trust them when they rise to be Ministers. Moreover, the alternation of power from one party to another provides in the leaders of the Opposition men who can criticize with knowledge the policy of their successors, and who if called upon to succeed those successors, bring in their turn some experience with them.

As the actual working executive has necessarily a party character, it is a merit of this system that the Nominal Executive, be he King or President, Should stand outside party, and represent that permanent machinery of administration which goes on steadily irrespective of party changes. An elected President cannot so easily fill this role as can a hereditary king, though some Presidents have filled it well in France. When a Cabinet falls, the transfer of power to another is a comparatively short and simple matter. The Executive Head (*i.e.* in England the Crown, in France the President, in Canada or Australia the Governor-General) commissions the leader of the Opposition to form a new Ministry; the occupants of the chief offices are promptly changed, and the ship, having put about, is soon under way on her new course, commanded by a new captain, and all this may happen without the worry and cost of an election.

These merits of the Parliamentary system are balanced by serious defects.

The system intensifies the spirit of party and keeps it always on the boil. Even if there are no important issues of policy before the nation there are always the Offices to be fought for. One party holds them, the other desires them, and the conflict is unending, for immediately after a defeat the beaten party begins its campaign to dislodge the victors. It is like the incessant battle described as going on in the blood-vessels between the red corpuscles and the invading microbes. In the Legislature it involves an immense waste of time and force. Though in theory the duty of the Opposition is to oppose only the bad measures and to expose only the misdoings of the Administration, in practice it opposes most of their measures and criticizes most of their acts. Legislation is either, as in France, apt to be sacrificed to "interpellations" intended to damage the Cabinet, or, as in England, to be delayed and clogged by the interposition of party conflicts.

Debates over measures admittedly good are often vexatiously protracted merely in order to prevent the Ministry from carrying other measures which are disliked, or an angry Opposition may seek to damage it by so obstructing all business as to force them to present at the end of the session a sorry harvest of statutes.

Crediting the close association of Executive and Legislature with the merit of avoiding friction, it is also true that where either organ dominates the other, the consequences may be unfortunate. In the eighteenth century the Ministry commanded a large section of the British House of Commons by means of pocket boroughs which the Crown held, or could obtain the use of from their owners. In England, whenever a Ministry has a strong party organisation at its beck and call, it can put pressure upon members through the local party committees in their constituencies; and it has happened in Italy that a Minister may in one way or another obtain control by unseen methods over a large section of the representatives. In France, on the other hand, it is Ministries that suffer, for members are able to extort all sorts of favours for their constituencies from Administrations whose instability compels them to angle for every possible vote; and in Australia a Labour Ministry is a passive instrument in the hands of a parliamentary caucus which is itself controlled by an organisation out-side Parliament. A subservient Ministry loses the respect of the nation, as a dominant one lowers the credit of the Legislature.

A system which makes the life of an Administration depend upon the fate of the measures it introduces disposes every Cabinet to think too much of what support it can win by proposals framed to catch the fancy, of the moment, and to think too little of what the real needs of the nation are; and it may compel the retirement, when a bill is defeated, of men who can ill be spared from their administrative posts.

The Cabinet system grew up in Britain when there were only two parties When between 1876-1906, there appeared a third and, somewhat later, a fourth, it worked less well. The same thing happened in Australia after 1900, has since then happened in South Africa, and is now happening in Canada. In Franc for many years past no Ministry has been able to hold office except by getting several groups to unite so as to form a majority of the whole Chamber. Group alliances are what chemists call an unstable compound, and when they dissolve, down goes the Ministry.

Lastly, the very concentration of power and swiftness with which decisions can be reached and carried into effect is a source of danger. There is no security for due reflection, no opportunity for second thoughts. Errors may be irretrievable.

The Presidential or American system on the other hand was built for safety, not for speed. Founded on the doctrine that the Executive and Legislative departments ought to be kept separate, because only thus could the liberty of the citizen be secured, it not only debars the Executive head and his Ministers from sitting in the Legislature, but in the United States permits the latter both to narrow by law the President's field of action and to refuse him the money needed for carrying out any policy they disapprove. He is helpless against them, except in the narrow sphere which the Constitution reserves to him, and in that sphere the Senate can hamper him in the selection of his high officials. These well-meant provisions, grounded on fears for liberty, have proved inconvenient by impeding the co-operation of representatives and administrators. The former cannot question the latter, except by means of Committees. The latter have not, unless through a Committee, the means of conveying the needs of their departments to the representatives. Delay, confusion, much working at cross purposes are the result: and this is particularly felt in the sphere of finance where the legislature may refuse money when the Executive needs it, and may grant money for no better purpose than to purchase the political support of powerful sections or clamorous constituencies. The "Separation of Powers" has for some purposes turned out to be not the keeping apart of things really distinct but the forcible disjunction of things naturally connected. There is, moreover, no certainty that the Legislature will carry out the wishers of the Administration, however reasonable. The may even decline to pass the statutes needed to give, effect to treaties duly ratified.

The Presidential system leaves more to chance than does the Parliamentary. A Prime Minister is only one out of a Cabinet, and his colleagues may keep him straight and supply qualities wanting in him, but everything depends on the character of the individual chosen to be President. He may be strong or weak, wise or short-sighted. He may aim at standing above party and use his authority and employ his patronage with a single eye to the nation's welfare, or may think first of his own power and his party's gain, and play for his own re-election. The re-eligibility of the President has so often been supposed to unduly affect his action that many Americans think he should be legally disqualified for a second continuous term of office. In some republics such a provision exists.

The United States has best shown the strength and weakness of the system, but just as it works differently in the hands of different men, so is it a different thing in different countries. In nearly all of the republics of Latin America racial and social conditions throw larger powers into the hands of the Executive chief than would be permitted to him in the United States. This has been seen in constitutional Argentina and Uruguay, as well as in those disorderly States where a President is usually a military dictator. Legally the powers may seem the same: Practically they are wider in the countries where constitutional traditions are still new and public opinion still weak or divided into sections by any economic or religious antagonism.

For administrative purposes it is a gain that the members of the Cabinet are not, like those of Britain, obliged to give constant attendance in the Legislature and that when a Minister starts a promising policy he can count on carrying it on without being upset by a sudden change of government. The Legislature, too, since it cannot displace the President, nor even a Minister, is not distracted from the work of legislation by debates intended to discredit the existing and instal a new administration.

Two other merits may certainly be credited to the Presidential scheme. Under it legislature are less dominated by party spirit than of Britain and France, of Belgium and Australia and Canada, for party discipline is not so strict at Washington as at Westminster, though the party organisations are stronger. Under it there is also a greater sense of stability, partly because a shifting of the political balance can take place only at elections, points fixed by law, partly because the legislature can by withholding funds check the Executive in any project thought to be risky, while the Executive can by its veto arrest the legislature in a dangerous course. In either case, the appeal is to the judgement of the nation, to be given, if not forthwith by public opinion, then before long at the next general election. The moderate elements in the country need not fear a sudden new departure: the demagogue cannot carry his projects with a run.

Is Responsibility to the People, a cardinal merit in every form of free government, better secured under the Parliamentary or under the Presidential system? Apparently under the former, because there is more unity, the Cabinet having over the whole policy and administration of the country that full power which their majority in the Legislature has granted them. If they err by omission or by commission, they cannot shift the blame to Parliament, for if they do not receive from it the necessary support they can either dissolve it or resign office, transferring responsibility to it or to their successors.

Under the Presidential scheme the President is responsible, except where the Legislature fails either to pass at his request the laws, or to supply the money needed to carry out the policy he recommends, in which case it is not he but the legislature that becomes answerable for any resulting evil. The majority in a Legislature which prevents a President from acting of course incurs a responsibility attaching to the party which has elected it: and a party may so suffer, but it is a responsibility far less definite than that attaching to a Cabinet, or to the leaders of an Opposition, in a Parliamentary country. When President and Legislature belong to the same party, it is to him that the nation looks, for he can ask the Legislature for all that the conjuncture requires, be it statutes or grants of money. But when he and the Legislature are at odds, and the country is not evidently with the one or the other, there is nothing for it but to bear with the deadlock and await the next ensuring election.

In the Presidential system the man chosen to be head of the Government becomes more definitely Head of the Nation than does a Prime Minister in a Parliamentary country like France, Canada, or England. The eyes of the whole people are fixed upon him even if he be a man of less than first-rate quality, whereas in Parliamentary countries it is only striking personalities such as Pitt or Cavour or Bismarck that excite a similar interest and exert a similar authority. An American President stands high above others, meaning more to the people than leaders in Congress do, and always sure to command attention when he speaks. He need not consult his Cabinet nor regard its advice as must a French or British Prime Minister. To his Cabinet he is a Master, to a French or British Cabinet only a Chief. A prime Minister may fall at any moment if the Assembly tires of him: a President stands firm, and has to be taken by the nation for better or worse while his term lasts. Hence the method of choosing the Irremovable Head becomes proportionately more important. No perfect method has been found.

but this much may be said for popular election, that whereas the method of natural selection from the Assembly in parliamentary countries gives a perhaps undue advantage to oratorical brilliance, the method of deliberate choice by a legal act of the whole people affords a wider field of choice for persons of other gifts, for men like George Washington, or of the type to which in their different ways such strong personalities as Grover Cleveland and Theodore Roosevelt belonged. It often fails to find the fittest men, but it has, at least in the United States, excluded the unworthy. American experience cannot, however, be taken as a general guide. There are in Europe, as well as in those Spanish American republics in which a popular election without violence is now possible, countries where election by an Assembly is the safer methods. This was the view of those who framed the present Constitution of France.

These two types of government so far resemble one another, having both sprung from the common root of a feudal monarchy, that it has been necessary to consider them together. The third or Swiss type has a very different source, for Switzerland was never ruled by a single sovereign, and its legislature grew out of the diplomatic conferences in which the delegates of thirteen little States met to discuss their common foreign policy. The main-spring of the Constitution is the National Assembly, which controls the Executive and in which the whole power of the People is embodied, except in so far as the Constitution limits legislative action and in so far as the people have a final voice in legislation by the Referendum and Initiative. The Swiss system has the advantage of simplicity and of a concentration of authority. The National Assembly chooses and supervises the small Federal Council which carries on administration. Both are watched by public opinion, and can be overruled if necessary by popular vote. Policy, both foreign and domestic, is continuous, moves with an even step, the ideas the same, the men the same. No time is wasted in party strife. Economy and efficiency are secured. The unchecked power which the people can exercise when by the Initiative their votes amend the constitution or enact a law, has not proved dangerous in a country with a population so shrewd. cool, and accustomed to the use of freedom. There are few prizes ambition can strive for beyond the respect and trust of fellow-citizens. A humdrum State, but it is prosperous and contented, and nowhere does patriotism glow with so steady a flame.

Can the advantages which this type of government has bestowed on Switzerland be secured elsewhere by like institutions? The conditions are peculiar: a small nation, its citizens not indeed poor, but very few of them rich, highly intelligent, long trained by local self-government, little distracted by party spirit. It is hard to suppose in any other country a coincidence of these conditions sufficient to give such an institution as the Swiss Federal Council a like chance of success. Nevertheless, we may imagine that even in a country twice the size of Switzerland, a small Cabinet Council appointed by an in the closest touch with the Legislature, and itself appointing and supervising the heads of administrative departments, might, in quieter times than the present, carry on public business with less friction and at less cost than has been found possible under either the Parliamentary or the Presidential system. An Administration not immersed in the whirlpool of party politics might devote itself to the task of bettering the condition of the masses of the people by measures none the less effective because they were not designed to win the momentary support of any section. Politics would be less spectacular : but after all politics were made for men, not men for politics. It would be hard to introduce such a system in any country where the passing of laws has been long associated with party strife, an where the distrust of opponents, intensified in our days by class sentiment, makes each side suspect whatever proceeds from the other; but since alike in France, in America, and in England the constitutional machinery that exists for investigating, preparing, and enacting legislation upon economic and industrial topics has failed to give satisfaction, light upon the problem of improving that machinery ought to be sought in every quarter.

Other schemes of government than the three here described might be invented, and one such, that of a series of local Assemblies, each sending one or more of its best men to a higher Assembly till they culminate in a Central Executive and a Central Council, has taken a sort of shape in the scheme of Russian Soviets.

Many paths might be cut in the forest, but for the present it is enough to indicate those that are well trodden.

If we return to the questions whence we started, it would seem that of the three types examined the people's will receives a fuller and prompter effect under the Parliamentary system and the Swiss system than under the Presidential. The distinctive quality of this last, which some would call a fault and others a merit, lies in the fact that by dividing power between several distinct authorities, it provides more carefully than does the Parliamentary against errors on the part either of Legislature or Executive, and retards the decision by the people of conflicts arising between them. The Swiss, guarding themselves against mistakes committed by the Legislature but placing no check on the direct action of the people, seem to take the greatest risks; but they are really the most conservative in spirit of all the nations, and make the least use of the wide powers reserved to the citizens. Efficiency is most likely to be secured by the Parliamentary system, because whatever the Executive needs it is sure to obtain from its majority in the Assembly, subject, of course, to any check which the existence of a Second Chamber may provide.

As between these two systems the parliamentary seems to be preferred by the new States which have arisen in Europe during the last hundred years, the newest adopting it in the French rather than in the British form. The Presidential system has found favour among the Latin American republics which drew their ideas of self-government from the United States, and has in most of them allowed the Executive a wider power, going so far as in the Argentine Federation to permit a President to supersede the elected officials of a State on the ground that this is necessary to secure a fair election, no party trusting its adversary to conduct elections fairly. So far as the experience hitherto acquired warrants any general conclusion, that conclusion would be that while the Parliamentary has many advantages for countries of moderate size, the Presidential, constructed for safety rather than promptitude in action, and not staking large issues on sudden decisions, is to be preferred for States of vast area and population, such as are the United States and Germany.

Those who hold the chief merit of a scheme of government to lie in the amplitude of its provisions for the expression of the popular will may observe that the Swiss system is the only one which brings out that will in an unmistakable and unpervertible from, viz. by an Initiative or Referendum vote, whereas under the other two systems a vote given at an election, being given primarily for a candidate, not for a law or executive act, does not convey the people's judgement on any specific issue.

That is true, that the cumbrousness and cost of any frequent use of the Referendum in a large country are practically prohibitive, and the party which possessed a strong and ubiquitous organisation would have an unfair advantage at a voting. The opinion delivered would be for half or more of the citizens not their own, but an opinion imposed upon them by others. If the Will of the People means the personal mind and purpose of each individual citizen, to search for it is to search for the pot of gold at the foot of the rainbow.

—James Bryee

7

Localism, Centralism and Federalism

No modern government, not even the smallest, can transact all its affairs in one place. Because the territorial range of the state is coextensive with society, wherever individuals have contracts, situations will arise which call for government on the spot.

Thus a modern political system, whatever its nature, requires a local administration. Two questions must then be settled:

What functions should be assigned to which level?

Which authorities should be preponderant, the central or the local?

The issue posed in these questions has several ramifications which are fundamental to statecraft. Ever since governments were organised territorially, their structure has necessarily been influenced by area. The state is conditioned by geography as much as by history. Its operations extend not only through time, but through space. Hence the problem recurs of relating its functions, institutions, and jurisdiction to the area it occupies. This is no easy puzzle to solve because the fittest boundaries from the standpoint of one function are seldom appropriate for another. A large city will obtain its water supply from one place; its electricity and other forms of power may come from a second; its sewage will, or should, be disposed of in a third. A transportation system connecting the sections of a city and linking it with adjacent suburbs will assume one shape; but the organisation of districts for schools or the prevention of air pollution or crime may require yet other contours. Food for the urban population will be drawn from nearby farms, and from distant flour mills, stockyards, fruit orchards, and fishing grounds. The livelihood of the city dweller, who must find employment in a factory, business office, or retail store, depends on the intricate relationships of complex economic mechanisms whose boundaries may be national or international. Finally, the military defense, which in the Middle ages was provided by stout stone wall around the city's perimeter, depends today on submarines or on satellites encircling the globe. In short, each function of government, plotted geographically, projects itself on a map corresponding to its own needs; and if the maps were superimposed, no two would coincide.

How can we best adapt the structure of the state to interests and services which are spread out in such different patterns? The answer is a common-sense solution. Since it would be impossible to organize separate governmental systems with different areas for every function, and since identical areas would be unworkable, a compromise must be adopted. This consists in distinguishing needs or problems of general concern from those whose range is essentially limited. Hence the familiar division between a central agency and units of more circumscribed range.

THE COMMUNITY OF INTEREST

Besides this argument of convenience, the case for separating local authorities from central is reinforced by further considerations. It is undeniable that proximity creates a community of interests. People who live in the same neighbourhood have many ties. They are equally concerned about sanitation and public health, about water and similar essentials, about transportation to and from their work, about shopping and recreational facilities. The inhabitants of the same area are in constant contact. They meet face-to-face and communicate directly. Their daily activities bring them together; their children go to the same school or playground; most of their friends live within easy reach. In such circumstances, many elements basic to the community are present, for a community consists in a sense of solidarity evoked by common interests and shared experience.

But it is also possible for that feeling of oneness to extend beyond the finite area of face-to-face relationships, provided common interests exist and similar experiences are perceived. People are united, for instance, by the problems of growing and selling the same crop. Thus the Old South paid homage to "King Cotton," as do Canadian prairie farmers to wheat an Sao Paulo *Fazendeiros* to coffee. Membership in the same religion may serve as a bond, as with Catholics, Jews, or Moslems, who are scattered among different localities, nations, or continents. So may people be drawn together who speak the same language, or have similar systems of government, or belong to one cultural tradition. Politically, all such wider unions—or extended communities—are reinforced when the territory they occupy forms a physical continuum. What gave the Old South its strength and made secession seem practicable was the compactness of the cotton kingdom. What consolidates the French-speaking Canadians, besides their church, is their concentration in the Province of Quebec. An extended community is always stronger when its members are contiguous than when they are dispersed. For like reasons, because proximity makes organisation easier, a concentrated minority is generally more effective than a scattered one of the same size. If this were not so, it would be impossible to explain the separation of Ulster from Eire, Norway from Sweden, Israel from the Arab states, or Pakistan from India.[1] Pakistan itself broke up after two decades, its eastern portion becoming the state of Bangladesh. This occurred because Bengal and the Punjab, though united by religion, differed in language and other aspects of culture as well as in economic development. It was impossible to organize a common government for two distinct regions separated by a thousand miles of Indian territory. Community depends on communication. "Decentralisation," "local autonomy," "states' rights"—such terms and all that they imply are derived from that in politics proximity makes a difference.

BOUNDARIES AND PSYCHOLOGY

Moreover, a political boundary itself contributes to a sense of solidarity. It would be erroneous to assume that a community of interests is a result, transferred to politics, of causes that always originate in other social groupings One of the most important of the experiences that unite a group is that they share the same government. The Structure of the state has no less intimate an effect on the organisation of society than society has on the state. When territorial areas are demarcated so that jurisdictions and services may be organised, symbolic associations tend to cluster around the same boundaries. Cooperative sentiments of pride and loyalty, along with competitive attitudes of jealous rivalry, attach themselves readily to spatial units. Both large and small cities can evoke in their inhabitants a city-centred patriotism. People then become conscious of their identity as Londoners, Parisians, New Yorkers, Bostonians. Or they may identify themselves with some wider, yet politically articulated, areas. A county, perhaps , or a province, or a state within a union acquires an individual character: Witness the traditions and folklore of the Vermonter, the Texan, the Bernese, the Gascon, the Castilian, the Yorkshireman. Or the area may broaden out into regional dimensions, as long as it is endowed with recognizable features, real or supposed; for example, New England, Dixie, the Highlands, the Midi, the *Serttho*,[2] the Outback.[3]

It is the purpose of boundaries to divide. Physical separation lends itself to psychological alienation. All who are on "your" side of the line belong to "your" group; those beyond it do not. This feeling is heightened by the opposition that can arise mutually between different communities. A pair of cities may develop a rivalry, as in the cases of San Francisco and Los Angeles, Toronto and Montreal, Sydney and Melbourne, Madrid and Barcelona. So may a pair of counties like Yorkshire and Lancashire in England; or two cantons, such as Bern and Zurich; or two provinces, like Ontario and Quebec; or two sections, like North and South. It is precisely because of the psychological significance of boundary lines that common speech confers a symbolic meaning, of deeper import than their literal one, on such terms as "crossing the Rubicon,"[4] "beyond the Pale,"[5] "the Chinese wall," "the Mason-Dixon line," and "the Iron Curtain."[6]

LOCAL LIBERTIES VS. CENTRALISED DICTATORSHIP

Local loyalties, regional rivalries, and separatist sentiments, where they exist in force, are barriers to unity and therefore to centralisation. But a further factor, sometimes working in conjunction with these influences and sometimes operating independently, also produces a decentralizing effect. It is the fear that power is always susceptible to abuse, and that any accumulation of power not counterbalanced by an independent power can become dangerous. This is the core of the argument against monism, since the net result of ecclesiastical or business autonomy way to create social structure largely exempt from the control of the state and therefore capable of resisting or obstructing it. This is equally the logic of the separation of powers, since there can be no omnipotent state to fear if the institutional structure of the government is dispersed in the form of coordinate branches. Likewise, this is the rationale of a preference for federalism and for "local liberties," the assumption being that Leviathan's grip is weaker when its skeleton is loose jointed. Local or state governments, on this theory, can be made partly independent of the centre, so that they may provide focuses of resistance if tyranny should ever be established there.

The nature of such tyrannies has been too vividly exemplified in modern times to doubt their character, Modern dictatorships are a product of aggressions, attaining control by violence. Because their regimes are founded primarily on force, not on right, they remain insecure even after they have come to power. Hence they continue to vent their aggressiveness against their opponents and any institutions where opposition can rally. If the government at the centre is dictatorial, it is obvious that local parties can become a medium for criticism and local government a vehicle for opposition. To prevent this from happening is important to the modern dictatorship, which never feels safe unless its control is total. Thus the authoritarian regime eliminates any traces of local autonomy and subordinates all local authorities to the central will.

That autocracy is unlikely to permit decentralisation is exemplified equally in both extremes of Right and Left. Before Mussolini's supremacy was established in Italy, the system of local self-government, despite its shortcomings, was an outlet for local feeling. This was particularly so in the regions of Tuscany and

Lombardy, where famous cities flourished, where geniuses had lived and worked, and where historic events were cradled. The dictator, however, prizes dependence in his fellow citizens, not independence. The Municipal Council of Milan, for instance, had been controlled by Mussolini's political opponents, the Socialists. This he could not permit. So he abolished the locally elected councillors and substituted an official, the *Podesta*, appointed from, and responsible to, the centre. The same practice commended itself to Adolf Hitler, an authoritarian centralist by temperament and conviction. In the German Empire, which Bismarck made by blood and iron, and in the Weimar Republic, which the moderate left and center parties created after World War I, the structure of the state was federal. But Hitler would have none of it. As he consolidated his power after the summer of 1934, he proceeded to abolish the Lands (or states) that has composed the federal system. Then, applying the *Führerprinzip*, he organised the German Government from the top downward, appointing in each region and district a hierarchy of officials (*Gauleiters* and other) whose power derived from his.[7]

In the case of the Soviet Union, a form of federalism as noted earlier, was embodied in Stalin's constitution. Several factors combined, however, to make the reality utterly different. One was the imprint of Stalin's personality, being as intolerant of opposition as was Hitler, and the legacy which his long and merciless tyranny bequeathed to his successors. Centralism was further reinforced by the series of economic Plans, all imposed from Moscow. From these, no component republic or "autonomous" region could deviate. In addition, the Russian Republic, one of fifteen units so styled, actually contained over half of the country's population and three-quarters of its territory. This alone precluded any genuine balance in the distribution of powers between the Republics and the Union. Finally, it must be emphasised that true federalism always involves the possibility that one of the units (a republic, state, canton, or province) my be politically opposed to the government at the centre. In other words, federalism pre-supposes democracy. That did not exist in the Soviet Union while the Communist Party retained its monopoly. Only since the Gorbachev revolution has a genuine federal system come within the bounds of possibility.

THE CASE OF YUGOSLAVIA: BREAKTHROUGH AND BREAKDOWN

Prior to the late 1980s the exception among Communist regimes was Yugoslavia, and it is worth examining. When Tito Proceeded to govern Yugoslavia after the defeat of the Nazi invaders, he first sought his inspiration in Moscow and imitated the Stalinist model. In practice, however, Stalinism broke down for reasons both economic and political. With their diversity of cultures, languages, and religions, the Yugoslavs did not take readily to the centralism which Stalin's methods demanded. Industrial production did not revive as expected, and the attempts at enforced collectivisation of the peasants were a failure. Politically, this proud and independent people resented the domineering attitudes of Russian "advisors" in Belgrade. In 1948, when three-quarters of his foreign trade was directed East and the Red Army was on the Romanian border less than a hundred miles from Belgrade, Tito had the courage to dismiss the Russians and break with Stalin. The Georgian despot declared that he would bend his little finger, and Tito would fall. But in this instance he had not correctly assessed either the man or the situation. Since then, aided by the United States after 1950, the Yugoslavs experimented along their own lines.

The essential feature of their experiment was the requirement that every social activity or economic enterprise—be it a factory, hotel, orchestra, or housing development—should belong collectively to, and be managed by, the persons who work in it. This principle of ownership and control by the producers of a commodity or service was the Yugoslav version of socialism.[8]

In order to convert this principle form theory to reality, they concluded that their system needed maximum decentralisation. Popular ownership and operation would be more genuine if the local community—not the central government—were in charge. Consequently, the system they introduced was built, some what like the Swiss, from the local level up.

It is rare of practice to conform to principle. What then was the situation in Yougoslavia? Did the realities match the theory? The answer is that the match was only partial. If traced on paper, the actual evolution of policy would not be a straight line, curve, or spiral, but a zigzag. The Yugoslavs experimented with something which would be difficult anywhere and was novel in the light of their past traditions. To encourage the citizens of a local area or the members of a particular enterprise to share personal responsibility for policies and to supervise their administration intelligently and conscientiously is a tremendous task in civic education. The public must be well informed, and the directors of enterprises require training and experience. Since Yugoslavia was deficient in both respects, mistakes were made. But making mistakes and learning to draw the right lessons from them are aspects of the process of self-government. At any rate, the country faced up to the implications of transforming a mass of subjects into communities of citizens.

Besides the problems of converting theory into practice, the Yugoslav system contained inherent contradictions. There were political factors which militated against some of the intentions previously described. Although the avowed aim of the regime was to decentralize and to rely on local initiative, centralised planning continued. Nor was this avoidable. In various aspects of its social and economic development, Yugoslavia had far to go before it caught up with the countries of Western Europe. The responsibility for adopting measures to strengthen the country as a whole necessarily fell on the government at the centre. At the same time, internal conditions varied considerably because of the contrasting legacies that Yugoslavia inherited from the Hapsburg and Ottoman empires and the destruction of different areas in two world wars. Slovenia and Croatia, for example, were considerably more advanced then Macedonia and Montenegro. But to achieve an internal redistribution, using the resources of the more developed regions for the benefit of the less developed required central power, central planning, and central budgeting. Under these circumstances, the desire for control of economic enterprises at the local level was not readily reconciled with the priorities and programmes that the national government sought to establish.

A similar contradiction permeated the politics of the system. Communist parties have been centrally disciplined and were directed from the top. Also, in Communist practice—Marxist theories not withstanding—the subjective cult of an individual personality often loomed larger than objective laws of historical development. How did this fit in with the Yugoslav emphasis on community initiative, Flexible, experimentation, and local responsibility? The answer is that their experiment was neither one thing nor the other. For three and a half decades, one man and one party were politically preeminent. Tito emerged the victor in a war which was civil as well as foreign, and after it was over, he conducted a genuine revolution. During those periods and when Stalin was seeking his destruction, his government dealt roughly with opposition. But once his power was consolidated and his position was secured, his rule underwent a subtle evolution. He gained wide respect and popularity for the valid reasons that he had defied both Hitler and Stalin, preserved his country's independence, and accomplished more than anybody else to unify it. In addition, as a Croat, he was sensitive to the internal diversities of so complex a society and well understood that centralised uniformity or domination by a single group would be inconsistent with Yugoslav realities.[9] Hence he, the autocrat, encouraged the policy of decentralisation.

Under these conditions, the Communist party also modified itself. To express it distaste for a centralised monolith of the Stalinist type, it changed its name from party to league. Within its ranks, distinct groups evolved in the 1960s arguing—even in public—for different policies. Some contended that the Communists should retain their monopoly as the unifying, directing force in the government, the economy, and society at large. Others believed they should withdraw from positions of control and increasingly share their power, functioning as a source of ideas, enthusiasm, and criticism. Tito himself responded to these discussions in a manner that not only showed extraordinary flexibility for a man in his seventies, but also indicated a statesmanlike resolve to safeguard the future. When he ousted Rankovic and his entourage, he stopped a tendency that could have restored the Stalinist model of an authoritarian police state. Then after the Soviet occupation of Czechoslovakia, he reorganised the personnel and structure of the Communist party by promoting younger individuals into the top leadership.

Subsequently, however, his course against zigzagged in reverse. When dissident Croats, operating in and out of Yugoslavia, launched an overt terrorist campaign against his regime, Tito reacted with vehemence, discerning a threat to the fragile unity of Yugoslavia as well as to his personal authority. In the course of that reaction, much of his earlier tolerance was sloughed off. Critics were punished; the Communist leadership in Croatia was purged; questioning intellectuals among the professors and students found their freedom severely limited.

After 35 years of continuous supremacy, Tito in 1980. The system which he bequeathed was designed for two purposes: to prevent any other one individual from wielding as much power as he had, and to institutionalize at the top the internal diversities of Yugoslav society. Leadership would be collegial as in Switzerland. The members of the executive committee would represent the component republics and they should rotate in the chair.

"Things Fall Apart"

As it turned out, this difficult experiment, which only the Swiss have operated with success, could not have been launched at a worse time. In much of the world, the 1980s were a decade of adverse economic conditions whose effects brought hard times to Yugoslavia. Whenever that happens, people are wont to express their discontent by voicing any other dissatisfactions which trouble them—and those in the Yugoslav case never lie far below the surface. The country which was artificially tacked together in the Versailles Treaty after the Austrian and Ottoman Empires had collapsed was a congeries of diversities—ethnic, religious, and linguistic. Specifically, the two northernmost republics, Slovenia and Croatia, which had been ruled by the Hapsburgs, were the most highly developed and their religion was Catholic. Annually, the central government took a portion of their wealth and redistributed it for the benefit of the poorer, less developed south where the religious preference was either Orthodox or Muslim. Between north and south lay Serbia, the largest of the republics in terms of population and Orthodox in religion, which before 1914 had been independent of both Hapsburgs and Ottomans. The ancient enmity between Serbs and Croats was intensified in World War II when Croat Fascists sided with the Nazis and killed many of the Serbs in their midst. With Tito gone, there was no one whose political power was sufficient to transcend the internal divisions and maintain Yugoslav unity.

The separatist tendencies came to a head early in the 1990s, when both Slovenia and Croatia proclaimed their independence, and their governments took measures (such as control of their frontiers) to indicate that these were "sovereign" states. A resistance to their would-be secession was immediately organised by Serbia. This republic had come under the control of Slobodan Milosevic, a Communist Party leader and ardent Serbian nationalist. His designs for a "Greater Serbia" involved extending Belgrade's sway to the adjacent areas where clusters of Serbs were intermingled with other ethnic groups, as in the provinces of Kosovo and Vojvodina. Since there were Serbian enclaves within Croatia, Milosevic was determined to place those areas under his control. Hence in the autumn of 1991 a tragic civil war erupted between Serbs and Croats, with the Yugoslav military, which was largely officered by Serbs, deployed on their side. After several months of brutal hostilities an vain attempts at conciliation by both the European Community and the United Nations, It was evident that Yugoslavia had disintegrated. Early in 1992 Croatia and Slovenia were accorded international recognition as independent states. As in the case of the Soviet Union, the failure of the Yugoslav experiment demonstrates that Marxist concepts of the classless society were unable to transcend ancient ethnic enmities. If federalism is to function successfully, the component units must be willing to tolerate diversity within a framework of consensus on shared values. In the Yugoslav case, neither the tolerance nor the consensus emerged. Hence "Balkanisation," as it was traditionally called, ensued.

FREEDOM AT, OR FROM THE CENTER?

Wherever a single party or individual is politically dominant, it is customary for centralism to prevail. One wonders, therefore, whether this combination reflects a natural affinity and whether centralism and liberty are incompatible. Some argue that political freedom demands substantial decentralisation. Both statesmen and scholars have developed the theme that local self-government spells local liberties, which add up to the sum of national liberty. History supplies evidence for this view. In England, for example, the grant of corporate privileges to London and lesser cities, and the growth of a rural administration in which the country gentry (as distinct from the higher nobility) played a major role were factors that encouraged a sturdy spirit of resistance to anything smacking of oppression from the centre. Moreover, in local politics and administration many persons discovered a preparatory training ground where they were initiated into the art of government before deploying the experience thus gained at the national level. These are considerations too important to be overlooked.

But in a broader perspective one notes that sin is no monopoly of the centre, nor virtue of the localities. Examples of despotism emanating at the centre can be matched by as many cases of local dictatorship. "There are village tyrants as well as village Hampdens."[10] People have often sought the aid of a distant protector to defend them from a nearby oppressor. The local bully—whether landowner, bishop, captain of industry, or political boss—could not always be resisted by the people of the locality where he dominated. If they were to be freed, he had to be overawed by some greater power from outside. In short, dictatorship can reign at the centre; but so can freedom. There can be local tyrannies; or alternatively, local liberties. Local independence may defy a central dictator: and freedom, centrally organised, can defeat a local autocrat. Political chemistry is a rich amalgam of the same basic elements in diverse formulas that are ever being combined in new compounds.

UNITARY AND FEDERAL STATES

Though modern dictatorships prefer a centralised structure,

it does not follow that contemporary democratic states are decentralised to the same degree. Wide differences exist and are expressed in contrasted institutional patterns. The most familiar is the distinction between unitary states and federal. In the former the government is organised on two levels only—national and local, the latter comprising both urban and rural authorities. A federal state has three levels instead of two, since between the national government and the local ones there is an intermediate layer, designated as states in the United States or Australia, as provinces in Canada, or as cantons in Switzerland. Intergovernmental relationships are therefore more complex in federal systems than unitary. In the latter, only central-local relations and inter-local exist. But in the former, the relationships are federal-state, federal-local, and state-local, as well as federal-state-local and interstate and inter-local. Hence, delimiting thc jurisdictions and meshing them together is far more intricate. Federal systems are thus more legalistic, more "jurisdiction-minded," and slower to act.

But caution is needed, lest these generalisations become over simplified and inaccurate. Besides the distinction between federal and unitary, further differences occur within each category. Unitary states can be highly centralised, for example Denmark and New Zealand; or centralised to a lesser degrec, as is Britain. A federal union can be decentralised in the manner of the United States or Switzerland; or it may distribute powers in favour of the centre, as was the original intention in Canada.

CENTRALISATION IN BRITAIN

A review of some contrasted types well make these points clearer. Great Britain is a democratic state whose structure is both unitary and centralised. How important are its local governments and what functions do they perform? A product of ancient traditions continuously readapted to social change, the design of British local government has never been uniform, simple, or logically consistent. Its outline combines the practicable and the desirable, the old and the new. Certain features in this blend endow the system with its general character. One is the differentiation between the metropolitan areas, where population and industry are highly concentrated, and the rest. A second dominant trait is the dependence of local government on financial aid from the centre, and their legal subordination to Parliament. A third factor is the principle by which functions are distributed between the two levels. Let us see what bearing this has on the dispersion or concentration of power in the British system.

Even when the structure of the state is specifically designed to avoid excessive centralisation, it is impossible to determine the best allocation of powers with certainty. In Britain decisions about what functions "belong" to the national or local level have been influenced by social clustering, political pressure, fiscal resources, and historical tradition. In certain cases a dividing line between local and national concerns can be drawn without too much difficulty. Maintaining a fire brigade, for example, or providing public transport for an urban population inside municipal limit is clearly appropriate to local authority. On the other hand, the organisation of a police force to protect persons and property—a function which could be either central or local—has remained under local control,[11] largely through a series of historical circumstances hardening into tradition. Modern social and economic changes have evoked a national concern in matters where the original emphasis was primarily local. In a complex of contributing factors, the root cause can be traced to the expansion of industry with its consequent stimulus to population growth and urban concentration. Britain has almost one quarters of the population of the United States in an area equal to the state of Oregon. Even within that small space, a high proportion of the people are densely congested in the London area, the Midlands, the industrial North, and the "waist" of Scotland. The larger cities not only increased in size, but their suburbs and satellites sprawled into the nearby countryside. Their economic urgencies and opportunities, acting as a magnet, drew the rural economy into their orbit. The culture of the capital, transmitted by newspapers,[12] magazines, books, radio, and television, pervaded the village. The automobile—that "magic carpet" of the modern family—brought urban tourists, sightseers, and vacationers to "Ye Olde Tea Shoppe" and the parish church. Equally, it permitted Farmer Giles to take his wife and children for an outing so that they might savor the throngs, hubbub, and sooty air of city streets.

Economics, congestion, and mobility have necessitated many readjustments in central-local relations. Programmes of public assistance to the poor, for example, were once regarded as a local responsibility. But when it became evident that poverty (especially if associated with inadequate education or prolonged unemployment) was mainly a function of the national economy, and when the areas hardest hit by a business depression were unable to offer sufficient public relief to needy families from local resources, the conclusion followed that the responsibility for assistance must by spread over the entire community. For these reasons, many a governmental service has literally been "nationalised." Some functions have been wholly transferred from local to national jurisdiction. In other instances a partnership has evolved whereby national and local governments cooperate in a specific activity (for example, education or housing).

Under such a system the partners are not, and never can be, equal. A government of the whole is inevitably more powerful than those representing segments, irrespective of whether it deals with the parts severally or collectively. The realities of their relationship, as these exist in political power and financial resources, are mirrored in the law of the United Kingdom. Only one institution in Britain has the legal authority to decide how to distribute governmental functions between the centre and the localities, and when to add or take away. That institution is necessarily the supreme lawmaking body, Parliament. At law, every local government is subject to the Parliament—which created most of them, can reorganize any of them, and has clothed them all with their legal authority and defined their areas and powers. In this sense, because of the legal omnipotence of Parliament, the form of the British system is highly centralised. Moreover, the need to finance the social services has reinforced the centralizing principles of constitutional law. The increase in governmental functions has been felt at both levels, local as well as national. But many of the newer local activities cost more than local resources can afford.

particularly in the less wealthy areas where the need for government aid is greater. With most sources of taxation engrossed by the national treasury, there is a limit to the revenues of local bodies, which must thus depend on annual grants from the centre. These are given with conditions about programmes and standards determined in Westminster and Whitehall.

In the quarter of a century since 1985, the basic question of what kinds of local government were appropriate and what their relations should be to the centre was fully reexamined. As a result, the basic pattern was redesigned, although not in such a fashion as to reduce the grip which the capital maintains over the rest of the United Kingdom. The need for some kind of restructuring was linked with Britain's economic decline in comparison with other leading industrial societies. That was itself reflected internally in the depression which has overtaken the major industries of an earlier period—namely, coal mining, steel, railways, ship building, and textiles. Since these tended to be concentrated geographically, certain cities and regions (particularly in the Midlands and the North) were falling behind the more prosperous South. The bases of power of the two major political parties were also linked to these shifts, since Labour had traditionally derived much of its voting support from the strongholds of the older industries, while the Conservatives had a bigger following in the southern region. As it turned out, ideas for reform which were initiated under a Labour government were later carried out by Conservative governments, with modifications which suited their policies. After a Royal Commission, appointed by Labour, had reported in1969, the Conservative Heath Ministry put through Parliament the Local Government Act of 1992.

Under the new design, the dominant unit became the county, with broad powers extending to general planning, coordination of transport, most highways, police and fire fighting, education and so on. Counties were subdivided into smaller districts which were responsible for housing, building regulations, garbage collection, and the protection of the environment. London and six of the counties where people and industry are most congested were designated as metropolitan. There, the subordinate districts had some of the powers (education for example) assigned elsewhere to the counties. Below and within the districts were the smallest units, 8000 parishes, created to safeguard local interests. At the opposite end were regional authorities, broader than countries, exercising responsibility for public water supply and sewage.

The issue of central power versus decentralisation received a new twist in the sixties and seventies. Public opinion crystallised around the fact that so much of the power and wealth of the United Kingdom was concentrated in the London area. The proposed remedy was to redistribute some of the capital's perquisites to other parts of the country. The natural place to begin was in the component parts which had been united to form the kingdom, a notion reinforced by the distinctive historical and cultural traditions of Wales and Scotland plus their distance from the southeast. Thus the ancient drama of Celtic resistance to the Anglo-Saxon was reenacted once more in modern dress. Sentiments of Welsh and Scottish nationalism acquired a political momentum with which the two major parties and the central government were forced to reckon. In Wales the main impetus for nationalism was the demand to revive the Welsh language. But in Scotland, where the burden of the complaint was economic, nationalist sentiment pointed to the North Sea oil, laying in latitudes parallel to the Scottish coast, which the Scots would control if independent of the English. In the general election of October 1974, the Scottish Nationalists gained 31 per cent of the votes cast in Scotland. After that, however, their current slackened. When Parliament enacted a measure of devolution,[13] and separate referenda on this issue were held in 1979 in Scotland and Wales, too few voted affirmatively for an Assembly to be set up in Edinburgh or Cardiff.

After mid-1979, however, not only did the Conservatives regain control of Parliament, but Margaret Thatcher's reactionary policies became ascendant within the Conservative Partly. Political hostility soon developed into open warfare between the central government and the governments of London, and the six metropolitan counties which had Labour majorities. Thatcher responded by demonstrating unequivocally where power lies within the British system—to wit, at the centre. Her method of dealing with the political power of her opponents in the big cities was ruthless and thorough. Using her parliamentary majority, she simply changed the law, abolishing the metropolitan authorities and transferring their functions to smaller units with more limited jurisdiction. Her other big weapon was the power of the purse. Being hostile to various of the social services which city councils under Labour control were providing in their localities, she proceeded to impose a cap, or limit, on what revenues they might raise and how much they might spend.

That done, in order finally to win her war against local government, she dropped her nuclear bomb. Parliament at her bidding devised a wholly new system for raising local taxes (or rates, as they are called in Britain). Hitherto, these had consisted of a graduated tax on property, which meant that the wealthy paid more than the poor. Thatcher introduced a poll-tax, levying the same amount on everybody. What she miscalculated, however, was the public reaction. A sense of outrage at this inequity spread across the country. It soon found expression in anti-Conservative majorities at by elections and in massive demonstrations of protest, some of which resulted in violence. In this case, the wielding of central power turned out to be counterproductive, since it recoiled on the head of its perpetrator. When Margaret Thatcher fell from office, one of the principal factors contributing to her growing unpopularity was the poll-tax. Wisely, her Conservative successor, John Major, scuttled it and restored what was essentially a property based tax, although with certain modifications of the original system.

The lesson of that episode is clear and convincing. In the *realpolitik* of British government, whatever be the historic traditions of local liberties, the balance of power is tilted in favour of Westminster and Whitehall. However, since the country is democratically governed, the voters have the last word. When central power is exercised with an arrogant disregard for social justice, the people will rise in revolt.

AMERICAN FEDERALISM, THE START OF AN INVENTION

Far more decentralised in form and fact is the government of the United States. In this respect, as in separating the three branches, the framers of the Constitution clearly expressed their preference for a dispersion of powers. Their accomplishment was the novel and ingenious one of federal union, undoubtedly the most distinctive, enduring, and influential contribution of America to the art of government. In what did the novelty consist? Prior to 1776 the 13 colonies were bound to Britain, severally and separately. In no way were they linked together. But to declare independence, to win a war, and build a new nation, required union. The first framework designed for this purpose by the Continental Congress was experimental, and its construction was imperfect. Under the Articles of Confederation a government was organised for the United States, but the problems of postwar development exposed its powerlessness. The Congress resembled not so much a legislature as a conference of ambassadors, acting under the instruction of the state governments. Its most important decisions required a majority of at least nine states; and the Articles themselves could not be amended without unanimity. The central authority was weak in its executive arm and altogether devoid of a judicial branch. For revenues and for troops it depended on what the states contributed.

A few years of experience with that system soon exposed its inadequacies. The Congress lacked the authority to weld the states into a unity, to mitigate their commercial rivalries, to establish a sound currency, to remove, the causes of domestic disorders,[14] and to foster American interests abroad. The delegates to the Philadelphia Convention of 1787 were sent for the purpose of revising the Confederation. Fortunately they exceeded their instructions and drafted the Constitution of a federal union. As Hamilton saw it, the flaw in the Articles was that the parts predominated over the whole. The principal weakness, in his diagnosis, was the dependence of the government at the centre on the states which served as intermediaries between it and the individual.[15] It was this defect which the Constitution removed, thereby inaugurating a more perfect union. The new central government was equipped with a Congress which could legislate and tax; an executive, with its own agencies of enforcement; and a judiciary, with authority to preserve an equilibrium between the whole and the parts and to uphold the supremacy of the Constitution. Above all, the federal government now derived its mandate directly from the people as voters and carried its services directly to them as individuals.

When George Washington became president, with him was inaugurated the principle of a new type of federal union, the like of which was unknown earlier and was unfamiliar to the generation which created it. Leagues were no novelty, nor were confederations. But all of them, and the Articles of Confederation, were alike in the essential feature that power lay with the parts, while the central institutions provided machinery for cooperation, not for government. What distinguishes a federal union from leagues, confederations, and unitary states is that everyone in it is subject to and is served by three levels of government, because every parcel of land in the United States falls under three jurisdictions—federal, state, and local.[16] what further distinguishes a federal union is that its constitution makes it impossible for the federal government to abolish the member states or for then to eliminate the federal government. The governments at both higher levels are derived directly from the people, and the constitution not only creates a national authority, but guarantees to the states their permanent position within the union. Thus, after the Civil War, Chief Justice Chase described the American System as "an indestructible union composed of indestructible states."[17] This meant that the states could not break up the federal union or the authority that unifies it, nor could the latter destroy the states and substitute a unitary system.

CENTRALISATION IN AMERICAN GOVERNMENT

The virtue of federalism is its flexibility in extending a single jurisdiction to a larger area and to more people, while permitting diversity and decentralisation. But federalism, like any enduring system, does not remain the same. In the United States, for example, it had to adapt to the expanding numbers and power of the American nation; to industrialisation and its social aftereffects; to the migration of millions from Europe; to participation in two world wars; to the growth of national sentiment and the exercise of international leadership. Such events led to changes which were called in the 1930s "the new centralisation" and "the new federalism." The immediate cause of modifications in the federal structure was the assumption by governments of new functions at all three levels.[18] However, the rate and degree of growth have differed from one level to another, so that the former equilibrium among the three has altered. Until 1932, more than half of the government in the United States was local, in the sense that local revenues and expenditures exceeded those of the federal and all the state governments combined.[19] What happened thereafter was a spectacular extension of federal activity in response to the depression of the early 1930s and the resulting demands for unemployment relief and social security. In the traditional mode of distributing powers under the federal system, on the local governments fell the first responsibility for finding remedies. Their fiscal resources, however, were insufficient for their legal and political obligations. Consequently, the cities and counties turned elsewhere for aid—first, to their state legislatures, which gave what help they could, but in most cases were themselves too weak financially to underwrite the whole bill. Eventually it was the federal government under Roosevelt's New Deal which mobilised the resources of a nation to alleviate a catastrophe of national scope.

Six years (1932-1938) of legislative debate, electoral decision, and judicial review brought a federal commitment to such policies as the regulation of agricultural prices along with subsides, unemployment relief and public works, social security, the public generation and sale of hydroelectric power, fixed maximum hours and minimum wages in industry, control of the securities market, insurance of bank deposits, and more. For some of these programmes, limited precedents had been established earlier. In other instances federal intervention was entirely new. In every case, however, the scale of these federal undertakings was unprecedented. Nor during Roosevelt's presidency was any amendment made in the text of the Constitution, save the one which, ironically, reduced

Table 1: Public Finances and Public Employees in the American Federal System, 1902-1988

	Government Revenues (000,000'S Omitted)			*Government Expenditures (000,000'S Omitted)*			*Government Employees (000'S Omitted)*		
	Federal	State	Local	Federal	State	Local	Federal	State	Local
1902	653	183	858	565	136	959	-	-	-
1913	962	360	1,658	958	297	1,960	-	-	-
1932	2,634	2,274	5,381	4,034	2,028	6,375	-	-	-
1938	7,226	4,612	5,646	7,687	3,082	6,906	-	-	-
1944	51,399	6,714	6,665	99,448	3,319	7,180	3,365	-	-
1950	43,527	11,480	11,673	42,429	10,864	17,041	2,117	1,057	3,228
1956	81,294	18,903	19,453	72,644	15148	28,004	2,410	1,268	4,007
1962	106,441	30,115	31,506	105,693	25,495	45,053	2,539	1,680	5,169
1968	153,676	68,460	70,171	178,862	66,254	72,357	2,984	2,495	6,884
1972	223,378	112,309	113,162	242,186	109,243	116,913	2,795	2,937	7,872
1980	564,000	213,000	156,00	526,000	173,000	259,000	2,988	3,753	9,562
1984	752,000	316,000	240,000	829,000	243,000	356,000	3,021[1]	3,924[1]	9,685[1]
1988	1,012,000	542,000	498,000	1,215,000	485,000	496,000	3,112	4,236	10,240

1985 Figures.

Sources: Historical Statistics on Government Finances and Employment: Census of Governments, 1962; U.S. Statistical Abstracts: and data from Bureau of the Census. Blanks indicate that the data are not available for these years. Grants from one level to another are included as expenditures, at the level that spends the money; and, as revenue, at the level that collects it. Trust fund data are also included. On this general subject the reader should consult Frederick C. Mosher and Orville F. Poland, *The Cost of American Government* (New York: Dodd, Mead & Co., 1964), to whom I am indebted for advice in preparing this table.

federal authority by restoring the control of the liquor industry to the states.[20] Central jurisdiction was extended by elastic interpretations of the interstate commerce and general welfare clauses and by the liberal use of the doctrine of "implied powers."[21]

Equally important for the working of federalism were some techniques adopted more systematically than before. The New Deal inaugurated a new era of intergovernmental relations. The older federal system has been compared to a three-layer cake with icing thinly spread around the horizontal layers. Most of the work of government was conducted at one level with little or nor reference to the others. The states, it is true, exercised some controls over the localities within their midst. But federal-state relations were few and loose, while federal-local relations were non-existent. After the New Deal, everything changed. Federal–state-relations became Closer. Federal-local relations were established. Federal-state-local cooperation was frequent. Much of this was done by expanding a device employed sparingly before the 1930s—the conditional grant-in-aid. For running the new model federal machine the fuel and lubricant were the financial grants which a government of wider jurisdiction and broader taxing powers allocated—on conditions—to smaller units. Thus, the modern three-layer cake is cut and consumed in vertical slices. Various functions (for example, social security or the regulation of agriculture) are performed nowadays by the governments of all three levels acting in unison. The cause of these readjustments is clear. When government is decentralised, functions must be assigned to the levels where they are appropriately conducted. How do we determine "appropriateness"? The problem is to find a working conformance between people areas, resources, and services. Theoretically, each unit of government should give service to an area whose people need it and have the money to pay for it. In practice that would result in gross inequalities between areas. Most of the modern changes in federalism were caused by social needs for which the political boundaries drawn in preindustrial society were inadequate. When business corporations and trade unions are organised nation wide, producing goods which move across state line, labour relations can no longer be confined to the states' jurisdiction. When a metropolis requires a daily supply of fresh milk of certified quality to be sold at a price which remunerates producers, processors, and distributors, agreement is needed among the authorities of the city and counties, of the states whose farms supply the milk, and of the federal government which supervises interstate compacts and regulates farm production. When factories and automobiles pollute the air, when industrial waste or domestic sewage contaminates a river, lake, or ocean, the remedies require strong government and the reciprocal efforts of separate jurisdictions. When welfare recipients move from an impoverished to a prosperous region, becoming charge on the latter's budget, their assistance retraining, and employment are partly a national problem, not wholly state or local. When a river valley in a backward area suffers from floods and erosion, only an authority wider and wealthier than the affected states and localities can raise them nearer to the national average. In today's world, people are more mobile. New industries choose the most advantageous among a variety of sites. Cities attract people by the work they offer, but many of the well-to-do commute from the suburbs. The economy and its human material are flexible, but political boundaries are rigid. A jurisdictional line, once drawn, is hard to erase. To eliminate a city or county is all but impossible; to abolish a state is unthinkable. The Structure retains its decentralised form. In theory, powers continue to be distributed as constitutional law ordains. But the transformation of our society and the pressures on modern government have remoulded their relationships.

THE NATIONAL ENFORCEMENT OF EQUALITY

The effect of these pressures can be observed in two major policy developments since the 1950s. One of these has concerned our social relationships at home; the other, out relations with other governments. One is primarily a moral question; the other is military. Both have had a centralizing effect.

The domestic issue has been the controversy about school integration. The problem of winning acceptance for the principle that children of different races may be educated together is especially relevant to the issue now under discussion. Both aspects of the choice between concentration and dispersion of powers have come to the fore in the conflicts that erupted in so many areas. Through the tortuous episodes of this struggle to enforce equality under law, all three branches of government at all three levels were compelled to participate and did so. The record illustrates what can happen when the political process uses government as a catalyst to speed a social revolution. Under a system where powers are dispersed, built in structural cleavages facilitate the tactics of obstructions. Significantly enough, the leadership came, and had to come, from the centre. There, it was the Supreme Court that took the initiative, affirming the principle of equality and instructing the federal district courts to apply it in local areas. Congress originally gave the Court no help, being paralysed by the capacity of southerners to filibuster in the Senate and by their control of key committee chairmanships through seniority. Eventually, however, the national pressure of majority opinion squeezed out of Congress the two Civil Rights Acts of 1957 and 1964. successive presidents grappled with the problem of enforcement, although neither Eisenhower nor Kennedy seemed to relish what he had to do. At the local level and in the capitals of the states concerned—more particularly Arkansas, Alabama, Mississippi, Louisiana, and Virginia—opinions were divided. Moderates believed that some integration had to be accepted and argued in favour of obeying the law, however distasteful its terms But generally the extremists prevailed, and they pushed the legislators and governors into impossible defiance of the United States—witness the postures of Governors Faubus of Arkansas, Barnett of Mississippi, and Wallance of Alabama.

As far as these events concern the issue of concentration or dispersion, two conclusions emerge. One is that a system of divided jurisdictions permits the passing of ticklish responsibilities from one agency to another. By default of the other branches, the judiciary exercised leadership and, by interpreting the law, was in reality helping both to make and enforce it. The other result has been to strengthen central power. Even the Eisenhower administration, which by policy and conviction favoured less government in general and less central government in particular. was impelled politically to impose the authority of the nation on the affairs of a school board. The long-accepted principle that school education was strictly a local, or at most a state, concern gave was before the greater principle that fundamental human rights (for example, the dignity of the individual that flows from equal treatment) form a national obligation. Local discrimination had to be abolished in this case by central authority.[22]

THE MILITARY IMPACT ON FEDERALISM

Besides these domestic developments, the tendency to centralize was rein forced by what happened on the international front. The two would wars of this century were such that no major power could remain outside the struggle. On a federal government the effects of participating in a conflict for survival are drastic. War is always a centralizer. It increases the control of the state over society, since protection and security become a people's paramount concern and these are preeminently the responsibility of the state. In addition it concentrates in the capital city the authority to plan, decide, and execute in order to promote a speedy and unified direction of military operations. Evidence for this is contained in the nation's budget. In 1916 the expenditures of the federal government amounted to $734 million. By 1919 the figure had risen 25 times, to $18.5 billion. With the "return to normalcy" under Harding that amount was cut back by 1922 to $3.4 billion. The same story was repeated in World War II. In 1940 federal expenditures stood at $9 billion. The effort to defeat Germany and Japan cost the United States, in 1945 alone, the unprecedented sum of $100.5 billion of which over $80 billion represented appropriations for the war and navy departments. Victory over the Fascist powers was again reflected in a reduction of expenditures, especially for the military services. Thus in 1948 federal outlays were under $34 billion. After that years, however, the strained relations with the Soviet Union and Communist aggression in Korea in 1950 sent the federal budget soaring once more to the higher altitudes of public finance. In 1952 federal outlays approximated $80 billion, of which some four-fifths was directly attributable to the obligations incurred in past wars, the cost of operations in Korea, aid to friendly foreign governments, and military preparedness as insurance against another world war. In 1968 federal expenditures reached a total of $178.9 billion. Of this amount, as much as $79 billion was spent by the Department of Defence alone—in addition to war-related expenditures of other agencies—and $30 billion of that sum (that is, $3.5 million in every single hour) was the immediate price of the involvement in Vietnam, the subsequent cost being the inflation of the 1970s which that war set in motion.

But even those amounts were dwarfed by the size of the military expenditures from 1982 onward under the Reagan Administration. Federal agencies which served domestic needs were placed on a slimming diet, amounting in some cases to starvation, while the Pentagon waxed fat. More that two trillion dollars were allotted to defence during that presidency, with the result that the proportion of the federal budget related to war rose from 25 per cent to almost 40 per cent. This was the more curious because it revealed an inherent contradiction in the professed aims of the right wing. Hostile to government in general, and therefore most hostile to Washington as the strongest, the Right was bent on cutting down the federal agencies and transferring many of their functions to the states. But the amount available to the latter was consolidated into block grants totaling less than the separate grants previously given for specific programmes.[23] The aim of restoring to the federal system an equilibrium which it had lost had much to commend it. In this instance, however, the attempt was flawed by the huge escalation of the military budget and by the conservative dislike for the social services.

When a modern state is preoccupied with military tasks, irrespective of whether the political system by democratic or autocratic, the framework of its institutions will be skewed to the performance of this primary function and the mobilisation of the requisite power. Because of the military need for coordinated planning, unified command, continuous vigilance, and speedy action, a system concentrated on its own defence is unlikely to maintain either checks and balances between branches of government or the powers of state governments vis-a-vis the nation.

Separation and dispersion are difficult policies to practice in a world scarred by the ward of the past and scared about those of the future.

THEME AND VARIATIONS: CANADA, AUSTRALIA AND INDIA

The example of American federalism has set a precedent for others. The Swiss Confederation was convulsed in 1847 when seven Catholic cantons sought tc secede, but were defeated by the Protestant majority in a short civil war. Next year, the victors rewrote their constitution and created a federal union patterned closely on the United States. For the first[24] time since 1291, when the cantons of Uri, Schwyz, and Unterwalden launched the confederation with a mutual defense pact, the Swiss organised a genuine central government which has lasted for 14 decades.

One may speculate whether the Swiss would have followed the American model if the Civil War had already broken out in the United States. A possible clue is provided by what happened in Canada in the 1860s. There, a federal union was formed for three reasons. Economic depression had struck the maritime settlements of Nova Scotia, New Brunswick, and Prince Edward Island, and recovery was sought within a wider framework. A unitary government had proved unworkable for the French and English inhabitants of Quebec and Ontario. Cool relations with the United States[25] and a determination to hold the West for Canada enforced the argument for a national authority. Federal union seemed the obvious solution, since it would permit the incorporation of the Atlantic seaboard with the upper St. Lawrence region, the separation of Quebec from Ontario, and the eventual inclusion of western territories when adequately peopled. But the recent experience of the near-dissolution of the American union in the Civil War convinced the British and Canadian statesmen that the central government of Canada must possess more powers than belonged to its counterpart in the United States. Thus, whereas the federal government of the United States was organised on the principle that its powers are delegated to it by the Constitution while the states retain the residue, the Canadians reversed this by delegating powers to the provinces and reserving the rest for the

Dominion.[26] In Canada, moreover, the national government (in effect, the cabinet) was granted the authority to veto provincial legislation , an ultimate weapon clearly intended to bolster national supremacy. The framers' intentions, however, were not borne out by subsequent result. Until 1981 the Canadian Constitution, in its legal status, remained an Act of the British Parliament, and it was a British court, the Judicial committee of the Privy Council, which finally decided whether legislation adopted in Ottawa or in a province was constitutional or not. Fro several decades prior to World War I the Judicial Committee interpreted the Constitution by giving priority to "property and civil rights in the province." Over the powers of the Dominion, thereby twisting inside out the plain language of the document and reversing the objectives of its architects. From the 1970s onward, many of the French-speaking inhabitants of Quebec supported a political movement which sought either considerable autonomy or outright independence. This threat succeeded in extracting major concessions from the English-speaking majority. Indeed in the early nineties, not only was the future distribution of powers in Canada still to be determined, but it was even uncertain whether Quebec would continue as part of the Dominion.

Even so, the Canadian case has demonstrated something else of importance: namely that it is possible to fuse the American and British patterns by combining federalism with the cabinet system. Concentration of powers, or integration, at the centre along with dispersion of powers, or decentralisation, in the field of Dominion-provincial relations—that is the Canadian compromise. This solution is also workable elsewhere, in the South Pacific as well as in North America. When the Australian states federated to form their present commonwealth in 1900, the same pattern was followed in the sense that federal-state relations were modelled on those of the United States while the British preference for a fusion of legislative and executive powers was continued in the cabinet.

More remarkably, what was done in Canada and Australia has also been tried in India. To provide a workable structure of self-government for a people of over 800 million is a formidable task, especially when they comprise a medley of ethnic, religious, and linguistic diversities and the wealth is distributed with appalling inequality. The constitution which the Indian's adopted on becoming independent owes much to the experience of Britain and America. From one, they took the cabinet; form the other, federalism. Both institutions have survived thus far, but with major departures from the norms which are acceptable in the West. More than once, "President's rule" (i.e., direct control from the centre) has been invoked with dictatorial effect. Nehru ousted the feely elected government of a state, which was communist, and imposed one to his liking. His successors have followed this example in other states whose governments opposed the centre, but were not communist. His daughter, Indira Gandhi, suspended civil rights from 1975 to 1977, jailed her opponents, intimidated the courts, and muzzled the press. The electorate retaliated by voting her out of office, but later, disillusioned by the alternative, voted her back in . But the authoritarian side of her personality, revealed in her resentment of those who would not bow to her will, impelled her into a course of action toward the Sikhs in the Punjab which recoiled on her own head, ending with the tragedy of her assassination. The Congress Party then chose her son, Rajiv Gandhi, to succeed his mother as Prime Minster. But he too, after winning one election and losing a second, was assassinated during a third campaign, thus putting an end for the time being to the family dynasty which ruled India almost continuously after the British departed. As for the country's venture in federalism, Rajiv Gandhi had decreed "presidential rule" (i.e., control from Delhi) over the Punjab in 1986. Considering the character of India—its size and diversity, and the inequalities between regions and social classes—it is amazing that the outward forms of democracy and federalism have thus far been maintained. That they function imperfectly in such a context is only to be expected.

FEDERALISM UNDER STRAIN: BRAZIL, FOR EXAMPLE

The difficulty in applying the federal principle under the pressures of the twentieth century has been an experience common to many countries. The depression of the early 1930s produced untold strain in federal systems, some of whose component units became, in fact, insolvent. Zurich, Ontario, and New South Wales could afford what Graubunden, Nova Scotia, and Western Australia could not. It made no sense for a constitution to assign functions to a level of government, but to withhold the fiscal means of supporting them. If this was true in countries whose economies were relatively developed, *a fortiori* the imbalance was compounded among peoples still burdened by a colonial past. This general truth can be illustrated by the case of Brazil.

Since becoming a republic in 1889, the Brazilians have experimented three times with constitutionalism, a federal regime, and a limited democracy. The constitution of 1891 was modelled after the United States and attempted a dispersion and separation of powers. Indeed, there were grounds for hoping that the balance between unity and diversity required by federalism was adaptable to the Brazilian reality. In the huge area of the Estados Unidos de Brazil—much of it in Amazonas, Mato Grosso, and Para, still uncharted and unoccupied—the contrasts will satisfy the most meticulous devotee of a pluralistic society. The history, folklore, and contemporary attitudes of Brazil abound with the distinctive traits of cities, provinces, and styles of life. This is not a country of uniformity but of a diversified social base, and its politics reflect that character. For some time the two largest states, São Paulo and Minas Gerais, shared the lead and alternated in occupying the presidency.

But that equilibrium was too precariously poised to withstand the centralizing forces which transformed society and politics in the first half of the twentieth century. When the worldwide depression struck Brazil in 1930, the political systems collapsed along with the economy. Getulio Vargas then emerged as the man who discarded the constitution, and imported from Italy a new regime (*Estado Novo*) of fascist style. His power lasted until the end of World War II when, like most dictators, he fell. Accordingly in 1946 the Brazilians redrafted their constitution and resumed their interrupted experiment in federalism, constitutionalism, and the beginnings of democracy. That second attempt lasted almost two decades, but broke down in 1964. What happened, and why?

The essence of the answer can be summarised in three points. First, the principles of a federal system appeared as an alien import and were never fully incorporated with the inherited tradition. In adapting itself of modernity, Brazil suffered the disadvantage that its Portuguese past could not help it the present. Therefore, Brazilians have had to search outside for other models to emulate. But whatever they introduce—be it in American federalism, the British parliamentary system, Italian fascism, or communism in either the Russian or Chinese variety—is vulnerable on the ground that it is foreign. Second, although federalism accords properly with the size of Brazil and its social diversity, the component units, or states, are grossly unequal. The majority are still so backward and lacking in financial resources that they are unable to support the services a modern government must provide. The states that do possess the wherewithal are São Paulo, Guanabara (the city of Rio), Minas Gerais, and Rio Grande do Sul. But of these, the one state of São Paulo, embracing the city of the same name exceeds the rest in population, capacity, and power. With 18 per cent of the country's populace, in the early 1960s the state of São Paulo alone accounted for one-third of the national income, supplied 45 per cent of the revenues collected by the union, and produced 55 per cent of the industrial wealth. Its government collected 46 per cent of the total revenue of all states combined, and its local authorities took in 47 per cent of all local revenues in the country. Under these conditions, the balance between the centre and the part which federalism presupposes was utterly lacking, and the great majority of the state depended on grants from the union.

Finally, this centralizing tendency was reinforced by the requirements and results of a rapid industrial development. The entire order was convulsed by the changes that industrialisation set in motion. But the other needed revolutions—agrarian, social, and political—did not keep pace with the industrial. In fact, they were deliberately postponed by the prevailing oligarchy which did not wish to lose its privileges and share them with a larger number. Mismanaged by successive presidents and congresses, the Brazilian economy floundered in a chronic position of internal inflation and external insolvency. Matters came to a head in 1964 when President Goulart advocated radical ceconomic and political changes which the left supported. That was the signal for the Right to mobilize.

A grouping of property holders, governors of leading states, and army commanders ousted the president, installing a retired marshal in his place. The latter governed by decree, postponed elections, and deprived opponents (including two ex-presidents) of their civil rights.

After the *golpe*, the military secured their grip on the Brazilian people, five successive presidents being army generals. In the first decade their rule was repressive in the extreme. They banned political parties, censored the press, tortured prisoners, and governed with police-state terror. In the economy they drove ahead with a rapid industrial expansion which was reckless of human and social cost. Profits, production, and exports soared, as the rich became ever richer. The gap between them and the poor continued to widen, and the physical environment, urban and natural, along with the Indians of the Amazon, were crushed under the juggernaut of "Order and progress." Resistance to this inhumanity was led by the Church, which underwent a revolution from below and abandoned its earlier stance of buttressing the power structure. Civilian opposition increased in the late 1970s as society began to pay the price for its headlong economic development and mounting disparities. Realizing at last that a majority of the public had had enough of being stamped on by military heels, after two decades the soldiers returned to their barracks. Elections were then held in which the candidate favoured by the military was defeated, and in 1985 an electoral college installed as president the first civilian in 21 years. After that a new constitution was adopted—the seventh since the country became independent in 1822. Once again, the basic principles are those of democracy, federalism, and a presidential system. But it remains to be seen whether these will be more consistently followed than on previous attempts. Although its development has made the Brazilian economy the world's eighth largest, much of the population has yet to receive any significant benefit from the growth which the military regime encouraged and which was directed by the rich for their own advantage. What is the true meaning of equal voting rights (extended under the new Constitution to illiterates and to those aged 16) in an economy so glaringly unequal that the wealthiest one-fifth earn more than 30 times as much as the poorest fifth?

THE INDIVIDUAL IN REVOLT

When the dominant influences of this century in politics, economics, and technology are considered in unison, ours would appear an era of integration and centralisation. Many of the driving forces in modern society combine in this direction—the demand for human rights and greater equality of conditions, the extension of the market and standardisation of its products, the quest for social security and economic stability, the continuous reiteration of identical messages in the press and on radio and television. True enough—and the evidence is all around us in whatever direction we turn.

But in politics a trend in any one direction always produces a countertrend toward the opposite. Hence in the sixties a contrary tendency began to manifest itself. It consisted in resistance to our contemporary society, to its professed values, as well as to the structure and style of its operation. Since the political system is enmeshed in the social order, those who reject the leading characteristics of society have attacked the leaders of its government, seeing in them the personification of the power that sustains the structure. This swelling chorus of protest, taking on the dimensions of a political force, is not simple in its origin or single-minded in aim. Its assault has been levied on certain traditional elements as well as on other of recent date. Most significant of all, it is worldwide in scope and is not confined to any one species of political system or culture. Its effects have already been felt in communities as varied as the USA and the USSR, Great Britain and France, Yugoslavia and Czechoslovakia, Germany and Canada, Mexico and Japan.

The nature of this movement can be deciphered by noting the objects of its attack. Certain targets are broad conditions or trends—for example, depersonalisation, materialism, established authority, centralisation, "the system." Others are more specific—the war in Vietnam, racial or cultural discrimination in housing, or employment: Authoritarianism in universities and schools, and in organised religion.

That today's urban-industrial environment breeds anger and anxiety should surprise nobody. Such feelings stem from the conviction that our social structure has grown too cumbrous and that its organisation and procedures are too complex. Countless individuals view their institutions with incomprehension. The result is a sense of helplessness. People feel lost—caught within the toils of a social mechanism which, in their experience, becomes ever more distant, impersonal, and routinised. Our lives are controlled by huge, distant systems, public and private, which are faceless and unresponsive. If you have a complaint an pick up the telephone, to whom do you speak? You write them a letter and receive the standard answer from the computer. Those social scientists and behavioural psychologists, who obscure the obvious with fancy jargon (of Greek or Latin derivation), label the results "alienation" or "anomie", or they say that institutions are "dysfunctional." Translated, this means that things are working badly and people are fed up.

The topic of this chapter—the relationship between central and local authorities and the distribution of power between them—supplies abundant examples to fortify that feeling. Most modern states have been conspicuously less successful in local government than at the centre. The transformation of the physical environment alone has created new conditions affecting individual lives and extending over areas for which traditional boundaries are obsolete. We are endangered by the damage to our habitat—the poisoning of air and water and the rape of the land. Millions are victims of social disorganisation, especially apparent in the largest metropolitan centres whose streets are choked with traffic, fumes, and crowds, which reverberate with noise, which generate crime and violence, and which resemble jungles of concrete and glass. When, in addition, these monsters become insolvent, as happened to New York City and Cleveland, they cannot even be justified as efficient purveyors of needed services. Hence, the resentment against centralisation and bigness in general is now expressed as a new search for the small community.

Beyond these general conditions from which we all suffer, there are the special grievances of those situated on the outer fringe of a community or at the base of its society—the poor, the young, and any minorities identified by race, religion, or language. Together, these react against what they designate Collectively as "the system." Frustration turns to rage and rage to violence when remedies come with glacial slowness or not all; the resort to violence is then triggered by the instant communication supplied by the mass media. The television screen in particular brings to the eyes of the underprivileged the daily images of an affluence they do not share, at the same time as it reports with contagious effect the explosive outburst from any corner of the world. Hence, although the occasion, dimensions, and immediate protest may vary, the same thread connects Watts and Londonderry, Mexico City and Tokyo, Columbia University and the Sorbonne; hence, too, the reassertion of cultural identities which differentiate a person from the majority or redefine one's remoteness from the centres of power. This takes the form of the nationalism, particularism, or separatism of Scots, Welsh, and Bretons; and French-speaking Canadians; of Croats and Slovaks; of Tartars, Kurds, and Sikhs.

When injustices are ignored or condoned by those who have the power to change them, an emotional revulsion arises which ends with an ethical challenge. Established authority is then endangered by the repudiation of its moral claim. As people question its legitimacy, the process begins in which authority will be stripped down to power, and power degenerates to brute force.

All of this is involved in the issue discussed in this chapter, the ever oscillating relations between the small community and the great society. To which unit do we our primary allegiance? If citizenship requires participation, at what level do we participate the most? With what unit do we feel identified? Those questions bring us to the fifth issue.

—L. Lipson

References

1. However, the geographical concentration of the minority, though vital in all these cases, is not the sole explanation of such splits. Sometimes the resistance which the local minority offers to the majority is fortified by a potent group outside. The support of

Protestant Britain was indispensable to Ulster: that of the Moslem peoples in the Middle East, to Pakistan; that of American and British Jewry, to Israel.

2. The arid area of northeastern Brazil.

3. The Interior of Australia.

4. This river formed the boundary line between Italy proper and the province of Cisalpine Gaul. In 50 B.C., Caesar led his army south across it, which the governor of a province was forbidden to do. Thereby he declared war on the central authorities in Rome.

5. When English power was expanding in the Middle Ages, the area where English law and jurisdiction prevailed (for example, in France, Scotland, to Ireland) was called the Pale. Those outside it were not subject of England. The same term was used to describe to the area in Russia where Jews were allowed to settle by the edict of 1792.

6. Compare the expression that used to describe the gulf between social and economic classes in an urban community, "the other side of the tracks." Nowadays, when freeways cut a swath through a city, they divide its population as the railroad used to do.

7. It should be noted that in the Italian Fascist and German, Nazi cases, this excessive centralism represented in part a reaction to the lateness of both countries in achieving national unification. See chapter 12, section on "The Problem in Europe."

8. As distinguished from its interpretation in Russia, where the owner was the state.

9. I once head a Yugoslav scholar say: "Yugoslavia is a country with six republics, five cultures, four languages, three religions, two alphabets, and one party."

10. Justice Jackson, in *West Virginia State Board of Education V. Barnette*, 319 U.S. 624 (1943). Gray in his "Elegy Written in a Country Churchyard" spoke of : "Some village Hampden that . . . the little tyrant of this fields withstood."

11. The nature of modern crime detection, however, and the problems, of apprehending criminals have enlarged the activities of Scotland Yard as a nationwide police service. In addition, through its grants to local bodies the Home Office prescribes general standards to which the local police must conform.

12. Britain's small territorial expanse and the integration of the railways, motorways, and air routes that radiate from the capital permit the London morning newspapers to circulate throughout the country.

13. Under this proposal, there were to be Assemblies for Scotland and/or Wales, elected by the voters of these regions, with powers to legislate in certain spheres and administer services financed annually by appropriations from the central Parliament.

14. Such as Shays's Rebellion in 1786.

15. *The Federalist*, no. 15.

16. Except for the district of Columbia, which comes solely under federal jurisdiction.

17. *Texas v. White*, 7 Wallas 725 (1868).

18. See chapter 7, Section on "Emergence of Big Government."

19. Consult on this point the figures in table 3.

20. The Twenty-First Amendment, Repealing the Eighteenth

21. Formulated in the opinion of the court in *McCulloch v. Maryland*, 4 Wheat. 316 (1819).

22. In 1979 the federal government brought suit against the Chicago schools on this issue. See also chapter 5, section on "Education Equality."

23. The figures tell their own story. In 1953 federal aid amounted to a little over 10 per cent of state and local expenditures. That had risen to 18 per cent by 1968, and to 26 per cent in 1978. In 1984 it had dropped to 19.5 per cent; in 1988, to 13.3 per cent.

24. A partial exception is the unitary state Napoleon imposed on the Swiss. This was accepted, however, only under foreign duress and proved so unworkable that Napoleon himself aided the Swiss in restoring confederation.

25. These were due to the British governments' unfriendliness to the North during the Civil War, and to intimations of possible expansion by the United States in the north and northwest.

26. On this point compare the Tenth Amendment to the U.S. Constitution with the British North America Act. 1867, Sec. 91-93. The Swiss copied the American pattern in their federal Constitution, Article 3, as did the Australians later. Commonwealth of Australia Constitution Act. Secs. 51, 52, 107.

8

Is Our President Like the British Monarch?

Strange though it may look, our Constitution, which contains 395 Articles and eight Schedules, 'has created a curiously ambiguous picture of the Executive branch of government'[1] and his not clearly defined the real position of our President. The executive power of the Union has been vested in the President[2] who is elected by the elected members of the Union Parliament and the elected members of the State-Assemblies.[3] The Constitution requires him to exercise the executive power either himself or through the officers subordinate to him.[4] At the same time, there is a Council of Ministers to aid and advise the President in the performance of his functions.[5] Its has nowhere been said in the Constitution that the President is the Constitutional head of the state and as such bound to accept the advice tendered by the Council of Ministers. It has been, some point out, deliberately left vague[6] to be determined by political practices as they crystallize under the stress of circumstances of the time.[7] The result of this vagueness is that there is no unanimity of views as regards the real position of our President under the system of our government and, ever since the Constitution was inaugurated in 1950, different views have been expressed about his real position.[8] At one extreme is the view that our President, notwithstanding the letter of the Constitution, is, as Dr. Ambedkar said, 'only a figure head' or 'merely a nominal figure head'[9] and at the other extreme it is held that our President, as R.S. Ruikar said. 'is super Hitler.'[10] Other views range in between these two extremes.

However, ever since the Constituent Assembly passed the Constitution the most popular view held about the position of our

President is that he is like the British King (or Queen). This view carries the weight of great prestige because it has been supported by such eminent persons as the late Dr. B.R. Ambedkar,[11] the father of our Constitution, the late Pt. Jawaharlal Nehru,[12] the first Prime Minister of India, and M.C. Setalvad,[13] the first Attorney General of India.

If we look a little deeper into the problem, we shall not fail to see that to equate the position of our President with that of the British King is neither to define nor clarify his position; it is rather to confuse it. Dr. B.R. Ambedkar was never precise about what the real position of the Indian President was, though, a number of times he said that the President was like the British King.[14] It was natural for him to say so, at least for one reason because the position of the British King himself is not clear in absolute terms,[15] and different writers and constitutional lawyers have expressed different views regarding the exact place of the British King in the British system of government.[16] Hence, when we say that our President occupies the same position in our system as the British King in U.K., we tend to admit tacitly that his position is not clear.

As a matter of fact there is no solid ground for holding this view about the position of our President except that, as Dr. Rajendra Prasad said, we have adopted the British model as our Model.[17] The hollowness of this view cannot be demonstrated more clearly by anything than the fact that even though we have adopted the British model, we have introduced many things which are not British in their nature as, for example, Fundamental Rights. or the Federal Principle, or the Supreme Court. Then, even the executive government of the British type has taken different forms in different countries[18] and the British political institutions have seldom been imitated truly in any country of the world. Our experience shows that, of all the political institutions of Britain, the Cabinet is the most difficult and Head of the State almost impossible to imitate, Even in monarchies like Japan and Denmark, leave alone the Dominions Like Australia and Canada and the Republics like France and Ireland, it has not been found possible to have a head of state exactly on the same pattern as in England.

It has, rightly, been asserted, therefore, that no doubt we have decided to adopt the cabinet or the parliamentary form of government, in contrast to the presidential type of government of the U.S.A. , but it does not necessarily follow that the Head of the State in India occupies the same position as the King in England.

The real reason why we have been so much inclined to equate the position of our President with that of the British King seems, to many, to be that 'political thinking in this country has fallen so deeply into ruts cut by exclusive study of the British constitutional history that few are willing to make the extraordinary efforts needed to get out of them.'[19] We have been so much impressed by the Constitutional practices of England that we unquestionably regard them as the best. There is, therefore, a tendency among us Indians to quote British practices with reference not only to the Head of the State but also to other institutions like Cabinet, Prime Minister, Parliament etc., and it seems sacrilegious if one goes beyond what is British.

In the very nature of things, we, as also other nations, cannot mould and shape our institutions on the pattern of England. To justify any institution or practice of India, without reference to Indian conditions and mentality, is simply untenable. And yet during the last fourteen years, our President hast not only functioned as a prototype of the British King, but also the belief is common that his functioning like the British King is a matter of convention and, as such, part of our Constitution. Not only that some would like to go a step further and treat this question as settled for all time to come. It is true that this notion has held sway so far but it would be unrealistic to hold that the matter is closed because all these years since the attainment of independence the impression has persisted that, because of the overwhelming majority of one political party, i.e., the Indian National Congress at the Centre and in the States, the Constitution is not being worked out as it should be. Dr. Rajendra Prasad, to whom the credit goes for having functioned just like the British King, is known to have raised a number of times the question of the real powers and position of the President[20] and, ultimately in 1960, he expressed grave doubts whether we are right in importing the conventions of the British constitution, particularly in reference to the President.[21] Jawaharlal Nehru, the then Prime Minister, termed this remark of the President as casual,[22] but there are people like Rajgopalachari, the last Governor-General of India, who think that there was something deeper in it.[23] Some have even criticised Dr. Prasad for acting just like a figure-head, thereby laying down wrong precedents which might damage the prospects of democracy in our country.[24]

The fact, however, remains that the President during the last 14 years has chosen to function under the notion that he was only a figure head. We cannot ignore the fact that the political conditions obtaining after independence, the historically evolved personalities of Jawaharlal and Rajenda Prasad and the all-embracing character of the Indian National Congress which made for the success of that notion, will not be available in the future. When we make any study of this problem, we should first be free from the political bias or consideration of circumstances that have affected, undermined or atrophied the position of our President during the past 14 years.[25] It is, therefore, necessary to examine, in some detail, how far it is correct to hold the view that our President is like the British King. If we examine the various constitutional provisions, we shall see that it is impossible for our President to occupy the same position in India as does the British King in England. We shall, in the main, examine the following provisions to show that they would continuously tend to make our President different from the British King.

1. The British king holds a hereditary office whereas the office of our President is elected one. This very fact introduces the follow-points of difference between the two offices:

    (a) The British King does not depend upon the support of any electorate for coming to his post and, hence, it is possible for him to remain aloof from political controversies. This enables him to remain not only above party politics but also neutral politically. Our

President, holding an elected office, on the other hand, cannot be completely free from political arguments,[26] because election, direct or indirect, means choice and choice necessarily involves controversy. The very fact of his election will give rise to all sorts of controversies about his work and conduct, character and personality, and achievements and services in the various fields. Thus, it will not be possible for our President to remain absolutely neutral in politics like the British King.

(b) The British King represents the entire British people and is the symbol of their unity, culture and civilisation. Our President, on the other hand, represents the electorate that has elected him, and nobody else;[27] he cannot represent the entire Indian people in the same way in which the British King does. The entire British nation treats the King as their own; the entire Indian nation will never treat our President as their own in the same sense.

(c) The allegiance that the British King commands from his people lies deep in sentiment and history.[28] The allegiance that our President would command from the Indians will depend upon his worth and achievements and not on sentiment. It is significant to note in this connection that the respect that President Rajendra Prasad commanded from the Indian People depended, apart from official pomp and show, more on this services to the nation and his saintly character and sweet temperament than his holding that high office. Similarly, the high respect in which our President, Dr. Radhakrishnan, is held, is, for the most part, due to his character and eminence as a great philosopher and scholar and less to his high office.

(d) The personal ambitions of a British King are always kept under control by his devotion to his dynasty. He will always be unwilling to take any such step as is

likely to jeopardize the fate of this dynasty. This factor does not operate in case of the Indian President.[29]

(e) In England, the King is not a representative of the people and hence an undemocratic institution in the otherwise democratic set-up of the governmental system. People in England would get alarmed if the King were ever to try to interfere with the working of democratic and responsible institutions like the Cabinet and the Parliament. In India, the President, the Cabinet and the Parliament are all democratic institutions in that they are all elected authorities. Hence, in India, people would not be alarmed in the same way if the President tries to check undemocratic and unconstitutional actions on the part of either Parliament or Cabinet. People look to the President, in certain circumstances, to uphold the people's rights and see that the spirit of the Constitution is faithfully observed by the party in power.[30]

Keeping the above points of difference in mind one cannot but agree with P.G. Ramamurti that it is difficult to reduce an elected President to the position of a mere titular or formal constitutional Head of the state.[31]

2. Our Constitution is a written constitution while the British Constitution is an unwritten one. This in itself is a very important factor introducing important points of difference between the position of our President and that of the British King. The following points may be noted:

(a) The status and authority of the King are based on conventions and traditions; the status and authority of our President are based on the powers that he exercises under the Constitution.[32] The British King has little power but the whole show is maintained on a level so as to make it appear as if he still possesses all those powers which he ever did. In the case of our President, if he has no power, he will have no authority moral or otherwise.

(b) Since the powers of the King are not written, legally there is no limit to the powers of the King. But there is a definite limit to the powers of the Indian President and the limit is prescribed by the Constitution. The Indian President cannot exercise those powers which have not been given to him under the constitution, or which have been given to some other authority by the Constitution.

The British Constitution is based on the theory of parliamentary sovereignty. Our constitution, on the other hand, recognizes itself as supreme. This means the British parliament can change the powers and position of any organ of the government including the King; it can increase or decrease the powers of the King, subject of course to the public opinion prevailing at the time; it can even abolish the kingship if it so likes. Our Parliament cannot do so unless the Constitution itself is amended. In England it is the Parliament in which have been reposed almost all the powers that were exercised by the King in the hey day of monarchy. In our country, unlimited powers are reposed in no organ. The arbitrary powers that were exercised by the British King have been snatched from the King from time to time. Now, any interference by the King with the powers of the Parliament would be treated as an encroachment of autocracy on democracy—the last thing which the British nation would ever tolerate. In India, the powers of the Parliament are as much granted by the Constitution as those of the President. Hence neither can interfere with the other. Politically, therefore, the British Parliament is far superior to the British King, whereas our Parliament is not so superior. The President is, even if indirectly elected by the same electorate as the Parliament. Hence, he may be expected to be even equal to Prarliament.[33]

4. In England the King is above the law and can do not wrong. In India, nobody is above the law; the President does enjoy certain immunities under the Constitution[34] but that does not mean that he is above the law. He can be impeached for the

violation of the Constitution.[35] He is under oath to protect and defend the constitution.[36] That means he can be impeached if he fails to protect the Constitution.[37] There is no such responsibility devolving on the King of England. This means that if the King is allowed any discretion, it would tend to make him autocratic and irresponsible. On the other hand if our President is allowed some discretion, it cannot make him autocratic because, after all, two-thirds of the members of each House of Parliament can always impeach and remove him.[38]

The existence of impeachment provisions in our Constitution also means that our President will always try to see that the majority required to impeach and remove him is never set against him which, in its turn once again, shows that whereas the British King can afford to be disinterested in party politics, our President cannot. Therefore, it is more than doubtful whether our President would remain disinterested if the party in power at the centre tries to change the fundamental principles of our Constitution because as defender of the Constitution, he does possess certain powers which the British King does not possess. In the face of this provision for impeachment, it does not seem to be possible to develop a convention in India to the effect that the President will be bound in all cases to accept the advice tendered by the Cabinet; such a convention can develop only if it is provided either in the Constitution itself or made a convention that the President shall not be liable to be impeached if he acted on the advice of the Cabinet. In the absence of any such provision in the Constitution, or, a convention to this effect, the British convention that the King is obliged to accept the advice of the cabinet in all cases, has absolutely no validity in India. To accept an advice which is against the Constitution is a greater violation of the Constitution than not to act according to the conventions of parliamentary government, Which were developed in other countries and which were never constant and always changing.

5. In England, they have a unitary government; we, on the other hand, have a federal polity. There is thus no occasion, in England, for the Central Government and the local authorities

to be politically opposed to each other. A general election in England give general power to rule over the entire field of the county's life, to the party that wins at the polls, that is, the decisions of the Cabinet, backed by the Parliament, are the decisions of the nation with regard to anything and everything. This is not so in India. Here we may face a situation, in which the government at the Centre and the governments in some States may be totally opposed to each other as the political parties running the respective governments at the Centre and in the States, may be believing in different ideologies. Hence, there may arise occasions of political, as different from legal, clashes between the two and the President may be called upon to arbitrate between the two. The demand of justice is that the President should not be bound on such occasions to act on the advice of the Central (Union) government as they themselves would be a party to the dispute; he should rather be free to adjudge the issue on merits. Hence our President functions in two capacities—as constitutional Head of the Union Government and as Head of the Federal State—whereas the British King functions only as the constitutional Head of the Central Government in England. It has therefore, been aptly said that 'the British Parliament and Cabinet exhaust the whole of British polity while our Union Government is only a part, albeit a large part, of the governance of our country.'[39] Although no serious situation has arisen on this point because the central leadership of the Congress Party was in a position to decide any dispute that arose between the Union Govt., and the governments of the States, yes the States, it is significant to note, has not been completely free from stress and strains on this point. On the occasion of the Central intervention in Kerala, the then President, Dr. Rajendra Prasad, is reported to have expressed the view that on such occasions the President should not be guided completely by the advice of the Union Cabinet.[40] A Similar voice was raised in the Parliament also were a communist Members, H.N. Mukherjee, suggested that on such occasions, the President should not treat the advice of the Union Cabinet as sufficient but should also take advice from the members of Parliament.[41] In England the King is free from such situations, but in India the President has to face such situations. Such situations have been rare so far but this will increase with the decline of the Congress majority in the Union Parliament and the State Legislatures.

6. Position of the President vis-a-vis Ministers

The position of our President is not the same as that of the British King vis-a-vis their respective Ministers. This would be clear from the following:

(a) In England the portfolios are allotted by the Prime Minister and the orders of the King are countersigned by a responsible Minister. In India, it is the President who allocates the portfolios among the Ministers and frames rules to prescribe as to how his orders are to be authenticated.[42] The rules framed in this behalf require the President's order to be authenticated by the permanent Secretaries etc., and not by the Ministers.[43] The difference to be noted is that the British King cannot do without Ministers, whereas it is, technically speaking, possible for the Indian President to act without Ministers, at least for some time. This also means that in England the King can do nothing against the wishes of the responsible Ministers. In India, again, it is possible for the President to issue orders without the advice of the Ministers or even against their advice, under the signature of a permanent Secretary.

(b) The Constitution itself does not say that the advice of the Council of Ministers is binding on the President. All that the Constitution says is that there shall be a Council of Ministers with the Prime Ministers at its head to aid and advise the President in the exercise of his functions.[44] Some writers and constitutional experts, notably Dr. Ambedkar. M.C. Setalved, D.N. Banerjee and D. D. Basu, read so much behind the

expression 'aid and advise' that they regard the advice tendered by the Council of Ministers to be binding on the President. They seek to justify this contention of theirs on the basis of the fact that the expression 'aid and advice'[45] or 'aid',[46] has led to the growth of responsible government of the British patterns in some countries, particularly the Dominions like Canada, Australia, South Africa etc., where the Governor-General has come to occupy the same position as the British King, accepting the advice of the Council of Ministers in all cases. But it is forgotten in this connection that the story of growth of responsible government in those countries is not so simple as it is made out to be. Many other factors than the expression 'aid and advise' have made for the growth of responsible government in those countries. For instance, take the case of Canada. Besides the expression 'aid and advice', it was also provided in that Constitution that the constitution was based on principles similar to those of Great Britain.[47] Then that constitution was guided by the conventions of the British constitution through the instrumentally of the Governor-General. Even then troubles arose in the course of development of that Constitution with regard to the position of the Governor-General whose position could be made clear only after years of practical experience. Above all, it should be remembered for all times that an elected President cannot be equated with a Governor-General who is appointed by the King of England and has no electoral backing.

Hence, it maybe, at most, a pious wish, and not a constitutional mandate that this expression should lead to the growth of such conventions as would render the advice of the Council of Ministers binding on the President. Even the late Dr. Rajendra Prasad, the former President, disputed this point and counselled that sufficient research should be done to determine the exact meaning of this expression.[48] It would, therefore, be wrong to suggest that this expression has acquired a fixed meaning which is applicable to India, binding the President to accept in all case the advice of the Council of Ministers.[49] In short, the British King is bound to accept the advice of the Cabinet according to the conventions well-established there were as our President is not. While our President is normally expected to act according to the advice of the Prime Minister and the Cabinet, he is, at the same time, required to exercise his powers in accordance with the Constitution.[50] 'It would seem then, that he would be entitled to reject advice if it involved taking a line of action which he believed to be unconstitutional.'[51] He is, therefore, obliged at the most to accept the advice of the Cabinet only so long as he is not asked to commit a violation of the Constitution.

(c) Then, there are certain matters in which the Constitution itself requires the President to act on the advice or opinion other than that of the Council of Ministers. The President, for instance, is empowered to seek the advice of the Supreme Court on any issue in which any question of law or fact is involved.[52] It should be reasonably expected that the President should act on the advice of the Supreme Court even if it goes contrary to that of the Council of Ministers. Similarly, the President has a duty to consult the Election Commission for deciding whether any member of Parliament has become subject to any of the disqualifications. It is required of him to obtain, in such matters, the opinion of the Election Commission and to 'act according to such opinion.'[53] In England, it is significant to note, the King accepts, in all matters the advice of the Ministers.

(d) Lastly there are certain other matters in respect of which, the advice of the Council of Ministers will not be available to, let alone be binding on, the President. Special mention may, in this connection, be made of the following matters:

(i) The President has been given the right the send messages to either House of Parliament 'with respect to a Bill then

pending in Parliament or otherwise.'[54] In contrast to this, the British King hardly requires to send message to Parliament when his Ministers are present there. The existence of this right in our Constitution only means that our President has been given powers to send such of his views to the Parliament as may not be in agreement with those of the Council of Ministers. Obviously the Council of Ministers is hardly competent to give advice in such matters.

(ii) The President has also power to address either House of parliament, or both Houses assembled together.[55] It would be well to remember that this power is in addition to his power to address both Houses of Parliament assembled together at the commencement of the first session after each general election to the House of the People and the first session of each year.[56] The British King does possess this latter power but not the former. The latter power in India as well as in England is exercised on the advice of the Council of Ministers so much so that the addresses of both the President and the King are actually prepared by the council of Ministers. But what about the former power? No occasion has so far risen in India for the President to exercise this powers. However, it was in the air at one time that the former President, the late Dr. Rajendra Prasad, intended addressing the Parliament on the issue of the Hindu Code Bill against certain of its provisions but the occasion did not arise because its introduction was, as he wished, postponed till after the general elections of 1952. It is the considered opinion of many eminent persons that whenever there arises an occasion, it will, in all probability, be exercised not only against the advice of the Council of ministers but also to take a stand against some course of action of theirs. The British King can hardly think of addressing the Parliament against the advice of the Cabinet because it would be treated as something entirely unconstitutional.

(iii) The President can send for any information regarding the affair of the Union government from the Prime Minister, besides and above that which the Prime Minister himself send

to him.[57] If we follow the British convention, it should be on the advice of the Prime Minister that the President should send for any information from the Prime Minister but it looks anomalous. It is difficult to see how the Prime Minister can advise the President as to what information the latter should send for from the former. This clearly points out that the President would necessarily decide for himself on this point.

(iv) The President can ask the Prime Minster,. Who may not refuse, to place before the whole Council of Minister for its consideration any matter on which decision has been taken by an individual Minister.[58]

This raises very important constitutional questions. First, it fetters the discretion of the Prime Minister in that he might consider it politically inadvisable to bring a particular question before the Council of Ministers at a particular time but under this provision he is duty-bound to do so. By doing so the President may, in certain circumstances, bring the Prime Minster into trouble, and, if the question referred to by the President is one on which there is strong controversy, it may divide the whole Council of Ministers. Secondly, while this provision in intended to ensure collective responsibility, it gives in fact power to the President to interfere with the working of the Cabinet. The British King, let it be remembered, has nothing to do with the internal working of the Cabinet. It is totally foreign to the British way of thinking that the formal head of the State should have authority to interfere with the working of the Cabinet. Thee has, it appears, been no occasion when this power has been exercised so far. But its very existence shows the difference between the British King and our President.

7. The British King is known to have little discretion. The only discretion, which he, if at all, enjoys, is with regard to the appointment of the Prime Minister and the dissolution of the House of Commons in certain special circumstances. As against this, our President, as many constitutional provisions suggest, enjoys personal discretion on many occasion. 'In this,' says K.M. Munshi, 'it is noteworthy that the Constitution uses a variety of words in relation to the powers

and functions, some of which necessarily involve the use of personal discretion. They are 'is satisfied' (Article 123, 347, 352, 356, 360), 'is of opinion'(Article 124 (3), 'consent' (Article (127), 'determine' (Article 128), 'deem necessary' (Article 124 (2), 'notifies intention' (Article 108), 'decision' (Article 103), 'pleasure' (Article 72 (2) etc.[59]

The question of using discretion has not arisen so far because, speaking constitutionally, it has been held by those at the helm of affairs that the President means the Government of India[60] and, speaking politically, there was no occasion for it on account of the predominance of the Congress party in the affairs of the country.

However, the above provisions in the Constitution, says Valmiki Choudhary, are enough to show 'that no provision has been made in the Constitution for the President to exercise his powers only on the advice of Ministers.'[61] The above analysis of the powers of the president goes to prove, if anything, that there are powers in the exercise of which he must take advice of the Council of Ministers will not be available to him at all; and finally, there are powers in the exercise of which he can used his discretion,[62] without violating any provision of the Constitution, of course in such a way as not to have to face impeachment. It is, therefore, that N.C. Chatterjee, a noted constitutional lawyer, is of the view that the President is not, in every case, bound to act according to the advice of the Council of Ministers.[63] The obvious conclusion, as K. M. Munshi, another constitutional lawyer of repute says, is that, althought our President is a constitutional Head of the state, he is not bound by the Cabinet's advice like the British King.[64] In fact, says K.M. Munshi, the President has, in the form of emergency powers, in the opinion of the Supreme Court and that of the Attorney-General, been provided with a constitutional machinery enabling him to act independently of the Ministry to prevent the Constitution from being twisted out of shape by political pressure or constitutional mishaps.[65]

After analyzing the above constitutional provisions, it becomes sufficiently clear that the position that our President occupies in our system of government is different from the one occupied by the British King, both in form and content. As a matter of fact, any elected President can never be fully equated with a hereditary king like that of England. He will be either more than a king or less than a king, but in no case, just equal to him. Fortunately or unfortunately, our President is both more and less than the British King. He is more than the British King in so far as (i) he heads a federal government in which he may, on certain occasions, be called upon to arbitrate between the Union and the State Governments; (ii) his powers are expressly written in thc Constitution: and (iii) he can act without, or even against, the advice of the Council of Ministers, if the needs of the nation demand and or the political situation in the country so permit.

He is less than the British King in that (i) he can never command that sentimental devotion and allegiance. from the Indian people which the British King does from his people; (ii) he can be impeached and removed from office for violation of the Constitution; and (iii) he cannot represent the Indian people in the way in which the British King does.

It would, thus, be a vain attempt to equate the position of our President with that of the British King. Even if we admit, for a moment, that he can be so equated, it would be undesirable as it would be dangerous, may be even fatal. It we treat our President just like the British King, we may face the following dangers:

(i) Our cabinet will become a dictator[66] unparalleled in history. The British Cabinet which possesses only normal powers has, under the pressure of the political developments, become a dictator. Our Cabinet, which possesses many abnormal powers, will, exercising those powers, beat many a dictator.

(ii) It will place the President in a very awkward position in certain circumstances and render the functioning of that office impossible. For instance, what has the President to do if a defeated Ministry refuses to resign? Whether he dismisses the Ministry or allows it to continue, he would be liable to be impeached in either case, if the conventions were given more weight than the letters of the Constitution for, some

may hold that it is unconstitutional for the President to dismiss a Ministry and others may, with equal, if not greater force, hold that it is the violation of the Constitution if the President allows a discredited ministry to continue in office.

(iii) It will destroy the quasi-federal character of our Constitution, and reduce the principles of a federal government embodied in it, [67] For whatever they are worth, to a mockery because the Union government, exercising all the powers of the President and treating him just as a formal Head of the State, can very easily treat the State Governments as municipalities. Besides, if we treat our President as if he were like the British King, our Constitution and the whole system of government embodied therein will prove inadequate in certain situations inviting dangers not only to democracy but also the Constitution itself. One such situation has been visualised by K. Santhanam. He says:

'... there may be no stable Ministry there may be a change of Ministry every day. No remedy has been provided in the Constitution for such a contingency.... If a general election does not result in the emergence of a stable government, he (President) is helpless.'[68]

As a matter of fact, the unfortunate effects of this notion, under which our President laboured and acted during all these years just as the British King, are already before our eyes. He has been treated, during these years, as a Post Office[69] to convey the decisions of the Cabinet of the day; the Cabinet exercising all the powers of the President has come to acquire a position which was never intended. The position of the President during all these years has been in no way different from the position of the French President in the third and the fourth Republic.[70] The powers of the President have been used in a way that has given the impression that the Cabinet was working to advance party interests over and above those of the nation. This may be particularly seen in the case of appointments to the high posts of Governors, Ambassadors etc., which have often gone to such members of the ruling party as were rejected by the people in the elections. This charge, according to

K. Santhanam, stands in the case of some High Court Judges also.[71] Again according to K. Santhanam, the Nanavati case has demonstrated only too clearly how the Executive has been tempted to interfere with the judicial process.[72] There have also been complaints that the Emergency powers of the President, particularly those relating to the breakdown of the constitutional machinery of the States, were used for party purposes.[73] On the whole, the Executive Government, pointed out an M.P. in the Lok Sabha, has tended to act in a way which has had a corrupting influence on our institutions.[74]The Constitution itself has been amended again and again without any specific mandate from the people. Our President has been a silent spectator to all this all the time because he was working just as the British King. The result is that an unfortunate feeling has been created that our President has no political value.[75]

However, this notion has not been able to do much harm because the Congress to do much harm because the Congress party which ran the Union and State Government during almost the whole of this period, was a democratic party, and, containing divergent elements as it did, could not be tyrannous to any one section of the People. But if a different party with a different complexion, comes to form the government at the Centre, and, treating the President just like the British King exercises all his powers, it will, there is reason to fear, create havoc and may bid good-bye to democracy itself. Thus, this notion is fraught with dangerous possibilities. There is a constitution limit to the dictatorial tendencies of a President but none to those of the Council of Ministers at the Centre if we treat the President as being just like the British King.[76]

We can therefore, say that its is neither constitutionally possible nor politically desirable to equate our President with the British King. Hence, K.M. Munshi is right in holding that our President's position is different from the British King.[77] To say that our President is just like the British King is simply a myth. Like all myths, it will be exploded. That it has not been exploded so far is mainly due to the character of the Congress party band its predominance in the Parliament and the State legislatures. The

President has so far been elected through the pleasure of the party in majority at the Centre.[78] The President and the Cabinet both belonged to the same party or depended on the same party for their continuance in office. It was, naturally, the Congress party which had complete control over both and therefore it mattered little whether a particular power was exercised by the President or the Cabinet. As soon as this predominance of the Congress party withers, or even diminishes, this myth would not stand even for a moment and would be exploded.

The position of the President during all these years has been standing under the shadow of the powerful personality of Jawaharlal Nehru backed by an overwhelming majority in the Parliament and immense popularity and support in the country. If no party gains a majority, the President may, says K. Santhanam, used all the powers allowed to him by the Constitution.[79] It is, therefore, wrong to judge the position of the President on the basis of the practice of the last 14 years.[80] It is too much to expect that in future, in case the President belongs to a party different from that which has formed the government at the Centre, he will be content to be guided entirely by the Central Cabinet in all matters.[81]

Sometimes, it is suggested that our system with a President enjoying a position similar to that of the British King is already established and there is nothing to worry about it. Nothing can be farther from the truth. We may advance the following considerations to show that the country has not finally accepted this notion:

(i) There have been demands that the President should act independently of the Cabinet, consulting somebody other than the Cabinet on certain occasions.[82]

(ii) C. Rajagopalachari has on one occasion suggested that the Cabinet should act on the advice of the President, and not the President on that of the Cabinet.[83]

(iii) During the Chinese invasion, there was a demand from many responsible quarters that the President should dismiss the Cabinet which had failed to protect the frontiers of the country.

(iv) Finally, Dr. Rajendra Prasad, the first President was not happy with the position assigned to him.[84] He raised questions regarding the powers of the President as apart from those of the Prime Minister from time to time.[85] and ultimately gave vent to his feelings publicly and urged rather pointedly that it should be seriously studied how far the President should be equated with the British King.[86]

Many other proofs can be given to show that the Indian people, as a whole, are not for treating the President just as a prototype of the British King.

Lest the notion should do more harm in changed situations and prove fatal to our system of government and the Constitution, we should do well to recognize in all sincerity that our President is distinctly different from the British King and that there are certain occasions when he, unlike the British King, is expected to protect the Constitution, defend the fundamental principles of our system of government and save the nation from party dictatorship, even if it involved taking a line of action unsupported by the Cabinet. For this, has been allowed sufficient discretion under the Constitution.[87] The argument that the use of any discretion of the part of the President would make him a dictator, does not stand to reason because there is sufficient guarantee against it, particularly in the provision of impeachment.[88]

However, if, on the basis of the experience of other countries, it is felt that the weapon of impeachment will not be very effective in checking a President from being an autocrat or using his discretion indiscriminately, the remedy does not lie in making him politically impotent and incapable of checking a Cabinet which, with the help of its majority in the Parliament, is bent upon changing the Constitution beyond recognition, by adopting policies which are against the best interests of the country and behaving undemocratically otherwise; it rather lies in rendering the President incapable of becoming a dictator. For that we can:

(i) either provide, on the pattern of the Irish Constitution,[89] that whenever the President chooses to exercise his discretion, he

shall do so only in with consultation with some authority, other than the Cabinet, to be provided for in the Constitution itself. (This authority may consist of the Chief Justice of the Supreme Court, the Chairman of the Council of States, the Speaker of the House of the People, all the former Presidents who are alive and the retired Chief Justices of the country, etc.)

(ii) or, do way with those powers of the President, which can be used in a dictatorial manner, as, for example, the power to declare an Emergency or issue Ordinances.

For either of the two, the Constitution may be needed to be amended, which should not be shirked. There is also a feeling in certain quarters that the Constitution should be amended while the Congress Party is in a commanding position both at the Centre and in the States. It will be easier for the Congress Party to make the necessary amendments in Constitution now, than for any party including the Congress in the future. To leave the things as they are, is not only to refuse to face realities but also to invite dangers to our system of government.

—Prof Jai Narain Lal

References

1. Neumann R. G. '*European and Comparative Government.*' 1960, Third Elition, p. 711.
2. Article 53 (1) of the *Constitution of India.*
3. Article 54, *Ibid.*
4. Article 53 (1), *Ibid.*
5. Article 74 (1), *Ibid.*
6. Palmer. N. D., *The Indian Political System,*' 1961, First Edition, p. 112.
7. Gladhill A. '*The Union Executive,' in Aspects of Indian Constitution*, (Edited) by Madan Gopal Gupta, 1956.First Edition, p. 150.
8. Banerjee D.N. '*Some Aspects of the Indian Constitution,*' 1962, First Edition, p. 49

9. *Constituent Assembly Debates*, Vol. VII pp. 998-1036.
10. *Hitavad*, Dated 12.2.50.
11. *Constituent Assembly Debates*, Vol. VIII p.32.
12. *Hindustan Times*, dates 8.7. 59.
13. Setalvad. M. C., '*The Common Law in India*,' 1960, First Edition, p. 173.
14. Munshi K. M., '*President . . . . India*,' 1963, First Edition, pp. 7-8.
15. Carter, Ranvey and Herz., '*The Government of Great Britain*,' 1953, First Edition, pp. 182-3.
16. Harvey James and K. Hood, '*The British State,*' 1958, First Edition, p. 69.
17. Hindu, dated 14. 8. 56.
18. Neumann, R.G. *European and Comparative Government,*' 1960, Third Edition, p. 712.
19. Srinivas, P.R., '*President's Powers*' *in Indian Express,* dated 8.12.60.
20. *Hindu*, dated 4.12.60.
21. *Hindustan, Times*, dated 29.11.60.
22. *Northern India Patrika,* dated 17.12.60.
23. *Indian Express,* dated 2.12.60.
24. Frank Moraes, '*President and Premier, Balance of constitutional Powers*' *in Indian Express,* dated 27.6. 59.
25. Munshi, K.M., '*President . . . . India,*' 1963, First Edition, p.27.
26. Michael Stewart, '*Modern Forms of Government,*' 1959, First Edition, p. 12.
27. Manshi, K.M., '*President . . . . India,*' 1963, First Edition, p. 14.
28. *Ibid,* pp. 12.3.
29. Gladhill A, '*The Union Executive*' *in Aspects of Indian Constitution*, (Edited) p. 158.
30. *Hindustan Times,* dated 7. 5. 52.
31. Ramamurti, P. G., '*The Draft Constitution of India,*' in Journal of Political Science, Vol. X, 1949.

32. Munishi, K.M., '*President . . . . India,*' 1963, First Edition, p. 13
33. *Ibid*, p. 24.
34. Article 361 of the *Constitution of India.*
35. Article 56, *Ibid.*
36. Article 60, *Ibid.*
37. Munshi, K.M., '*President . . . . India,*' 1963, First Edition, p. 13
38. Article 61 of the *Constitution of India.*
39. Srinivas, P.R., '*President's Powers*' in Indian Express, dated 8. 12. 60.
40. Told by a source which wishes to remain anonymous.
41. *Lok Sabha Debates.* Vol. 51, 1961 Col. 3673.
42. Article 77 of the *Constitution of India.*
43. The Authentication (orders and other instruments) Rules 1958, S.O. 2297, dated the 3rd Nov., in 'Rules & Orders under the Constitution of India,' 1960, p. 4.
44. Article 74(1) of the *Constitution of India.*
45. Section 11 of the *British North America India Act*, 1867.
46. Section 62, of the *Commonwealth of Australia Constitution Act,* 1900 & Section 12 of the *Union of South Africa. Act,* 1909.
47. Preamble of the *British North America Act,* 1867.
48. *Hindustan Times*, dated. 29. 11. 60.
49. *Ibid.*
50. Article 53(1) of the *Constitution of India.*
51. Alan Gladhill. 'The Republic of India,' 1951, First Edition, p. 101.
52. Article 143 of the *Constitution of India.*
53. Article 103 (2), *Ibid.*
54. Article 86 (2). *Ibid.*
55. Article 86 (1). *Ibid.*
56. Article 87 (1). *Ibid.*

57. Article 78 (b), *Ibid.*

58. Article 78 (c), *Ibid.*

59. Munshi, K.M., '*President . . . . India,*' 1963, First Edition, p. 45.

60. *Lok Sabha Debates.* Vol. 49, 1960 Col. 6920.

61. Valmiki Chowdhary, '*President's place in our Democracy,*' *Search Light,* dated 4. 10. 59.

62. Palmer. N. D., *The Indian Political System,*' 1961, First Edition, p.112.

63. *Statesman*, dated 17. 12. 60.

64. *Deccan Herald,* Dated 16. 1. 63.

65. Munshi, K.M., '*President . . . . India,*' 1963, First Edition, pp. 34-35.

66. *Ibid*, p. 53.

67. *Ibid*, p. 36.

68. Santhanam, K. '*Union State Relations in India,*' 1960, First Edition, p. 11.

69. *Amrita Bazar Patrika,* Dated 20. 7. 59.

70. Amar Nandi, '*The Constitution of India,*' 1959, VII, Edition, p. 122.

71. *Mail*, dated 25. 1. 60.

72. *Hindu*, dated 10. 4. 60.

73. *Parliamentary Debates,* (House of the People) Vol. II, Part II, 1953.

74. *Lok Sabha Debates.* Vol. 49, 1960 Col. 6899.

75. Bawa, T. S., '*Nehru's India,*' 1956, First Edition, p. 9.

76. *Deccan Herald,* Dated 16. 1. 63.

77. *Ibid.*

78. *Lok Sabha Debates.* Vol. VII, 1957 Col. 12459.

79. *Statesman*, dated 25. 2. 61.

80. Munshi, K.M., '*President ... India,*' 1963, First Edition, p. 27.

81. Santanam, K. '*Democratic ... Pitfalls,*' 1961, First Edition, p. 21.

82. *Lok Sabha Debates.* Vol. 51, 1961 Col. 3673.

83. *Hindustan Times*, dated. 10. 12. 62.
84. Sri Prakash, '*Rajendra Pd—As President's in Tribune*, dated 7. 4. 63.
85. *Hindu*, dated. 7. 12. 60.
86. *Hindustan Times*, dated. 29. 11. 60.
87. Munshi, K.M., '*President ... India,*' 1963, First Edition, pp. 44-45.
88. *Ibid.* p. 53.
89. Article 13(9) of the *Constitution of Eire,* 1937.

9

Indian Federalism

Polities is often defined in terms of the struggle for power. Democracy is a means of coming to terms with political powers, taming it and making it subservient to popular wishes. Federalism is a means of bifurcating it territorially.

A unitary system of government concentrates all legal power in a central government, with subordinate units of government being the creation of and subject to the will of that central government. In effect the lower units are administrative extensions of and have no legal status independently of the central government.

A confederation is an association entered into by a number of sovereign governments which retain most legal powers but cede some such as defence and foreign affairs, to the newly created confederal authority. A federation is a half-way house in which two sets of governments coexist with separate but not necessarily equal powers within their respective autonomous jurisdictions. A federal arrangement may be the result of an agreement by a number of independent countries motivated by shared attributes and goals, as in Australia and the United States. Autonomous governments cede a defined part of their sovereignty or autonomy to a new central organism. Or it may be the product of a devolution of power from a previously centralised system of government, as in Canada and India. In neither case did provinces have an existence independent of the colonial government; in both cases, a federal arrangement was imposed by British statute. British India comprised a number of provinces and 562 princely states. The latter, accounting for about two-fifths of the subcontinent's territory, were granted internal autonomy under the paramountcy of the British crown in defence and foreign affairs, and were therefore closer to the confederal model. The provinces on the other hand were essentially administrative units. And the colonial regime, serving the needs of the metropolitan rulers, was unitary in nature.

Federalism in India predates the constitution adopted in 1950. Certain legislative powers were delegated to the provinces as early as 1861. The 'nation-building' subjects of health, education, agriculture and irrigation, and public works, along with the financial ways and means appropriate to these subjects, were given to provincial assemblies by the India Act of 1919. The Government of India Act of 1935 set up a union with federal features. Following the Canadian precedent, the act created autonomous units and combined them into a federation. Provincial legislatures were given autonomous jurisdiction in specified subject and derived their powers directly from the crown. A practical legacy of the 1935 division of powers was the emergence of a group of politicians experienced in running provincial governments and with their power bases located at the provincial level.

A product more of geography and history than inter-unit agreement, federalism was given formal recognition in the 1950 constitution. It retained the tripartite classification of the powers of state and central governments. These are enumerated in the seventh schedule of the constitution. The central government is given exclusive authority in the 97-item Union List, including currency, income tax, foreign affairs and defence. The State List, embracing 66 items, includes health education, agriculture, land revenue and police. The 47-item Concurrent List gives shared Jurisdiction to the state and central governments in such subjects as civil and criminal law, and social and economic planning. However, state rights are qualified even in this list. The governor of a state has the power to reserve a state bill for consideration by the president, who may choose to disallow it (Article 201). Following the Canadian but departing from the US precedent, residuary powers (that is, those not included in the three lists) are given to the central government (Article 248). If there should be a conflict between the union and a state, then the union law shall prevail.

Thus both before and after independence, the solution to India's perennial problem of unity-in-diversity was sought in a modified model of federalism. The federal features were necessary to accommodate the considerable diversity of the country. The structure of government is clearly federal, and the structures and institutions of government in New Delhi have their counterparts in the state capitals. Article 1.1 of the Constitution affirms that 'India, that is Bharat, shall be a Union of States'. In 1993, the Union of India comprised 25 States and 7 Union Territories (see Table 1.1) Union Territories account for under 1 per cent of India's territory by area. Goa, having been liberated from Portuguese Rule in 1961, become India's 25th State in May 1987, and Daman and Diu, the other former Portuguese colonies, were made a Union Territory.

The very diversity of India, however, generated strong centrifugal pressures, and a powerful central authority was believed to be necessary to counteract them. The constitutional drafting committee preferred the term 'union' to emphasize two main points. First, unlike the American and Australian federations, the Indian federation is not the product of a negotiation by the constituent units. Second, and again conscious of the US civil war, the framers of the Indian constitution wished to make it clear from the outset that the component parts had no freedom to secede from the Indian union. (The 16th amendment of 1963 made even the advocacy of secession an offence). The need for territorial integrity and political stability was further underlined by the mass carnage of partition, the conflicts with Pakistan, the Communist insurrection in Telengana and the requirements of state-led economic development.

These are the reasons why the word 'federalism' does not appear anywhere in the Constitution of India. At the time that the constitution was drafted, debated and adopted. the issue of group rights of different religions and communities was rather more important and urgent than that of states' rights. Partition demonstrated the dangers of subordinating the national identity to parochial loyalties. The movement for India's independence was led by the Congress Party, which was itself highly centralised. Since the political units of the British Raj were constituted on the basis of administrative convenience, there was little opportunity for regional identities to coalesce around the existing political units. This was to change with the reorganisation of states along linguistic and cultural lines. Only then did the Congress Party's monopoly on the authoritative allocation of values come under serious challenge from strong regional parties promoting ethno nationalism. The rise of regional identities in many parts of the country is perhaps the development that has given most concrete expression to state rights. Yet it may also be the case that consciousness of regional identities has in many case been a reaction to over-centralisation of Indian Politics.

INDIAN FEDERALISM

The constitutional form given to unity-in-diversity has created some confusion among analysts. The system of government adopted by independent India has been described variously as cooperative federalism (Austin, 1966, p. 187), 'quasi-federal' (Wheare 1951 p. 28), and unitary in both concept and operation (Chanda, 1965, p. 124). The central government is so dominant in the legislative, administrative and financial spheres as to reduce states to being 'glorified municipalities' (Minoo Masani, quoted in Hanson and Douglas, 1972, p. 115). It may be debated as to whether India is a unitary state with subsidiary federal features, or a federal states with subsidiary unitary features.

No consensus exists among political scientists on a precise definition of federalism. However, one school has traditionally chosen the characteristics of the US political system as the measure of federalism in general, and evaluated other polities against this point of reference. On this arbitrary rather than logically derived basis, there are six correlates of federalism:

> The functions of government are divided between two sets of authorities, one exercising jurisdiction over the whole national territory, the other within its provincial borders;

- The legal status of both sets of authorities is co-equal. That is, the invasion of each other's jurisdiction is legally impermissible. Nor may one level of government, in discharging its own duties, override or veto the operations of the other level;

- The operations of each governing authority are usually conducted by its own set of officials;

- There is a written constitution detailing the above elements;

- The federal legislature is bicameral, with one of the chambers representing the constituent states; and

- The constitutional division of powers between the two sets of authorities is interpreted by an apex court.

India satisfies every criterion except the second (although the third is only partially satisfied, as we shall see). We should remember too that even in the United States, the Supreme Court has progressively enlarged federal jurisdiction at the expense of state rights, for example in civil rights, and that the revenue and expenditure of the federal government are vastly greater than that of state governments. Indeed the federal government gives financial grants-in-aid for specific projects within state jurisdictions, for example the construction of highways.

On the minimalist criteria, of the range of governmental activities being divided and shared between two sets of constitutional authorities, India is a federal state. But it is a flexible rather than a rigid federation, with the balance between the central and state governments varying to suit the changing circumstances. Where a rigid demarcation of powers might have made the Indian state too brittle, flexibility has given it resilience to absorb and overcome periodic strains and stresses. Under normal conditions, the authority of state governments is coordinate with rather than subordinate to the whishes of the central government. For it is derived not from laws made by the central government, but from the very same constitution which creates and legitimates the central government. Under abnormal conditions, the central government can override most state preferences. But it can do so only within constitutional limits and safeguards and for prescribed periods of time other than such temporary dispensations, the legislative and executive boundaries separating the federal and state governments cannot be altered unilaterally. The courts may give a broadening construction of existing powers (judicial verdicts have tended to enlarge the scope of central government powers in all federal systems). But even the courts cannot re-assign powers to one set of government that have been explicitly conferred on another.

The federal ideal has been seriously diluted in India by the constitutional bias in favour of the centre in normal times, the constitutionally permissible opportunities to set aside state governments under exceptional circumstances, the substantial state dependence on the centre for operating and capital revenues, the centralised bureaucratic, police and judicial services, and the centralised nature of the major political parties in India. States are subject to the legislative control of the union under exceptional circumstances and administrative control under normal circumstances). A further qualification to Indian federalism include the lack of dual citizenship (although most states distinguish between domiciles and aliens in the conferment of many rights and privileges, for example admission to medical colleges).

The essence of federalism is a territorially-based dual government. The US constitution prescribes the structure and powers of the federal government, leaving the states free to adopt their own constitutions. In India, only the state of Jammu and Kashmir has the right to determine its own constitution. Under Articles 3-4 of the Indian Constitution, the union parliament may reorganize the states or alter their boundaries by a simple majority in the ordinary process of legislation. The consent of the states concerned is not necessary. (Consent necessarily connotes the power of veto.) In the Australian and US conception, the union is indissoluble, the states are indestructible. The alteration of existing boundaries or the formation of new states requires the consent of the states concerned. In India, The President is enjoined merely to 'ascertain' their views and may prescribe a time-limit for them to express their views. The States Reorganisation Act of 1956 reduced the number of states from 27 to 14 by means of unilateral legislation by the Parliament of India.

By virtue of the theory of the equality of state rights, every state of the United States has two senators in the US Senate regardless of area or population. Representation in the Rajya Sabha — the second chamber designed to protect the status and interests of states in India – is weighted according to population, with the number ranging from 1 (the minimum for any state) to 34 (for U.P.) (Table 3.1). In addition, 12 of its 250 members are appointed by the President. Of the 238 Rajya Sabha MPs elected by the state legislatures, several can only euphemistically be said to be residents of the states from which they are elected. (In 1993 the Election Commissioner threatened to begin enforcing the residential qualification more stringently.)

Article 249 empowers parliament to enact laws with respect to any matter included in the State List, for a temporary (but renewable) period of one year, if the Rajya Sabha adopts a resolution by a two-thirds majority that it is necessary and expedient to do so for the whole or any part of India in the national interest. This is in addition to Article 252 which empowers Parliament similarly at the request of two or more states. Critics argued that Article 249 was superfluous because of Article 252, and pernicious in conferring unilateral powers on the central government. On the other hand, it is only the Rajya Sabha, the custodian of state rights in the union, that can so empower Parliament, for delimited periods and in order to cope with exceptional circumstances. The balance between states and the centre could be redressed by a more even division of powers between the Lok Sabha (embodying the democratic principle) and the Rajya sabha (representing the federal principle) in New Delhi.

Articles 256 and 257 of the constitution enjoin state governments to exercise their executive powers in conformity with union laws and without impeding union authority. The central government can also assume executive powers under the same two

Table 9.1: State-wise distribution of seats in Parliament of India (1992)

	House of People	Council of States		House of People	Council of States
Andaman &			Kerala	20	9
Nicobar Is[a]	1	..	Madhya Pradesh	40	16
Andhra Pradesh	42	18	Maharashtra	48	19
Arunachal			Manipur	2	1
Pradesh	2	1	Meghalaya	2	1
Assam	14	7	Mizoram	1	1
Bihar	54	22	Nagaland	1	1
Delhi[a]	7	3	Orissa	21	10
Goa	2	1	Pondicherry[a]	1	1
Gujarat	26	11	Punjab	13	7
Haryana	10	5	Rajasthan	25	10
Himachal			Sikkim	1	1
Pradesh	4	3	Tamil Nadu	39	18
Jammu &			Tripura	2	1
Kashmir	6	4	Uttar Pradesh	85	34
Karnataka	28	12	West Bengal	42	16

Note: [a] Union Territory.

articles in order to issue directives to state governments. If they fail to comply, then the union government can invoke Article 365 and take over the functions of the recalcitrant state government directly. The last point is even more relevant in regard to the vastly expanded powers of the central government when a declaration of emergency is in force. Again, though, the Indian Constitution effectively codified trends that had been emerging in other federal systems where courts had interpreted the war and defence powers of federal governments fairly broadly. In comparison to the United States, the procedure for amending the Indian constitution is weighted in favour of the central government. The US constitution was the product of a voluntary agreement between hitherto autonomous units; it cannot therefore be altered without their consent. Yet the Indian constitution does differentiate between the federal and non-federal features in the amendment procedures. While fundamental rights (which have nothing to do with federalism) can be altered unilaterally by the central government, changing the process for electing the president requires ratification by a majority of state legislatures.

In sum, the framers of the Indian constitution believed that a rigid conception of federalism would not be allowed to negate the national interest. Moreover, the constitution enshrined federalism in a political sense without bureaucratic and judicial correlates. In the United States, 'dual government' is accompanied by a double set of officials and courts. There are two levels of government in India, at the centre and the states. The powers and structures of both are laid out in the constitution. But, as we saw in Chapter 2, the judiciary in integrated into a single hierarchy. Similarly, we shall see in subsequent chapters that the bureaucracy and the police forces are dominated at the district, state and national levels by officers recruited and dismissible by the central government on an all-India basis. The officials administer both state and union laws within the states to which they are deployed. The electoral process too is under the control of a National Election Commission, and the machinery for accounts and audit is similarly integrated.

There has also been some attempt to institutionalize cooperation between states. The States Reorganisation Act of 1956 set up five zonal councils for contiguous states and union territories. A further council was established for the northeastern zone in 1972. Each zonal council comprises the union Home Minister as chairman, the chief ministers and two other ministers of each members-state, and up to two representatives from union territories. Its agenda consists of items of common interest, in particular issues of social and economic planning and border disputes, interstate transport and linguistic, religious or even caste minorities. The zonal councils were given merely advisory roles, and they failed to develop into significant political institutions.

The National Development Council had been a little more visible.

It was set up in 1952 for the purpose of promoting cooperation between the centre and the states, as well as among states, in economic planning. It seeks to do so by recommendations on how to achieve plan targets, by a periodic review of the plan, and by debating important question of social and economic development. It has been suggested that the federal principle could be strengthened if this body, reconstituted on a 1: 2 ratio between the central and state government and including all heads of government at both levels, could replace the Planning Commission as the apex agency for guiding national planning (Paranjape, 1990, p. 2480). Non-planning issues are discussed at the Conference of Chief Ministers with a view to promoting coordination and uniformity.

An analysis of the interstate disputes between Punjab and Haryana on the sharing of river waters or territorial adjustments, or between Tamil Nadu and Karnataka over the River Cauvrey waters, would be grossly distorted if it did not include 'Political' calculations as well as the merits of the disputes. The ability of the central government to arbitrate in such interstate disputes is ultimately a function of the respective bargaining assets and skills of the various parties involved in the complex and often protracted negotiations. The constitution confers upon the centre the power to settle interstate disputes, and a favourite mode of interstate dispute-resolution is through the appointment of tribunals. But one result of this is that the centre becomes the focus of demands and grievances from the states involved in the disputes, and the issue is converted into one of centre-state relations.

FINANCIAL RELATIONS.

The existence of two levels of government in a federal polity makes it necessary to devise an appropriate balance of financial powers between the central and state governments. This is true both for revenue collection and expenditure of the funds raised. That is, the taxing and spending powers have to be divided between the two levels of government to handle public money. The division of powers must be derived from the constitution in order to be authoritative, and must be clear in order to avoid overlap and confusion. At the same time, the existence, of two levels of financial authorities exercising separate jurisdictions may impede the creation and growth of an integrated national economy. Litigation between different governments would further retard economic development.

Another problem in India was the imbalance of resources and demands between to centre and the states. The most productive resources—income tax, excise tax, custom duty and foreign aid – are centralised. This was done partly to effect economies in collection and partly to avoid Economic distortions. For example, variable excise duties could lead to arbitrary and uneconomic location of industries, while state-based income taxes could bring into conflict the principles of origin and residence. Yet the primary responsibility for fulfilling the demands of a development state were vested in the state governments. The asymmetry between the taxing powers and spending responsibilities has led to what is called the problem of vertical fiscal imbalance. For example, although by the mid- 1980s the states were spending more the 60 per cent of all tax revenues collected by state and central governments, the share of the total money raised by the states themselves was only about 35 per cent (Mukherjee, 1989, p. 21).

Efforts by state governments to discharge their constitutional obligations with regard to the welfare functions of education, health, agriculture and so on would entail growing expenditure. State governments therefore had to be given adequate finance to enable the proper delivery of these essential public services. There was tension between the centralizing requirements of a developing economy and the devolutionary impulse of federalism. India sought to resolve the tension by concentrating revenue-raising powers in the centre, but providing formulas for the transfer of the monies raised to states. The meager financial resources of the states are supplemented by financial aid from the central government in the form of grants-in-aid. The difficulty with this, however, is the conditions that might be attached to their utilisation. eroding the autonomy of the states.

Taxing powers are divided between the central and state governments by means of specific entries in the union and state lists in the constitution. The most significant taxing powers are given to the union government: income tax, excise tax and customs duty. It was important to maintain a uniform income tax structure throughout the country. Customs duty had to be centrally controlled because of its repercussions for foreign exchange. Excise duty has an impact on the price level, so excise rates required central control in order to facilitate price stability. While sales tax is a state subject, taxes on interstate trade and commerce, as also on imports and exports, are central subjects. Some fine distinctions are made in the entries. While the power to levy estate duties in respect of agricultural lands is vested in state legislatures, that in respect non-agricultural property belongs to the union parliament. Residuary power of taxation are also vested in the union parliament. Article 289 of the constitution exempts union and state properties from mutual taxation.

By constitutional amendment and judicial interpretation, central taxes can be classified according to the collection and distribution of their proceeds:

- Some duties are levied by the union, but collected and appropriated entirely by the states, for example stamp duty;
- Some taxes are levied and collected by the union, but their proceeds are distributed entirely within the states in which they have been collected, for example estate duty on non-agricultural property;
- Some duties are levied and collected by the union, and the proceeds are then distributed between the union and the states, for example excise duties.

Even after states have been assigned certain shares in the taxes levied by the central government, their resources may be inadequate to their tasks. The constitution anticipates this contingency and provides for the provision of annual grants-in-aid to such needy states as shall be determined by parliament. The welfare needs of tribal areas are especially underlined. The constitution provides for the establishment at five-yearly intervals of a Finance Commission, an impartial and expert body to recommend what measures should be adopted for the distribution of financial resources between the union and the states. What proportion of income tax should be assigned to the states? In practice, the finance commissions have recommended between 55 per cent and 67 per cent of income tax proceeds as the states' share. What formula should be used to distribute the share assigned to the states among them? Should it be on be the basis of financial need and, if so, should this be determined on the basis of population or average income levels? Should it be on the 'source of collection' principle, that is the amounts of taxes collected by the various states, in order to encourage maximum efficiency in revenue collection? Or should it be on a mix of these two criteria? The finance commissions have recommended a mix, with between 75 per cent and 90 per cent of the states' share of income tax proceeds being distributed according to population ratios.

What should be the amounts and distribution of grants-in-aid to the states? Ideally, the allocation of grants-in-aid should be guided by budgetary needs, the capacity to absorb and utilize grants optimally, financial managerial efficiency, fiscal prudence in the tax and expenditure equation, the provision of social services, special circumstances, and national priorities. In practice, the primary determinant has been budgetary deficits: which can reward inefficiency and pensalise fiscal produce. Grants-in-aid can be provided under Article 275 (obligatory) or 282 (voluntary). Decisions in the former category are made as per the recommendations of the Finance Commission, and the aid is unconditional. Aid under Article 282 is at discretion of the Parliament of India and subject to conditions set by it. Similarly, under Articles 270 and 272, the assignment of income tax and excise duties to states is mandatory and discretionary respectively.

A third problem is imbalances, between different regions, and the need for the central government to rectify such imbalances. At the time of independence, Maharashtra and West Bengal were more economically advanced than Assam and Bihar. It was feared that the persistence of inter-regional differences would generate political tension and instability. This in turn would pose a threat to the stability of federal arrangements. On the other hand, India is a poor country with limited overall resources and an urgent need for optimum utilisation of all available resources. There was also the fear that some states could slide into financial irresponsibility, the costs of which would have to be borne by the entire nation. So a delicate compromise had to be reached between the competing demands of rapid and balanced development.

The finance commissions have tried to increase the solvency and self-reliance of states by widening the ambit of shared revenues and recommending transfers on an unconditional basis. Paradoxically, however, the states have become increasingly reliant on transfer of funds from the centre, with more than half of all state expenditures being financed through such transfers. The balance would be dramatically altered if India should progressively reduce union-based custom and excise duties, and move instead towards a broad state-based regime of value-added tax. We should note that the shift in the financial centre of gravity towards the central government is not unique to the Indian federation. Every federal system needs some institutional mechanism to oversee adjustments and reallocations of resources between the different units. This has to be done on a flexible basis in order to match the distribution of funds to the changing requirements.

Before leaving this subject, we should note also that efforts by successive finance commissions to allocate grants-in-aid to states, for such basic national purposes as expansion of primary education, have sometimes brought them into jurisdictional rivalry with the planning Commission. States in turn have not been averse to playing off the two bodies against each other. To the Planning Commission, states will stress their resource-mobilizing capabilities in order to persuade the body to sanction prestigious development projects. To the Finance Commission however states will stress the limitations on their resources in order to win a greater share of the revenue being transferred to them form the centre.

Considerable sums of money are given to states by the union government under Article 282 in pursuit of the annual plan objectives which include reductions in regional inequalities. The annual plan allocations are based on a mix of population and economic output of the various states. The Planning Commission has a long tradition of mediating between the central and state governments. But inevitably it was viewed as a creature of the central government, and therefore more deferential to the wishes of those in power in New Delhi than in the state capitals. The political credentials of the Planning Commission were underlined by the frequent changes in its membership with each fresh change of the central government.

The discretionary grants under Article 282 exceed the amounts transferred to states under Article 275. Since the former are based on the recommendations of the Planning Commission, in practice this extra-constitutional body has come to wield a more significant influence on federal-provincial financial relations than the Finance Commission set up by the constitution itself. The convention of appointing one member of the Planning Commission as a member of the Finance Commission helped to provide a link between the two bodies. But it does not rectify the imbalance of the Planning Commission being responsible for about 70 per cent of the total grants disbursed by centre to the states.

A fourth problem in fiscal federalism relates to emergency measures. If there should be a proclamation of emergency under Article 352 of the constitution because of a threat to national security, then Article 354 provides for the suspension of all provisions relating to the division of tax proceeds between the centre and the states. In addition, a financial emergency can be declared under Article 360 if the President (that is, the union government) is satisfied that the financial stability or credit of India, or any part of the country, is under threat. While a financial emergency is in force, presidential proclamations may order a reduction of salaries of states officials, and require all money bills approved by a state legislature to be reserved for presidential consideration. Interestingly Article 360 was not included in the draft constitution. Its insertion was prompted in part by the devaluation of the rupee in 1949. Although the article is open to the criticism that it erodes the federal principle even further, its incorporation into the constitution was justified on the argument that the economic structure of the country is one and indivisible, and that the promulgation of a financial emergency would be the exception rather that than norm.

If we move away from an institutional conceptualisation of federalism and examine its operational manifestations, then it becomes clear that India is a cooperative rather than a competitive federation. This is especially evident, for example, the process of planning that will be discussed. The formulation of plans is done mainly by the central government, but with an important consultative role for states. The implementation of plans is chiefly in the hands of the states, but with the help of central finances and with an important monitoring and oversight role for the centre. State politicians are particularly interested in those subjects that have the greatest electoral appeal, for example education and agriculture. This has taken on added importance since the existence of different party governments in the centre and the states.

PARTY-POLITICAL CENTRALISATION

The imbalance in favour of the centre India's federalism has one other interesting consequence. It provides a readier alibi for state governments to pin blame for their non-performance on a central government controlled by a different party. The Communist Party of India (Marxist) often points to the constraints of federalism in explaining its limited achievements in West Bengal. Since so much power has been vested in the central government, the Congress Party in West Bengal cannot profit as much from the failures of the of the CPI (M) government in West Bengal. State and national politics are more successfully delinked in other federal systems like Australia and Canada.

India's founding prime Minister Jawaharlal Nehru was a principal architect of the constitution adopted shortly after independence. During his tenure as head of government (1950-64), he tried to give 'flesh and blood' to the constitutional principals. His government was inclusive, representative of the myriad strands of Indian society, committed to promoting secularism, sensitive to conventions governing relations between the treasury and opposition benches and generally careful not to intrude upon state rights. Yet even Nehru's legacy to Indian federalism was somewhat mixed. On the one hand, he was determined that his Congress Party would rule not only at the centre but in all the states as well. If the people could not see the wisdom of this when electing state assemblies, then the goal could still be achieved by behind-the-scenes manipulation and the use of constitutional tricks for bringing about the downfall of states governments. On the other hand, for most of the Nehru period central and state politics were largely autonomous. Several states were ruled by strong chief ministers from within congress, and a sort of bargaining model of federalism operated to mediate between a strong government in New Delhi and strong government in states.

Developments under Prime Minister Mrs Indira Gandhi (1966-77, 1980-4) led to the interlinking of the fates of the central and state governments. The 24th Constitution Amendment Bill abolishing the privy purses of the princes was rejected in the Rajya Sabha in September 1970 when Charan Singh failed to deliver three Bharatiya Kranti Dal (BKD) votes. Mrs Gandhi's response was to break the ruling BKD—Congress coalition in Uttar Pradesh (UP) and bring down the state government. Under Nehru, the centre had functioned as an impartial arbiter of conflicts internal to state politics. Under Mrs Gandhi, the stability of state politics became increasingly a function of the struggle for power in the centre. Her position became dependent on having pliant chief ministers; their position was dependent on her pleasure, before, the surest route to political power at the centre was through building broad-based coalitions at the local and state levels. Henceforth, the competition to occupy a chief minister's chair would be conducted mainly at the prime minister's residence in New Delhi. Power and resources at the state level become a reward for loyalty of the prime minister.

Rajiv Gandhi (1984-9) commented that centre-state relations in India had been reduced to the connection between the Congress Party's headquarters in New Delhi and its branch offices, with the former exacting obedience in return for largesse (Datta-Ray.1991b).Congress Party politics became increasingly centralised in candidate selection for state and national elections, cabinet and chief ministerial appointments and distribution of patronage. As the autonomy and influence of state party organisations and leaders was progressively curtailed, and the process of building stable political coalitions was neglected, the need grew for more frequent interventions by the central government in order to cope with chronic instability in the states.

Indian federalism is distinctive for granting the central government the power to dismiss elected state governments and replace them with administrations run directly by the centre under President's Rule. Under Article 356 of the constitution, the President may declare an emergency in a state if satisfied that the government of the state cannot be carried out in accordance with the constitution. President's Rules was imposed infrequently under Prime Ministers Nehru and Lal Bahadur Shastri (1950-66) (Table 9.2). Recourse to it expanded exponentially under Mrs Gandhi (1966-77), Generally with partisan motives. The same was true of the Janata government (1977-9), which set the precedent of dissolving nine Congress-ruled state assemblies on the dubious reasoning that the federal elections were a vote of no-confidence in all Congress ministries. When Mrs Gandhi came back to power, she turned the tables by dismissing the assemblies of nine states in which her party had triumphed in the Lok Sabha elections; only Kerala and West Bengal were left untouched.

As democratic government has taken deeper root, political power has been devolved from the centre to the states and districts. As a results, even Congress states politicians have regained some of the bargaining leverage lost during the era of centralisation under Mrs. Gandhi. The inability of the central government to bend state governments to its will was demonstrated even during the dominance of both levels by the Congress Party prior to 1967. Some state governments, for example that of West Bengal, were successful in thwarting major union initiatives in land reforms and agricultural income tax. One the other hand, the multiplicity of

Table 9.2: The Imposition of President's Rule on States, 1952-92

1952-56	1957-61	1962-66	1967-71	1972-76	1977-81	1982-86	1987-91	1992
4	2	4	16	15	33	6	13	6

Note: The chronology refers to the dates of imposition, not termination of President Rule. The total for the 41-year period is 99. There is not one state that has not experienced President's Rule at least once. States to have had Presidents' Rule most often are Kerala (9 times) and Punjab (8 times).

Source: Basu, 1993, pp. 449-51.

powerful factions in Congress as well as non-Congress state units leaves considerable room to the central government to play the role of (dis) honest broker. Also, because politics in India has become increasingly distributive along sectarian lines, with politicians attempting to build up vote banks, the centre had acquired an enhanced ability to play patronage politics.

The Sarkaria Commission on Centre-State Relations was set up by Mrs Gandhi in 1983 under the Chairmanship of retired Supreme Court judge R.S. Sarkaria. (Mrs Gandhi Announced the setting up of the commission shortly after the formation of a regional council of opposition chief ministers of four southern states to buttress the demand for greater state autonomy). It inquired into the role of the governor, the relationship between state administrations and all-India services, the appointment of high court judges by the centre, the implications of the President's power to withhold assent from bills passed by state legislatures, and state financial dependency on the centre. Its report, published in 1988, recommended the creation of a series of independent federal bodies with constitutional status and advisory functions such as the National Economic and Development Council and an Inter-Governmental Council, as well as the Planning Commission and the Finance Commission. It sought to reduce the element of arbitrariness in the dismissal of state governments by the centre. The Sarkaria Commission also suggested ways by which the pool of revenue resources shared by the centre and the states could be expanded in order to place the sharing of revenues on a more equitable basis. Overall, although its spoke of 'Cooperative federalism', the trust of its report was in favour of a strong centre that could best preserve the unity and integrity of the country. It may perhaps have been influenced by the exceptional number and strength of challenges to the unity and integrity of India during the mid-1980s. The Sarkaria Report quietly buried and centre-state relations in the 1990s have settled into the familiar pre-Sarkaria mould of *ad hoc* responses to specific situations.

By the 1990s politicians have gradually become less cosmopolitan and more provincial even as federalism, has become steadily more complex, requiring bargaining and accommodation between governments run by various political parties. In 1991, in addition to its good performance at the national level, the Bharatiya Janata Party (BJP) won power in four states: Himachal Pradesh, Madhya Pradesh, Rajasthan and U.P. Ayodhya, site of the disputed Babri Masjid lies in U.P. The BJP was committed to rebuilding a temple on the site. But the BJP state government, have provoked a Hindu-Muslim polarisation before the 1991 election, realised after it that failure to maintain law and order would invite central government intervention and dismissal of the state government in U.P.

In the Lok Sabha debate on 21December 1992 Prime Minister P.V. Narasimha Rao argued that Article 356 was too restrictive to have permitted him to dismiss the U.P. government before the Babri Masjid demolition on 6 December, so perhaps, it needed to be amended. Students of Indian politics were thus faced by the novel situation of a prime minister justifying non-use of Article 356 to dismiss a state government. Constitutionalists rejected the Prime Minister's contention that he could not have acted sooner (Noorani, 1993a, p. 11). Under Article 355, the central government can deploy its own security forces to suppress any disturbances without having to impose President's Rule. The central government is charged with the responsibility to protect every state against external aggression and internal disturbance. The deployment of central forces can be ordered in a situation rapidly drifting towards anarchy and, if necessary, against the wishes of the state government. The National Integration Council had met on 23 November. The BJP had boycotted the proceedings. The central government had received intelligence reports warning of specially trained squads being organised for purposes inimical to the security of the Babri Masjid structure.

After the destruction of the Babri Masjid in December 1992, all BJP-run state government were dismissed and fresh elections held in the four provinces a years later. The fact that the BJP suffered significant reverses in the two important states of U.P. and Madhya Pradesh raised the prospect of the central government dismissing other non-Congress governments before the holding of state elections. Control of the reins of government at the state level gives considerable power of patronage during the holding of elections: incumbency is a decided asset. On the other had, there is a clear risk of generating sympathy for parties that are seen to have been harshly treated by the centre for purely political reasons. The optimum political strategy therefore is to engineer instability in non-Congress state governments so that they disintegrate about 6-12 months before elections are due, and then impose President's Rule for the interregnum.

THE GOVERNOR

Of all the constitutional functionaries, the governor has been the most controversial. Probably the most crucial reform in enhancing the confidence of states concerns the role of the governor. Specifically, he could be made responsible to the state rather than the central government. Justified originally in terms of providing a much-needed link between the central and state governments as well as a referee in the affairs of states, the office has been misused as an instrument of coercion and manipulation of individuals or parties that are unfriendly to the central government. As a result, the office of the governor has become the focal point of contested federalism. The office is probably one of the best examples of the decay of India's political institutions. At the same time, India is also noted for its resilience and its capacity for political regeneration: not just the rebuilding of enfeebled institutions but the creation of new ones that can cope with the continual pressures and challenges from society.

While every state must have governor, one person may be appointed the governor of more than one state. For example, the Assam governor has served as the governor of Meghalaya as well. Although no woman has as yet been elected to the presidency, several women have been appointed as state governors. For practical purposes in most instances the governor is the provincial equivalent of the President of India in ceremonial, executive, legislative and judicial functions. All four functions reflect the tension of the governor's split formal personality as representative of the central government and head of the state government. In the ceremonial functions, for example, the governor is a symbolic representative simultaneously of the President of India and of the state. The legislative functions include summoning, proroguing and dissolving the state legislature. The exercise of these functions can bring into conflict those commanding majority support in the central parliament and state legislature. Like the President, the governor too, acting on advice, may promulgate ordinances that have legislative force while the state legislature is in recess.

There are also some important differences, starting with the manner of coming to office. A state governor is appointed by and holds office at the pleasure of the President (Articles155-6). Once again the Indian Constitution followed the Canadian model while eschewing the Australian and US precedents. The draft constitution had called for an elected governor. An appointed governor cuts across the federal as well as the democratic principle; a governor appointed from outside the state my not be sensitive enough to the local needs and aspirations; and the office could become a point of friction if different parties were in power in a state and at the centre. Yet in the end the Constituent Assembly opted for an appointed governor chiefly to protect national interests against undesirable parochialism. On the one hand, the expense and effort of holding elections would not be justified for a ceremonial post. Yet on the other hand, an elected governor would also be a rival source of authority to the chief minister. Governors are usually appointed to states other than their own in order to minimize partisan involvement with local politics.

In practice, the office of the governor has been merely ornamental if the state government commands a clear majority on the floor of the assembly, and if it is of the same party as the central government. The interesting episodes concern exception to these two conditions. As is the case with the President at the centre, the governor can acquire considerable ability to influence the politics of a state if the majority party is immobilised by powerful rival factions, or if there is no single party with a majority in the legislative assembly. This has been only too common in India since the 1967 state elections, in which year five state governments were formed without a clear legislative majority. On these occasions, reflecting the power of patronage conferred by the manner of appointment and dismissal of the governor, the office-holder can become a mere tool of the central government. Even more unsavoury is the practice of dismissing state governments that still command a majority in their assemblies.

The scope for bending the affairs of states to the wishes of the centre through the governor comes from two sources: the discretionary powers of the governor and the emergency powers of the union government. Together, the two ensure that the governor functions as the 'eyes and ears' of the union government. Given the ever-present threat of disorder in several parts of India, the 'Constructive contribution' of the emergency powers of the union government to the maintenance of fragile political institutions should not be ignored (Manor, 1991, p. 146).

The governor of a state is required to act in accordance with the aid and advice of his chief minister and cabinet except in those provisions of the constitution that require him to exercise his functions in his discretion': the question of whether the matter is one requiring his discretion is in turn at the absolute and unquestionable discretion of the governor (Article 163). Such discretionary power extends, for example, to administering the affairs of a union territory adjoining the state for which the governor is responsible, or to certain areas (usually tribal or hill areas) for which the governor of a state may be designated as having special responsibilities (Article 371). The discretionary latitude of the governor, whose scope is greatly expanded during President's Rule, is in marked contrast to the binding requirement that the President must always act on the aid and advice of the prime minister and the central cabinet. A President cannot therefore call on gubernatorial precedents to guide his own actions when making delicate decisions.

Under Article 356, the President may dismiss a state government if he is satisfied, on the basis of a report from the governor 'or otherwise', that the constitutional government of the state has broken down. For obvious reasons, such a report may have to be communicated against the wishes of the state government. Similarly, a governor may his her own judgement on whether to reserve a bill that has been duly passed by the state legislature for presidential consideration. A governor would be constitutionally remiss if he did not do so, for example, in the case of a bill seeking to erode the powers of the state high court.

One set of controversies that have swirled around the office arose from gubernatorial judgements that have anticipated, and sometimes even disregarded, the likely vote on the floor of a house rather than testing the majority of a government. The practice became commonplace during the prime ministerial reign of Mrs Gandhi and after the loss of Congress monopoly over state governments from 1967 onwards. Yet the first example of the dismissal of a state by the central government occurred in 1959 during the Nehru era (although Mrs. Gandhi was party President at the time). The Communist government of Kerala was dismissed by the governor on his instinctive conclusion that the minds and feelings of the people had experienced a tremendous shift against the communist ministry. (No. actual or public opinion poll was held to document such a shift of electoral opinion.) The post-1967 developments institutionalised the practice of using the governor to pursue the interests of the ruling party at the centre in installing the government or chief minister of its choice. Governor Gopala Reddy dismissed the Charan Singh ministry in U.P. in 1970 without awaiting the assembly vote that was due within a few days. When faced between equally unstable alternatives of divided non-

Congress coalitions and a factionalised Congress, governors restricted their options to asking a Congress chief minister to prove a majority on the Legislative floor within a generous period or imposing President's Rule. In tandem with the centre, state units of the Congress Party followed the strategy of 'divide or join': divisions would be encouraged within non-Congress coalitions in order to bring about their disintegrations, or else an alliance would be formed with one powerful group against another.

We have already discussed the events of 1997 and 1980. In both years, six of the nine dismissed governments commanded a majority in their respective legislatures at the time of their dismissals. On 16 August 1984, Governor Ram Lal would not give Chief Minister N.T. Rama Rao 48 hours to prove his majority in the Andhra Pradesh assembly and replaced him with Bhaskara Rao, a defector from the ruling Telugu Desam Party. Despite all sorts of bureaucratic and police harassment by Bhaskara Rao and Physical impediments to rail and air travel by the Congress government in New Delhi, Rama Rao managed to parade a majority of members of the legislative assembly (MLAs) before the President in New Delhi on 21 August, at which point the central government distanced itself from the actions of the state governor.

It is clear then that sate governments are dismissed more for party political reasons than any other. In effect the collective legal responsibility of the state cabinet to its legislative assembly under the conventions of parliamentary democracy has been displaced by the individual political responsibility of the governor to the central government under the imperatives of a centralizing federalism. As a corollary, in effect the governor has usurped the constitutional prerogative of the legislature to make and unmake governments in parliamentary democracies.

A second set of controversies has involved the dismissal of state governments independently of reports from the governor recommending such action. One of the most notable of such instances occurred in 1991 in state of Tamil Nadu (see Tummala, 1992). The Dravida Munnetra Kazhagam (DMK) government was in power after the 1989 elections. In 1990, the National Front central government collapsed. Chandra Shekhar became prime minister because, although he controlled less than 10 per cent of the Lok Sabha MPs, he had the support of Rajiv Gandhi's 197 Congress MPs.

The pro-Congress All-India Anna DMK (AIADMK) opposition in Tamil Nadu began to urge the dismissal of the DMK government. Pressure during 1990 turned to an ultimatum in January 1991. The governor of the state at the time, appointed by the National Front government, was Surjit Singh Barnala, whose own Akali government in Punjab had been dismissed by Gandhi in May 1987. Despite representations from intelligence agencies purporting to show the DMK's entanglements with Sri Lankan Tamil Terrorists, Barnala refused to submit a report to the President recommending a dismissal of his state government. The dismissal was effected over his objection on 30 January 1991 on grounds of the State government's inability to maintain law and order—even though New Delhi had earlier declined the DMK government's request for the deployment of central paramilitary forces for assisting with the maintenance of law and order. (Barnala had always argued that President's Rule in Punjab had actually worsened the law-and-order situation there after May 1987.)

A duly elected state government still in command of a majority in its assembly, and with the law-and-order situation considerably better than in many other states, was thus dismissed by an unelected central government. Analysts were divided as to which was greater violation: of the norms of democracy or federalism. There was a further twist to the strange affair. Governor Mohammed Yusuf Saleem of Bihar resisted pressure from the Chandra Sekhar government to dismiss the state's Janata Dal government. On 10 February 1991, his address to the joint session of the state legislature, written by the state government, included a passage critical of the dismissal of the DMK government in Tamil Nadu. (The governor was physically manhandled by angry opposition legislators during his entry into the assembly building.) He in turn was dismissed by the union government on grounds of 'Constitutional impropriety', thereby raising the question of whose rubber the governor should stamp: that of the central or state government? Barnala was offered the Bihar governorship instead. He refused the Bihar appointment and rsigned his Tamil Nadu post.

The above comments indicate the degree to which the office of the governor has been politicised into serving the interests of the party in power in New Delhi. The practice has been underlined by appointing party candidates who have been defeated in elections to the office of governor, as well as retiring bureaucrats and military officers who have been loyal to the prime minister or the ruling party. The Sarkaria Commission recommendation, that a governor should not belong to the party in power in New Delhi in the case of a state with a different party in power, has been ignored by all governments. In 1990, V.P. Singh's National Front government asked 18 Congress-appointed governors to resign. Home Minister Mufti Mohammad Sayeed openly declared that the governor was a representative of the centre and as such should enjoy the confidence of the centre (*HIE*, 27 January 1990, p. 1). This despite a Supreme Court ruling in the *Raghukul Tilak* case that the governor, occupying an independent constitutional office, is not subject to control by the union government. The relationship between the central government and a state governor is not that of employer-employee, said the court, in its verdict delivered on 4 May 1979. There was an interesting variant on the theme in 1992. On 27 March, Governor M.M. Thomas of Nagaland accepted his chief minister's advice to dissolve the Legislative Assembly and hold fresh elections, on the ground that no stable government could be formed because of a fluid party situation. The governor's recommendation was taken as proof that constitutional government in the state had broken down, and on 2 April Nagaland came under President's Rule under Article 356 of the Constitution.

An insistence on appointing person who are regarded as unacceptable by state governments can strengthen the suspicion that the governor is an agent of and imposed by the union government. The office of the governor will be less controversial and less politicised if conventions are established that persons appointed to the post should be acceptable to the state governments, and should be continued in office for their full term except for incompetence or proven incapacity to function. The appearance of nonpartisan consensus is vital to the smooth functioning of all non-executive constitutional figureheads. This will also ensure that governors are more sensitive to the need to avoid controversy and to act evenhandedly. For while impartial conduct and devotion to constitutional propriety has been the norm with presidents, the same cannot be said of governors.

THE SPECIAL STATUS OF KASHMIR

Intolerance of provincial governments and recourse to sectarian politics by successive central governments in New Delhi have produced steadily deteriorating problems in the two key states of Punjab and Kashmir. The two together are also a good illustration of the increasing intertwining of religion and politics in modern India (Mansingh, 1991, pp. 308-9).

About two-thirds of the six million people of Jammu and Kashmir are Muslim. Kashmir (as the state is commonly known) has a unique status in the Indian federation conferred on it by Article 370 of the constitution. It is a full-fledged state and part of the 'territory of India as defined in Article 1 of the Constitution. Under the British Raj, it was one of several princely states. While the people were mainly Muslim, the hereditary Maharajah, Sir Hari Singh, was Hindu. A popular movement led by Sheikh Abdullah agitated against the maharajah's autocratic rule. Its secular nature attracted support from Congress but opposition from the Muslim League. There was also an embryonic movement to keep Kashmir free of any external attachment. The Kashmir problem thus crystallised into a struggle between three competing versions of nationalism: the religious nationalism of Pakistan, the secular nationalism of India and the ethnic nationalism of Kashmiris (Varshney, 1991).

Attempts by the Maharajah to remain independent in 1947 came to nought when the state was attacked by armed tribesmen wishing to force the issue of Kashmir's merger with Pakistan. India made its help in repelling the invasion subject to the accession of the state to India. The Maharajah acceded to the Indian Union on 26 October 1947 and Indian troops were flown in on the next day. Pakistani troops crossed the border openly in November and the ensuing first war over Kashmir was ended with a UN-mediated ceasefire on 1 January 1949. Kashmir remains the symbol of the Indo-Pakistan conflict. The military situation in effect partitioned the province between Pakistan and India on a 1:2 basis. The area under Indian control has three parts: Buddhist-Majority (51 per cent) Ladakh, Hindu-Majority (66 per cent) Jammu, and the Muslim-majority (95 per cent) Jhelum valley. Because of the peculiar history of Kashmir's accession to India, Delhi declared that the Indian government's responsibility would be limited to defence, foreign affairs and communications. Other parts of the constitution would apply to the province only on a provisional basis until such time as the people of Kashmir themselves adopted their own constitution through a constituent assembly. This was done in 1954, embracing the applicability of virtually the entire range of the Indian constitution to the state.

But there were some significant exceptions. The state of Jammu and Kashmir retains its own separate constitution instead of the provisions of Part VI of the Constitution of India Which govern the administration of all other states in the union. The state constitution, which was promulgated in January 1957, cannot be suspended under Article 365 on the ground of non-compliance with a union directive. While the Parliament of India has jurisdiction in respect of Kashmir with regard to all matters in the Union List, residual powers are vested in the state government of Kashmir (other than for dealing with terrorism, territorial integrity and secession). Even the power of preventive detention has been vested in the Kashmir legislature. The state's consent is required for any alteration of its name or territory, and for the proclamation of an emergency under Articles 352 or 360 dealing with an internal disturbance and a financial crisis respectively. Rights to employment, settlement and acquisition of property in the state discriminate between 'permanent resident's and non-residents.

Despite a few ups and downs, after 1957 there was a growing web of linkages between Kashmiri nationalism and the Indian political mainstream culminating in a seminal accord between Sheikh Abdullah and Mrs Gandhi in February 1975. In this accord, the 'Lion of Kashmir' accepted the finality of Kashmir's accession to India while the prime minister guaranteed Kashmir's regional autonomy under Article 370. The accord was endorsed by the people in the 1977 elections, generally believed to be the state's first free and fair election. Kashmir became a place of beauty but not a joy forever. Peace and tranquility lasted until Sheikh Abdullah's death in 1982.

The mantle of leadership of the National Conference Party and the state government was inherited by his son Farooq Abdullah. Mrs Gandhi then subjected the state to her familiar tactics of manipulative politics. She campaigned against the National Conference in the June 1983 elections, and the state unit of the Congress Party refused to accept its loss in the elections. The Prime Minister began to employ the rhetoric of 'anti-national elements in Kashmir. She succeeded in splitting the National Conference in 1984 and installing a pro-Congress faction in power, but at the price of the political destruction of her 1975 accord with the Sheikh. Governor Jagmohan proved pliant in dismissing Farooq without giving him the opportunity to prove his majority in the assembly, and so initiated the most serious and sustained period of alienation of Kashmiris from the Indian mainstream.

Moreover, 'by manipulating the removal of an elected Chief Minister who acted as a useful buffer in a State that is of the utmost strategic and demographic importance, the Centre [came] directly to grips with the Kashmir question' (Datta-Ray, 1990, p.11). By the time that Farooq Abdullah teamed up again with the Rajiv Gandhi-led-Congress in the 1987 elections (which were rigged), Islamic groups were ready to assume the mantle of anti-Delhi militancy. By the end of the 1980s the Indian Army had in effect become an army of occupation, low-intensity insurgency gripped the entire state and the provincial administration had effectively collapsed.

Constitutionally, then, the federal balance is tripped slightly more towards state rights only in the case of Jammu and Kashmir. Kashmir is thus more equal than other states in the Indian union. The delicacy of its situation arises firstly from its geopolitical location at the crossroads of India, Pakistan, Afghanistan, Russia and China; and secondly from the fact that it is India's only Muslim-majority state. Loss of Kashmir would not just deprive Indian of the fertile and populous Vale of Kashmir; it would also render impracticable Indian claims to the Aksai Chin region of Ladakh and threaten control of Punjab. It attracts the attention of the BJP on both counts. Demands for the abrogation of Article 370- which was originally described as a temporary and transitional provision—have been voiced most vociferously by the BJP, on the argument that India is one country and Jammu and Kashmir is an integral part of India. A former governor of the province, Jagmohan, pointed to the 'farcical' situation that an Indian could get US citizenship after ten years' residence there, but could not get a similar status (domicile) in Kashmir (*SW*, 26 June 1993, p. 5).

In 1993, the Kashmir Pandits began to voice a demand for their own union territory, named 'Panun Kashmir', to be carved out of the state. They based their demand on the alleged history of the Muslims' refusal to live in peaceful coexistence with the Hindus tri of the province. To the Kashmir Hindus, the Indian government is guilty of failure to protect their lives and property from terrorists. To the Kashmiri Muslims. India is itself the enemy and Indian security forces the perpetrators of the worst outrages that have defiled an entire community. Whatever their religion, most Kashmiris are united in having lost trust in the Government of India.

The fact that Kashmir is the only Muslim-majority state in India, plus the controversial manner of its accession to India, plus the fact that about a third of the erstwhile princely province is under Pakistani occupation, combined to keep the Kashmiri problem alive as a national, regional and international issue. An armed uprising begun in 1989-90 had claimed some 13000 lives by the end of 1993.

About half a million Hindus (the Kashmiri Pandits) have fled their homes for the safety of Jammu and Delhi. India alleges that the militants are financed, armed and trained by Pakistan, and that without Pakistani complicity the insurgency could be contained. India believes that Pakistan has concluded that it is less costly, safer and more effective to wage a proxy guerrilla war than a real one. The worry in New Delhi has been that in backing terrorist violence in Kashmir (and Punjab), Pakistan was aiming to achieve by means of low-intensity proxy conflict goals that were unattainable by conventional military means.

The patterns of demands by religious and linguistic groups and government responses to them are familiar enough for us to be able to sketch a political profile. The groups' initial demands are couched in moderate language and their goal is usually no more than ensuing the preservation of political space guaranteed to them by the constitution. The state and central governments ignore them: they lack sufficient nuisance value to command the attention of hard pressed decision-makers. There is no discussion, let alone negotiations. Instead, the mettle of the movements' leaderships is tested by casual repression and harassment. This converts and 'evolution of rising expectations' of the groups into a sense of grievance and arouses them into mobilizing wider support for their cause. The government then resorts to the tactic of divide and rule. Intelligence agencies and agents provocateur are used to delegitimise the movements, while new radical leaders are promoted in order to outflank the movements' leaders, possibly to terrorise them and certainly to splinter their followings. Radical leaders promoted into prominence by the government then turn into fanatic secessionists in their own right, or else succeed in driving hitherto moderate leaders into increasingly hardline rejectionists. This is they story of Punjab, Kashmir and Assam as well as a variety of movements within states. The special constitutional rights given to Kashmir could have been used as a healthy precedent for re-establishing centre-state relations with all the other provinces, Instead the central government in New Delhi chose to rule through a series of rigged elections and puppet chief ministers.

CONCLUSION

The constitution attempts to establish institution and practices that would permit the preservation of distinct regional identities while maintaining a sense of Indian nationhood: a concurrent list of powers for central and state government, an independent Finance Commission, and a general institutional framework designed to facilitate voluntary cooperation. Within this framework, efforts have been made to make states realize that they do possess common interests, and that the central government is not a hostile power. In addition to the constitutional framework, there is considerable centre-states and state-state collaboration. That is, while the constitution emphasizes demarcation, practical politics place a premium on cooperative bargaining.

Politics is about the control and exercise of power. A political system is about the institutional distribution of power. Democracy and federalism are the two great institutions of India's constitutional structure. Democracy seeks to achieve a balanced distribution of power between the state and the citizens. Federalism seeks to strike a satisfactory balance between the central and state governments. A strong government is not inconsistent with democratic governance: the moral authority to govern based on constitutional propriety is more useful than authoritarian powers acquired by stealth and subversion. A strong centre is not incompatible with strong states: there is no reason why a union of strong states should not lead to a still stronger India. Under Indian conditions, centralisation of power will lead to an unnecessary nationalisation of local problems. If the government in Delhi were to try to rule the country as a feudal fiefdom, it would risk displacing the 'politics of accommodation' with the 'politics of manipulation' (Hardgrave and Kochanek, 1993, p. 135).

The most pressing requirement for India since independence has been economic development, pointing to an expansive role for the central government. The contrary permissive and restrictive pulls of democracy generate tensions between majority rule and minority rights; those of federalism generate tension between central dominance and provincial autonomy. India is effectively a bargaining, cooperative federalism, even though the channels, forums and outcomes of bargaining may change from time to time. The distinction between democracy and federalism is important also in understanding why the crises is Assam, Kashmir and Punjab are more accurately viewed as failures of federalism rather than of democracy. Moreover, the Congress Party, often identified as the key to the stability of the democratic order in India, can itself be a threat to the federal order because of its excessive centralisation.

As a half-way house between a unitary and confederal arrangement, federalism contains an inherent paradox: its units seek national unity but do not wish to lose their own identities. Federalism in India is a particular manifestation of the syncretic impulse in Indian society. People can be proud of their regional identities without any overt or implicit downgrading of their patriotism. The constitution has established institutions to promote a satisfactory blend of regional and national identities. These are buttressed by informal collaboration between the centre and the states, and between the states directly. State ministers sharing particular portfolios—health, education, agriculture, housing—can get together to discuss common problems and map out a common strategy. For example, although education is a state subject, all states have to have knowledge of the confidence in one another's certification process in order to recognize each other's qualifications. Indian federalism should not be evaluated by the standards of competitive, sometimes even confrontational, federalism in Western countries. All in all, India's efforts to preserve unity in diversity have so far successfully – if only just – withstood tensions strong enough to have split apart some other experiments in federalism in developing countries.

Perhaps inevitably, the reorganisation of states along linguistic lines was the prelude to fresh demands for greater autonomy on the one hand, and the subdivision of existing states into newer states on the other. We have already referred to examples of the former: by the communist governments of West Bengal, and the regionalist governments of Tamil Nadu, Andhra Pradesh, Punjab as Assam. A good example of the unsatisfied aspirations for ethno-national statehood within the Indian union is the demand for a separate state of Jharkhand to be carved out of the contiguous tribal districts of Bihar (manly) and Orissa, West Bengal and Madhaya Pradesh. Another example is the periodic demand for a separate Gurkhaland to be parcelled off from West Bengal.

The government has sought to accommodate linguistic diversity with a three-language formula that was recommended by the National Integration Council in 1961. The constitution declared the official language of India to be Hindi in the Devanagari script (Article 343). English, the language of the Raj, was to be retained as the 'language of administration' for no longer than 15 years. States were permitted to adopt languages other than Hindi as their official language (s). The three-language formula required all schools to teach English, Hindi and the regional language of the area; in Hindi speaking states, the third language would be an other regional language of India. Attempts to 'impose' Hindi on the southern states produced mass protests and agitations against 'Hindi imperialism', and the official languages policy has failed to alter the monolingual status of most Indians. But Hind did become the official language of India from 26 January 1965, with English becoming a 'subsidiary' official language. It is used for official communication between a non-Hindi state and the union or another state.

Opinion is divided on the cause of the unsatisfactory health of Indian federalism. There are some who argue that the constitutional framework is itself flawed, suited only to the same party being in power in the states and at the centre. The periodic proposal to give constitutional status to the Planning Commission, for example, is part of an overall demand for redefining centre-state relations. Others argue that the constitution as such is sound, but appropriate conventions to underpin it have yet to toke root (Palkhivala, 1983, p. 34). It has been argued with reference to Article 356) permitting the imposition of central rule on states) that 'The powers it confers are freely availed of. The conditions for their exercise are as freely ignored" (Noorani, 1992, p. 12). Clauses that were drafted in order to protect the territorial integrity of the country have been used in so arbitrary and capricious a way that they might well imperil national unity: identity-asserting, separatist and secessionist movements feed on a sense of grievance.

In an important decision on 11 March 1994, the Supreme Court upheld the validity of the Dismissal of the four BJP state governments on 15 December 1992. But the court also ruled also that presidential proclamations were subject to judicial review, and that the president could be required to submit to the court the material on which he had formed 'requisite satisfaction' in issuing a proclamation under Article 356. Assembly dissolutions could be set aside if the president's proclamation was 'malafide' or based on 'wholly irrelevant or extraneous considerations' (*HIE*, 19 March 1994, p. 2). Applying these criteria, the court held the proclamations of 21 April 1989 and 11 October 1991, dissolving the assemblies of Karnataka and Meghalaya, to have been unconstitutional. The political significance of the verdict is that henceforth, knowing that dismissals of state governments can be set aside by the courts, the central government will be hesitant about abusing Article 356.

There are several long-term trends that favour regionalism, pluralism and decentralisation (Brass, 1982). The best evidence of the reality of a bargaining model of federalism in India is the existence of a variety of parties in power in several states across the country. Brass (1990, pp. 110-18) has classified state party systems into one-party-dominant (the sole remaining example being Maharashtra); one-party-dominant systems with institutionalised opposition; and competitive, where there is some experience and possibility of alternation of government. It is an interesting affirmation of his thesis about the long-term federalizing trends that one year after his book was published, the states of U.P., Himachal Pradesh and Rajasthan moved from the second to the third, competitive, category. An equally dramatic example of the strengthening of 'fiscal federalism' came at the annual meeting of the World Economic Forum of government and business leaders in Davos (Switzerland) in February 1994. There were two delegations from India: a federal, headed by Prime Minister P.V. Narasimha Rao who gave a keynote address on the consolidation of economic reforms; and a state delegation from Maharashtra headed by Chief Minister Sharad Pawar, who tried to present a case for Bombay as an emerging global financial centre.

India can therefore best be described as a cooperative federalism with the paramountcy of the centre, being enshrined in the constitution. The elements of cooperative federalism are administrative cooperation between the central and state governments in the implementation of their respective public policies, partial dependence of state governments upon payments from the central government to help finance state projects, partial dependence of the central government on states for the administration of federal programmes, and the use of conditional financial transfers by the central government to shape policies in subjects that are constitutionally within the jurisdiction of states.

References

Bose (1987). A collection of papers analyzing a range of problems in Indian federalism.

Datta (1984). A useful set of readings exploring a range of issues in centre –state relations.

Fadia (1984). A discussion of Indian politics at the state level.

Prasad (1984). Examines the subject from the perspective of a constitutional lawyer.

Sarkaria (1988). The most recent and a comprehensive examination by a government commission of the framework and workings of Indian federalism.

Tummala (1992). A critical examination of the dissolution of the state government of Tamil Nadu in 1991.